# The Rise and Fall of
# Zionism in the 21$^{st}$ Century

# Sean Hogan

# Dedication

*For the people of Palestine,*
*whose endurance has carried history on their shoulders.*
*And for my own children and grandchildren,*
*that they may inherit a world where justice is not selective,*
*and silence is never the last word.*

# Acknowledgement

No book is written in isolation. This one, especially, owes much to the voices, courage, and scholarship of others.

First, to the many historians, journalists, and human rights investigators whose work provides the foundation on which I stand. Their commitment to truth—often at the cost of their own safety— has ensured that the record cannot be buried, however much power tries to obscure it.

To Palestinian writers, poets, and witnesses whose words carried not only fact but humanity into this work. Their resilience is a reminder that history is not only archived but lived.

To colleagues, friends, and fellow readers who offered conversation, debate, and encouragement—thank you for sharpening my thinking and challenging me to push further.

To Ireland itself, whose memory of famine, partition, and colonial dispossession echoes through these pages, shaping how I see and why I write.

Finally, to my family, for their patience and faith. Writing about such a painful subject is not easy; living with someone while they do so is harder still. This book is as much yours as mine.

# About the Author

Seán Hogan is a seasoned board leader, strategist, and social scientist whose career has spanned governance, public service, and complex negotiations across Ireland and the UK. A Chartered Director with decades of experience navigating political systems, regulatory environments, and high-stakes decision-making, he brings to his writing a rare blend of analytical discipline and lived insight into how power actually functions.

His lifelong interest in geopolitics, colonial legacies, and global justice has shaped a body of work that confronts difficult truths with clarity and compassion. Drawing on a background steeped in Ireland's own history of dispossession and political struggle, Hogan offers a distinctive perspective on the modern Middle East and the collapse of long-held narratives about Zionism, democracy, and Western influence.

*The Rise and Fall of Zionism in the 21st Century* is his most ambitious project to date, a sweeping, human-focused examination of ideology, morality, and the unraveling of a geopolitical myth.

# Preface

This book was not written in comfort. It was written against the backdrop of bombardment, famine, and international paralysis. Each day brought fresh reports from Gaza—families starved, aid convoys attacked, children pulled from rubble. It is impossible to write in such a moment and claim neutrality. Neutrality, when faced with atrocity, is complicity.

My purpose here is not to rehearse tired debates but to confront the central paradox of our age: how a movement born in the ashes of genocide stands today accused of committing one. That paradox demands more than silence. It demands that we bear witness.

This is not a book only about Israel and Palestine. It is a book about power, myth, and the fragility of democracy when confronted by nationalism. It is about how trauma can be weaponized, how history can be distorted, and how colonial patterns re-emerge even in the twenty-first century. It is also about responsibility—of governments that looked away, of leaders who excused the inexcusable, of societies that preferred myths to truth.

I write, too, from Ireland, a country whose own history of colonization and partition sharpens its empathy for the Palestinian cause. Our memory is not theirs, but it rhymes. That parallel is not abstract. It is lived.

This book is offered, then, as witness and warning: witness to a history unfolding before our eyes, and warning that if we fail to confront it, the shadow it casts will darken not only Palestine but us all.

# Introduction –
# The Shadow of History

Zionism was born in the shadows — the shadow of European antisemitism, the shadow of pogroms and exile, the shadow of a Holocaust that seared itself into the conscience of humanity. It emerged as a promise: A promise that Jews could build a homeland of safety and dignity, free from persecution. To its earliest advocates, Zionism was not simply a political project; it was a lifeline.

But shadows are deceptive. They distort as much as they reveal. From its beginnings, Zionism carried contradictions that would grow with time. Its vision of refuge for one people was built on the dispossession of another. Its claim to democracy masked structures of exclusion. Its appeal to morality was tethered to military power. What began as a story of survival has, in the 21st century, become a story of domination — and, increasingly, of collapse.

This book is written in another shadow: the shadow of Gaza's ruins, of famine used as a weapon, of journalists and aid workers buried in unmarked graves. It is written as the world itself begins to reckon with the charge of genocide on its watch. To examine Zionism today is to confront not only Israel's history, but also the failures of the international community, the hypocrisies of Western democracies, and the long arc of colonialism in which Zionism is entangled.

**Promise and Betrayal**

The story begins with a promise. For Jews in late 19th-century Europe, facing waves of pogroms and institutional discrimination, Zionism offered a vision of liberation through nationhood. The Holocaust gave that vision an unanswerable urgency. In 1948, the state of Israel was declared, celebrated as the rebirth of Jewish

1

sovereignty after two thousand years of exile. Yet the same moment that symbolised refuge for one people meant catastrophe — *Nakba* — for another. More than 700,000 Palestinians were driven from their homes. Hundreds of villages were destroyed or renamed. From the beginning, Israel's triumph was entwined with Palestinian dispossession. Zionism was therefore never a story of one people alone. It was always a story of two peoples whose destinies became bound together in ways neither could escape. This tension, between Jewish safety and Palestinian freedom, between the dream of a homeland and the reality of occupation, lies at the heart of the conflict.

## The Arc of the Book

This book traces Zionism's journey through three broad movements.

- Part I – *The Promise* explores its origins, its triumphs, and the narratives that sustained it: democracy, morality, survival.

- Part II – *The Fracture* examines how those narratives broke down under the weight of occupation, corruption, and global scrutiny, culminating in charges of apartheid and genocide.

- Part III – *The Reckoning* looks at what follows: resistance, dissent, and the search for visions beyond Zionism.

I see this arc as not simply historical but moral. It asks whether a movement born of trauma can survive when it inflicts trauma on others. It asks how myths unravel when confronted by evidence, and what lessons Zionism's rise and fall hold for the 21st century — about nationalism, democracy, and the dangers of power without accountability.

**Why Now?** Why did I write this book now? Because the 2020s mark a turning point. For decades, Zionism enjoyed near-total protection from criticism in the West. To question Israel was to invite accusations of antisemitism. To speak of occupation was to be told of terrorism. To suggest apartheid was to court outrage. But Gaza changed everything. The sheer scale of destruction, the deliberate use of starvation, the killing of aid workers and journalists in numbers greater than both world wars and Vietnam combined, all forced a reckoning. The United Nations spoke of genocide. The International Court of Justice issued provisional measures. Even Israel's allies began to waver. A state born in the shadow of genocide now stood accused of committing one. That irony, that tragedy, defines the present moment. It forces us to ask whether Zionism, as a political project, has reached its moral end.

**The Irish Parallel**

As an Irish writer, I see that to many in Ireland, Britain's role in Palestine bore striking similarities to our own colonial experience: the imposition of control without genuine consent, the manipulation of communal divisions, the quiet arrogance of an empire convinced of its civilising mission. The echoes were not only abstract but literal. After the Irish War of Independence, many veterans of the dreaded "Black and Tans" — a force remembered in Ireland for its brutality against civilians — were redeployed into the British Mandate police force in Palestine. The same methods of collective punishment, raids, and repression tested on Irish streets were exported to Palestinian villages. Ireland and Palestine, in that sense, shared not only the shadow of empire but the very agents of its violence. These parallels have shaped Ireland's stance on Palestine in the 21st century. The empathy did not begin with Gaza; the seeds were sown in Ireland's own history of famine, dispossession, and partition. That memory explains why Ireland has become one of Europe's most outspoken critics of Israeli settlements and one of the first EU states to call occupation what it is: annexation. In May 2024, Ireland went further still, becoming one of the first EU member states — perhaps the very first — to formally recognise

Palestine as a sovereign state. It was a decision steeped not only in contemporary outrage but in historical memory. Ireland's shadow, like Palestine's, lingers. It reminds us that colonial wounds do not simply fade; they shape identity and political choices for generations. For Ireland, solidarity with Palestine is not a passing stance; it is the natural extension of its own history of resistance to domination.

### The Contest Over Narrative

To write about Zionism is to enter a battlefield of narratives. Every word is scrutinised, every critique labelled, every silence weaponised. For decades, Israel mastered this battlefield, controlling the language: occupation became "disputed territory", siege became "security", mass displacement became "voluntary migration".

But narratives fracture when reality becomes undeniable. When the world sees starving children, bombed hospitals, and bulldozed graves, the power of euphemism collapses. Truth asserts itself, however much states may resist. This book is written in that spirit — to strip away euphemism and confront the reality behind the words.

### Witnessing and Responsibility

This is not a neutral account. Neutrality is impossible in the face of occupation and genocide. But it is a fair account. It traces Zionism from its origins to its 21st-century crisis, examining both its promises and betrayals. It engages with defenders as well as critics, myths as well as realities. Above all, it treats the subject not as abstract geopolitics but as a moral question with global implications. The story of Zionism is also a story of the international community. It is about Western democracies that defended Israel while condemning similar actions elsewhere. It is about the United Nations, often powerless in the face of vetoes. It is about states of the Global South, from South Africa to Latin America, that increasingly refuse to accept double standards. To read this book is therefore to confront not only Zionism but ourselves: our complicity, our hypocrisies, our silences.

**The Central Question**

In the end, one question runs through every chapter: if a movement born in the ashes of genocide is now accused of committing genocide, what does that say not only about Zionism but about humanity itself? The answer will shape not only the future of Palestinians and Israelis but the moral credibility of the world. Zionism's rise and fall is not just a regional story. It is a parable about trauma, nationalism, and the dangers of power unmoored from justice. This is the shadow of history in which we now stand. The choice is whether we remain in it, or whether we find the courage to step beyond.

# PART I: THE PROMISE

# CHAPTER ONE

## Section 1: The Birth Of A Movement

Strangely, the story of Zionism does not begin in the Middle East. It begins in Europe — in the cities of Vienna, Paris, and Berlin; in the ghettos of Warsaw and the shtetls of Ukraine; in the salons of the assimilated bourgeoisie and the crowded tenements of the Pale of Settlement. It begins with a paradox: the simultaneous rise of Jewish emancipation and modern antisemitism, of opportunity and exclusion, of belonging and rejection.

By the late 19th century, Europe was in upheaval. The Enlightenment and the French Revolution had shattered old hierarchies, promising liberty, equality, and citizenship to those who embraced the new order. Jews, confined for centuries to segregated quarters and denied basic rights, began to step into public life. They entered universities, professions, and politics. In cities like Vienna and Budapest, they became lawyers, doctors, financiers, artists, and intellectuals. For the first time in modern history, Jews could imagine being Europeans in full — citizens, not subjects.

But the promise of emancipation came with conditions. Jews could integrate, but only if they left parts of themselves behind — if they changed their names, converted to Christianity, or shed overt expressions of their faith. In France, the first country to emancipate its Jews, the revolutionary slogan of liberty was accompanied by the warning of the National Assembly in 1789: "To the Jews as individuals, everything; to the Jews as a nation, nothing." This was an important distinction.

This tension, between individual acceptance and collective exclusion, became the defining feature of Jewish life in 19th-century

Europe. In Western Europe, where emancipation was more advanced, Jews believed assimilation could secure their place. In Eastern Europe, where they remained a despised and segregated minority, pogroms and persecution kept alive the sense of precariousness that would eventually fuel the idea of national revival.

## The Language of Hatred

The word antisemitism itself carries a telling history. Coined in the late 19th century by the German writer Wilhelm Marr, the term was designed to give a veneer of pseudo-scientific legitimacy to anti-Jewish hatred, reframing age-old religious prejudice as a racial, immutable condition. Although "Semitic" refers to a family of languages — including Hebrew, Arabic, and Aramaic — the term came to be applied almost exclusively to Jews.

This narrowing was neither accidental nor neutral. It reflected the racialised ideologies of the time, in which Jews were cast as a distinct and dangerous "race", and it set the stage for a century in which antisemitism would become a rallying cry for exclusion, segregation, and eventually genocide. Ironically, this linguistic distortion persists today, obscuring the fact that other Semitic peoples — notably Arabs — would also be subjected to racialised discrimination, albeit under different labels.

## Antisemitism Reborn

As nationalism swept Europe in the 19th century, antisemitism did not disappear; it adapted. In France, the Dreyfus Affair of the 1890s exposed the fragility of Jewish belonging. Captain Alfred Dreyfus, a Jewish officer in the French army, was falsely accused of treason. His trial, accompanied by a wave of public hysteria and virulent antisemitism, saw crowds chanting "Death to the Jews!" in the streets of Paris — the cradle of European liberalism.

In Germany and Austria-Hungary, pseudo-scientific racial theories redefined Jews not as a religious group but as a separate and alien race. Antisemitism became modern, rationalised, and respectable, its language infused with the vocabulary of biology and nationhood. Politicians like Karl Lueger in Vienna built successful careers on antisemitic populism, framing Jews as the agents of capitalism, socialism, and indeed, every ill that modernity seemed to bring.

In the vast territories of the Russian Empire, where most of the world's Jews lived, the situation was even more desperate. Confined to the Pale of Settlement — a vast stretch of land from Lithuania to Ukraine — millions of Jews lived in grinding poverty. Periodic waves of violence, or pogroms, swept through these communities with brutal regularity. In 1881, after the assassination of Tsar Alexander II, mobs rampaged through Jewish towns and villages, encouraged or ignored by authorities. Homes were burned, women assaulted, businesses destroyed, and men beaten or killed.

These pogroms seared themselves into collective memory, passed from parent to child in stories and scars. They convinced many Jews, particularly in Eastern Europe, that life in exile — the diaspora — would never offer safety or dignity.

The Failure of Emancipation for many Jews, the 19th century was an age of dizzying contradictions. In one generation, they had moved from ghettos to parliaments, from the margins to the centre of European society. Yet the promise of equality was always conditional, always fragile. They could be successful, but not secure; integrated, but never fully accepted.

Even in places where antisemitism was less overt, Jews often found themselves convenient scapegoats in times of crisis. Economic downturns, political instability, or the rise of populist nationalism all too often revived old prejudices in new forms.

This reality was not lost on Jewish intellectuals and leaders. For some, the answer lay in further assimilation — to be so indispensable to their nations that antisemitism would wither away.

For others, particularly the young radicals of the late 19th century, the answer lay in socialism and revolutionary politics, in the belief that class solidarity could dissolve the divisions of race and religion.

But for a small and growing number, the conclusion was different, and far more radical: the problem was not that Jews were too visible or too foreign. The problem was that they had no state of their own.

The First Murmurings of Nationalism The idea that Jews constituted not merely a religious group but a nation — a people with shared history, language, and destiny — was not new. It had deep roots in religious tradition and collective memory, in prayers that ended with the words "Next year in Jerusalem." But in the late 19th century, this idea began to take on a modern, political form.

Influenced by the nationalist movements sweeping Europe — Italian unification, German unification, Polish independence — Jewish intellectuals began to argue that the Jews, too, were entitled to self-determination. In Eastern Europe, movements like Hovevei Zion ("Lovers of Zion") emerged, advocating for Jewish agricultural settlement in Palestine as a way of reviving the nation. These early Zionists were often religiously traditional but politically pragmatic, seeking to create a refuge from violence rather than a fully realised state.

In Western Europe, where assimilation seemed more possible, the idea was slower to take root. But the rise of political antisemitism, coupled with the public humiliations of cases like Dreyfus, began to erode the optimism of integration. A younger generation of thinkers, most famously Theodor Herzl, would soon give this emerging consciousness its name and its programme: political Zionism.

A Precarious Identity By the final decades of the 19th century, Jewish identity in Europe was fractured and contested. Was the future to be found in full assimilation and loyalty to the nation-states they inhabited? In revolution and the destruction of the old order? In religious revival and messianic hope? Or in the creation of a state of their own, a place where they could live as a majority and determine their own destiny?

This uncertainty — this sense of both belonging and alienation — was the crucible in which Zionism was born. It was an ideology forged not in the soil of Palestine but in the contradictions of Europe, shaped as much by fear as by aspiration.

For millions of Jews, the longing for security and dignity remained abstract, even impossible. Few could yet imagine the political movements, wars, and upheavals that would, within half a century, make the dream of a state a reality. But the foundations had been laid: the belief that safety required sovereignty, and that sovereignty required a return — whether physical, spiritual, or both — to an ancestral land.

## Section 2: Herzl the Holocaust: Refuge, and Statehood

If the antisemitism of 19th-century Europe provided the conditions for Zionism, Theodor Herzl provided its architecture. A cosmopolitan journalist and playwright, Herzl was not an obvious revolutionary. Born in 1860 into a middle-class, assimilated Jewish family in Budapest, he grew up more comfortable with Goethe than with the Talmud, more Viennese boulevardier than rabbinic scholar. Yet by the end of the century, he had become the father of political Zionism, the man who transformed a vague longing for return into a concrete political programme.

### The Dreyfus Affair and a Crisis of Faith

The turning point in Herzl's thinking is often traced back to the Dreyfus Affair. As a correspondent in Paris for the Viennese newspaper *Neue Freie Presse*, Herzl covered the trial of Captain Alfred Dreyfus, a Jewish officer falsely accused of treason in 1894. What struck Herzl was not only the miscarriage of justice but the ferocity of the public response. Parisian streets rang with chants of *À mort les Juifs! — Death to the Jews!* — in the heart of what many Jews believed was the most enlightened society in Europe.

For Herzl, the lesson was stark and unambiguous: assimilation had failed. No matter how European, how cultured, or how loyal, the Jew would always remain the outsider, the Other. In his diaries, Herzl wrote bitterly:

*If France — bastion of emancipation, progress and universal brotherhood — can get caught up in a maelstrom of antisemitism and let the Parisian crowd chant 'Death to the Jews,' where can they be safe once again — if not in their own country?*

This crisis of faith propelled Herzl to search for a solution not in individual integration or quiet endurance, but in collective sovereignty.

### Der Judenstaat — The Jewish State

In 1896, Herzl published *Der Judenstaat* (*The Jewish State*), a slim but electrifying pamphlet that would ignite a political movement. Its argument was direct and radical for its time:

• The Jews are a people, a nation bound by history, language, and culture.

• Antisemitism is a permanent feature of European society and cannot be eradicated by assimilation or reform.

• The only viable solution is the establishment of a Jewish state, where Jews would be masters of their own fate.

Herzl's vision was both pragmatic and utopian. He imagined a modern, technologically advanced state, governed rationally and offering refuge to Jews everywhere. Palestine was the preferred location, given its historical and spiritual resonance, but Herzl was pragmatic about geography; he even entertained proposals for settlements in Argentina and later British East Africa (the so-called "Uganda Plan"). What mattered was not the soil but the sovereignty.

## The First Zionist Congress

In 1897, Herzl convened the First Zionist Congress in Basel, Switzerland. Over 200 delegates — rabbis, intellectuals, businessmen, and activists — gathered to debate the future of the Jewish people. The Congress adopted a programme that became the foundation of the movement:

*Zionism seeks to establish a home for the Jewish people in Palestine secured under public law.*

Herzl understood the power of symbolism. He orchestrated the Congress with theatrical precision, from the formal dress code to the rousing speeches, presenting Zionism as a modern, disciplined political movement. In his diary, he wrote presciently:

*In Basel I founded the Jewish state. If I said this aloud today, I would be answered by universal laughter. Perhaps in five years, and certainly in fifty, everyone will perceive it.*

The Basel Congress marked the institutional birth of political Zionism, giving it a structure, a platform, and an international presence.

## Early Debates and Divisions

From the outset, Zionism was a movement of competing visions and internal tensions.

• Practical Zionists argued for immediate settlement and agricultural colonisation in Palestine, even without formal statehood.

• Political Zionists, led by Herzl, insisted that international recognition and legal guarantees had to come first.

• Religious Jews were divided: some saw the movement as a fulfilment of divine prophecy, while others condemned it as heresy, a human attempt to pre-empt God's redemption.

• Socialist Zionists envisioned a new, egalitarian society built on collective labour, laying the groundwork for the kibbutz movement.

These debates reflected the diversity of Jewish experience in Europe and the multiplicity of aspirations within the emerging nationalist framework.

**Opposition from Within**

Not all Jews embraced Herzl's vision. In Western Europe, where assimilation had brought relative comfort and social mobility, many viewed Zionism with suspicion or outright hostility. Prominent Jewish leaders argued that the push for a separate state would undermine their hard-won acceptance and fuel antisemitic accusations of dual loyalty.

The Reform movement in Germany declared:

*Germany is our fatherland. We are Germans of the Mosaic persuasion.*

In Eastern Europe, some Jewish communities gravitated toward socialism and the labour movement, seeing class struggle, not nationalism, as the path to liberation. The Bund, a Jewish socialist party founded in 1897, rejected Zionism as a bourgeois distraction from the fight for workers' rights and equality in their existing homelands.

**Early Practical Steps**

Despite resistance, Herzl pursued his vision with relentless energy. He sought audiences with European monarchs and political leaders, lobbying for support. He met with Kaiser Wilhelm II in 1898 during the German Emperor's visit to Palestine, hoping to secure backing for Jewish settlement under Ottoman oversight. The meeting yielded little, but it signalled Zionism's emergence as a player in international politics.

Meanwhile, small waves of Jewish immigrants, the First and Second Aliyot, began arriving in Palestine. These pioneers established agricultural colonies, often on land purchased from absentee landlords. They drained swamps, planted crops, and built the foundations of what would become a Jewish presence in the land. But their arrival also created friction with local Arab communities, many of whom saw the newcomers as outsiders supported by foreign capital and protected by imperial power.

### From Idea to Movement

By the early 20th century, Zionism had moved from the margins of Jewish thought to a movement with global reach. Branches of the Zionist Organisation sprang up across Europe, North America, and the Middle East. Newspapers, pamphlets, and public lectures spread the message of national revival. Fundraising campaigns, such as the Jewish National Fund, were established to purchase land in Palestine.

Herzl himself did not live to see the future he imagined; he died in 1904 at the age of 44. But his organisational genius and unyielding belief in the necessity of a Jewish state had set in motion forces that would reshape Jewish history.

### A Pragmatic Visionary

Herzl was not without his critics, even among early Zionists. Some accused him of naivety, others of elitism. Yet his great strength lay in his ability to transform an ancient longing into a modern political programme, one that could engage diplomats, inspire ordinary Jews, and adapt to changing circumstances.

His pragmatism, his willingness to consider Uganda or Argentina as interim refuges, has often been contrasted with the messianic attachment to the land of Israel that would dominate Zionist discourse in later decades. Herzl's Zionism was less about sacred soil than about safety, sovereignty, and survival.

## Section 3: Early Immigration and Settlement

If Herzl gave Zionism its political language, it was the early pioneers, the immigrants of the First Aliyah and Second Aliyah, who gave it physical form. Long before statehood, before borders and armies, Zionism was a movement of people carrying little more than hope, tools, and a belief in return.

### The First Aliyah (1882–1903)

The First Aliyah, beginning in 1882, was driven less by ideology than by necessity. Pogroms in the Russian Empire following the assassination of Tsar Alexander II, combined with deep economic hardship, drove thousands of Eastern European Jews to seek refuge. Most emigrated to the United States or Western Europe, but a small minority turned to Palestine, then a distant, underdeveloped province of the Ottoman Empire, as their destination.

These early settlers were not political Zionists in the Herzlian sense. Many were religious Jews motivated by faith, seeking to live in the land of their ancestors. Others were pragmatic, hoping to escape violence and poverty by working the land.

They founded agricultural communities such as Rishon LeZion, Petah Tikva, and Zikhron Ya'akov. The conditions were brutal: disease, inadequate infrastructure, and lack of farming experience led to high mortality and frequent financial collapse. These colonies survived largely thanks to support from wealthy benefactors such as Baron Edmond de Rothschild, who provided funds, expertise, and management, often at the cost of the settlers' autonomy.

### The Seeds of Tension

From the very beginning, these early settlements encountered tensions with local Arab communities. Under the Ottomans, Palestine was a multi-ethnic, multi-religious land, populated by Arabic-speaking Muslims, Christians, and Jews who had coexisted, not always peacefully, but without the sharp national boundaries that would later harden identities.

Land purchases during the First Aliyah were often made from absentee landlords based in Beirut, Damascus, or Istanbul. The peasants, the *fellahin*, who had worked the land for generations, were frequently displaced, sometimes with little or no compensation. To many Arabs, the newcomers were not neighbours but agents of foreign powers, arriving with foreign money and foreign ambitions.

At this stage, resistance was sporadic and localised: theft of livestock, skirmishes, and occasional attacks. But the seeds of mistrust were being sown. As historian Rashid Khalidi has argued, this period marked the beginning of an Arab awareness that Jewish immigration, though small in number, carried the potential to alter the demographic and political landscape of Palestine.

### The Second Aliyah (1904–1914)

The Second Aliyah, beginning in 1904 after the Kishinev pogroms and continuing until the outbreak of the First World War, brought a different type of immigrant. These were not primarily religious Jews but young, secular, often socialist pioneers, the *halutzim* (pioneers), inspired by a blend of nationalism and utopian idealism.

They spoke of building a "new Jew" — strong, self-reliant, rooted in the land, and free from the passivity they associated with life in the diaspora. This vision was both romantic and harsh, requiring physical endurance and ideological commitment in equal measure.

These pioneers laid the foundations of the kibbutz and *moshav* movements, collective and cooperative agricultural communities built on socialist principles. The kibbutz, in particular, became a powerful symbol of Zionism: egalitarian, ascetic, and communal, a society in miniature that blurred the lines between labour and ideology.

### Labour and Exclusivity

A defining principle of the Second Aliyah was "Hebrew labour" (*avodah ivrit*). The pioneers believed that Jews must cultivate the land themselves, rejecting dependence on Arab labour. This principle was both economic, aimed at self-sufficiency, and ideological, tied to the transformation of Jewish identity through productive work.

But the policy of Hebrew labour deepened tensions with local Arabs. It excluded them from jobs in the new settlements and reinforced a sense of separation between the Jewish newcomers and the indigenous population. Where the First Aliyah had been more pragmatic, employing local workers as needed, the Second Aliyah was openly exclusivist, a shift that would shape future relations in profound ways.

### Cultural and Linguistic Revival

The Second Aliyah also ignited a cultural renaissance. Hebrew, long a liturgical language, was revived as a spoken tongue, an extraordinary feat of linguistic nationalism led by figures like Eliezer Ben-Yehuda. Street signs, newspapers, schools, and workplaces became laboratories for a new Hebrew identity, one that linked the modern state-in-the-making to ancient heritage.

This cultural revival gave Zionism an emotional depth and cohesion that political organisation alone could not provide. It created a shared language, literally and figuratively, that bound the diverse waves of immigrants into a nascent national community.

### Women and the Pioneer Ethos

Women played a complex role in the early settlements. The pioneers of the Second Aliyah often espoused ideals of gender equality, and women worked alongside men in the fields and in the kibbutzim. Yet in practice, traditional gender roles persisted, and leadership positions were overwhelmingly male. The tension between ideology and reality would persist, mirroring broader struggles within Zionism between lofty ideals and pragmatic compromises.

## The Yishuv Takes Shape

By the eve of the First World War, the Jewish population in Palestine, the *Yishuv*, numbered around 85,000 out of a total population of roughly 700,000. It was still a small minority, but it was organised, cohesive, and increasingly self-aware. Institutions like the Jewish National Fund, the *Histadrut* (labour federation), and the embryonic defence organisations *Bar-Giora* and *Hashomer* laid the groundwork for what would later become the structures of statehood.

The *Yishuv* of this period was still fragile, dependent on foreign capital and vulnerable to local hostility, but it had begun to take on the characteristics of a national movement with a territorial base. As the world lurched toward war, that base, and the alliances it would soon form with global powers, would prove decisive.

## Arab Responses

For the Arab population of Palestine, the early decades of Zionist immigration were a period of growing unease and gradual politicisation. Local leaders and newspapers began to voice concerns that immigration was not a temporary refuge but part of a larger plan to transform Palestine. Petitions to the Ottoman authorities sought limits on land sales and immigration, but enforcement was weak, and economic pressures often outweighed political caution.

This period also saw the emergence of an educated Arab elite — teachers, lawyers, and journalists — who would become key figures in the political movements of the coming decades. While coexistence remained possible in many places, the fault lines of future conflict were already becoming visible.

## From Settlement to Strategy

The First and Second Aliyot were small in number, tens of thousands rather than hundreds of thousands, but their significance cannot be overstated. They established a physical foothold in the land, developed the organisational and economic structures of the *Yishuv*, and created a culture of resilience and self-reliance.

They also set patterns that would endure: a sense of pioneering mission, a belief in the transformative power of land and labour, and an undercurrent of exclusivity that complicated relations with the land's existing inhabitants.

By 1914, Zionism had moved beyond an idea in pamphlets and speeches. It had a base, a language, a community, and increasingly, the confidence that history was bending in its direction.

## Section 4: The Politics of Empire

If Zionism was born in the streets and salons of Europe, it found its first battleground in the decaying margins of empire. At the turn of the 20th century, Palestine was a provincial backwater of the Ottoman Empire, a quiet, largely agrarian society under the loose control of a state struggling to modernise and to survive.

For Jews imagining their national revival, this imperial context was not a blank canvas. It was a political landscape already shaped by local power structures, religious hierarchies, and the strategic ambitions of global powers.

### Ottoman Rule in Palestine

The Ottoman Empire had ruled Palestine since 1517. By the late 19th century, the empire was in steep decline, the "sick man of Europe," beset by internal rebellions, nationalist uprisings, and the encroachments of European powers.

Palestine itself was divided administratively between the sanjak of Jerusalem (reporting directly to Istanbul) and the vilayets of Beirut and Damascus. Local governance was often mediated through notables, the effendi families, who wielded significant influence in towns and villages.

The Ottomans were not hostile to Jewish immigration in principle, but they were wary of political movements that might destabilise their rule. Early Zionist settlers were subject to inconsistent oversight: in some periods, local officials facilitated land sales; in others, restrictions were imposed on immigration and land acquisition. Enforcement, however, was often lax or circumvented through bribes and legal loopholes.

**Britain, Empire, and the Colonial Mindset**

As the Ottoman Empire weakened, European powers circled. For Britain, Palestine was less about faith and more about geography: a crucial corridor between the Mediterranean and the Red Sea, near the Suez Canal, and vital to imperial communications with India.

Britain's approach to Palestine mirrored its approach to other colonies, Ireland most of all. In both lands, Britain played factions against each other, balancing competing claims while maintaining ultimate control. In Ireland, the strategy had been to contain nationalist aspirations through coercion and selective concessions, while cultivating loyalist communities. In Palestine, similar tactics would emerge: offering promises to Jews and Arabs alike, encouraging dependency, and assuming that imperial authority could manage competing claims indefinitely.

The echoes of empire were not abstract. When Britain assumed control of Palestine under the Mandate, it did so with methods and men already tested elsewhere. During the Irish War of Independence, London had unleashed the notorious "Black and Tans" — ex-soldiers recruited into the Royal Irish Constabulary who became infamous for their brutality, collective punishments, and terror against civilians. Their legacy was so reviled in Ireland that their very name became shorthand for colonial repression.

After Ireland, many of these same men, or men trained in their image, found themselves redeployed in Palestine. The British

Palestine Police Force, established in the 1920s, was staffed with veterans of the Irish conflict. They brought with them not only combat experience but also the tactics of collective reprisals, punitive house demolitions, and indiscriminate force against communities deemed rebellious. In effect, Palestine became the next "laboratory" for imperial policing, just as Ireland had been.

For Palestinians, this meant that the "civilising mission" of the Mandate came cloaked not in law or justice but in the dark uniforms and harsh methods of men already notorious on the streets of Cork and Dublin. For the Irish, watching from afar, the parallels were unmistakable: a small nation subjected to imported violence, its population disciplined not by consent but by the mailed fist of empire. It is no coincidence that Ireland would later prove among the most sympathetic voices for Palestine in Europe.

The result in both cases was eerily similar: deepening mistrust, simmering violence, and the legacy of unresolved grievances that would outlast the empire itself.

**European Rivalries and Zionist Diplomacy**

The Levant was also a theatre of European rivalry. France leveraged its historic ties to Christian communities; Russia styled itself the protector of Orthodox Christians; and Germany, under Kaiser Wilhelm II, sought to expand its influence in the region.

For Zionist leaders, these rivalries offered opportunity. Herzl, understanding the value of imperial patronage, sought audiences with anyone who could advance the cause. His meetings with the Kaiser in 1898, though diplomatically inconclusive, signalled that Zionism was no longer a fringe idea but a movement capable of engaging the great powers.

**The Tanzimat and Changing Power Dynamics**

The Tanzimat reforms of the mid-19th century, a series of modernisation efforts aimed at centralising and rationalising the empire, had profound consequences in Palestine. New land laws codified ownership and registration, often to the disadvantage of smallholders who had farmed plots for generations without formal title.

These changes made it easier for Zionist organisations and wealthy patrons, such as Baron Rothschild, to purchase large tracts of land from absentee landlords in Beirut, Damascus, or Istanbul. To the *fellahin* — the peasant farmers working the land — these transactions often came as a shock: their fields sold without their consent, their tenancy precarious, their displacement sudden.

Such dislocations sowed early resentment. While initial tensions were localised, the pattern of dispossession and exclusion began to foster a sense among Arab communities that Zionist settlement was not just migration but a colonial project backed by distant, powerful interests.

**European Eyes on the Levant**

Palestine was not only an Ottoman province; it was a prize in the Great Game of European imperial rivalry.

Britain, with its growing empire in India and its strategic interests in the Suez Canal (opened in 1869), viewed Palestine as a critical land bridge between the Mediterranean and the Red Sea. A friendly presence in the region, or at least one that was not hostile, was seen as a strategic imperative.

To many in Ireland, Britain's role in Palestine bore striking similarities to its own colonial experience: the imposition of control without genuine consent, the manipulation of communal divisions, and the quiet arrogance of an empire convinced of its civilising mission. These parallels were not forgotten; the seeds sown in Ireland's struggle would later shape its solidarity with Palestinians and help explain why, in the era of Gaza's devastation, Ireland emerged as one of Europe's most vocal critics of Israeli settlement and occupation.

France, with its historical ties to Levantine Christianity and a missionary presence in the Holy Land, nurtured its own ambitions. Russia claimed to see itself as the protector of Orthodox Christians in the region, while Germany under Kaiser Wilhelm II sought influence as it expanded its global footprint.

For Zionist leaders, these rivalries presented opportunities. Herzl, ever the strategist, believed that international sponsorship was essential. The fledgling movement could not secure a foothold in Palestine without the blessing, or at least the acquiescence, of the Ottomans and the support of a major European power.

### Herzl's Diplomacy

Herzl's diaries reveal a man as much diplomat as ideologue. He courted the Kaiser, seeking German support for a Jewish chartered company in Palestine under Ottoman sovereignty. In 1898, Herzl even travelled to Palestine to meet Wilhelm II during the Kaiser's state visit to Jerusalem. The meeting, immortalised in photographs, produced no tangible results but elevated the movement's profile.

Herzl also sought to engage Sultan Abdul Hamid II directly, offering to help restructure the empire's crippling foreign debt in exchange for permission to settle Jews in Palestine. The Sultan rebuffed the proposal, reportedly declaring:

*"I will not sell even a foot of the land, for it is not mine but belongs to my people. My people have fought for this land and watered it with their blood."*

Despite such rebuffs, Herzl's efforts laid the groundwork for a more sophisticated diplomatic strategy: to align the Zionist project with the geopolitical interests of a major imperial patron.

### Early British Interest

Britain's relationship with Zionism in this period was tentative but not indifferent. British officials recognised the potential utility of a loyal, Europeanised settler population in a strategically sensitive region. Figures such as Joseph Chamberlain, the Colonial Secretary, floated proposals for Jewish settlement in British territories, including the infamous "Uganda Plan" of 1903, which offered a tract of land in East Africa as a potential refuge.

The proposal split the movement. Some saw it as a pragmatic interim solution to the immediate crisis facing Eastern European Jews; others viewed it as a betrayal of the centrality of Palestine. The plan was ultimately rejected, but the debate revealed two enduring currents within Zionism: pragmatism and messianism, often in tension but never entirely separable.

## The Balance of Power

As the 20th century dawned, Zionism remained a minority movement within the global Jewish population, and its presence in Palestine was still small. But it had achieved two critical things: a foothold in the land and a growing capacity for political manoeuvre.

The *Yishuv* — the embryonic Jewish community in Palestine — was learning how to navigate the complexities of Ottoman administration, local power dynamics, and imperial diplomacy. The movement understood that statehood, or even secure settlement, could not be achieved by migration alone. It would require leverage, alliances, and the ability to align its aspirations with the strategic interests of great powers.

However, the world was changing rapidly. The Ottoman Empire was weakening, nationalist movements were rising across its territories, and Europe was sliding towards the catastrophe of World War I.

For Zionism, the coming upheaval would be decisive. What had begun as a dream and a diaspora movement would, within two decades, be propelled to the centre of international politics, not through numbers or strength alone, but through a combination of organisation, opportunism, and the extraordinary transformations of global power that war would bring.

## Section 5: Narratives and Myths

The building of nations, even before a state exists, begins with the stories of its peoples. For Zionism, stories were not mere embellishment; they were central to its power and appeal. They shaped how Jews in the diaspora saw their mission, how early pioneers justified their hardships, and how Arab communities interpreted — and resisted — the arrival of newcomers.

These narratives, forged in the crucible of displacement, aspiration, and fear, would become the bedrock of identity and, in time, of a terrible conflict.

### "A Land Without a People for a People Without a Land"

Few slogans capture the early Zionist ethos more clearly than the phrase:

*A land without a people for a people without a land.*

Popularised in the late 19th century, the slogan crystallised a powerful idea: that Palestine was empty, neglected, waiting for its rightful heirs to return. It was an idea rooted less in empirical reality than in myth-making — a way to frame immigration and settlement not as colonisation but as restoration.

In reality, Palestine at the time of the First and Second *Aliyot* was home to hundreds of thousands of Arabic-speaking Muslims and Christians, as well as long-established Jewish communities. Towns such as Jerusalem, Jaffa, and Hebron bustled with commerce; villages tilled the land and tended olive groves; trade routes connected the Levant to Damascus, Cairo, and Istanbul.

Yet the narrative of an "empty land" served a purpose. It was an early example of the power of language that future Israelis could exploit. It erased the presence of the Arab population from the story of return, allowing early settlers to imagine themselves as pioneers reclaiming a barren, neglected land rather than newcomers entering a complex, living society.

## Redemption Through Labour

Another formative narrative was that of redemption through labour. For many of the pioneers of the Second *Aliyah*, the Jewish condition in the diaspora was defined by weakness and dependence. The cure, they believed, was physical labour — the transformation of Jews into farmers, builders, and soldiers.

The land itself became a symbol of rebirth. Working the soil was not just an economic necessity; it was an act of national and spiritual renewal. Collective farming communities — the *kibbutzim* — were celebrated as utopian laboratories where class distinctions were dissolved and the "new Jew" was forged.

This ethos fostered remarkable resilience and solidarity, but it also had exclusionary dimensions. The insistence on Hebrew labour — the discriminatory refusal to employ Arab workers — reinforced divisions between communities and planted early seeds of segregation.

## The Eternal Return

At the heart of Zionism was the narrative of return: the belief that Jews were not newcomers to Palestine but exiles returning to their ancestral home after two millennia. This idea drew on deep religious and historical currents — the biblical promise of the land to Abraham and his descendants, the destruction of the Second Temple, and the long exile marked by prayers ending with *Next year in Jerusalem.*

This narrative resonated powerfully across the diaspora, offering a sense of continuity and purpose. For religious Jews, it was the fulfilment of prophecy; for secular Jews, it provided a historical and cultural anchor in a rapidly modernising and often hostile world.

But this same narrative, while affirming for Jews, could feel erasing for Palestinians. To them, the idea that the land was waiting to be "redeemed" implied that their presence — their villages, their olive groves, their centuries of rootedness — was invisible or irrelevant.

This tension, between the redemptive narrative of return and the reality of an existing society, would become one of the defining fault lines of the conflict.

## The Arab Awakening

If Zionism developed its myths of return and renewal, so too did the Arab population of Palestine begin to craft its own narratives in response. Local newspapers in Jaffa and Jerusalem published editorials warning of organised immigration and land purchases. Religious leaders spoke of the land as an Islamic trust — a *waqf* — to be safeguarded for future generations.

To many Arabs, the newcomers were not refugees seeking safety but colonists backed by foreign powers, buying land through absentee landlords and displacing tenant farmers. Early petitions to Ottoman authorities and local protests framed the movement as a threat to social and economic stability and, increasingly, to political sovereignty.

This early politicisation did not yet amount to an organised nationalist movement, but the seeds were there: a sense that the land was not empty, that its people had a claim, and that their future was being rewritten without their consent.

## Myth, Reality, and the Power of Narrative

Myths are not lies; they are simplified truths that organise complex realities into stories people can hold and share. For early Zionists, the myth of an empty land and the promise of redemption provided cohesion and purpose. For Arabs in Palestine, the emerging narrative of resistance provided identity and urgency in the face of change.

But myths, once entrenched, have consequences. They shape perceptions, justify policies, and harden identities. The early Zionist belief that Palestine was "empty" or "underutilised" allowed settlers to downplay the moral implications of displacing existing communities. Conversely, the Arab narrative that saw Zionist immigration as an imperial plot set the stage for resistance that would soon take on organised, militant forms.

### The Collision Course

By the eve of World War I, these competing narratives were on a collision course. Zionism was gaining international traction, buoyed by its organisational strength and diaspora networks. Arab communities were becoming more politically aware, if not yet fully mobilised.

The gap between perception and reality — between a land imagined as empty and a land experienced as home — would only widen in the decades to come, as war, diplomacy, and mass migration turned a contest over land into a contest over history itself.

## Section 6: The Road to Balfour

By the early 20th century, Zionism was still a minority movement among the world's Jews. The majority were focused on survival, assimilation, or emigration to places like the United States. But history was about to intervene.

The collapse of empires and the seismic shifts unleashed by the First World War would propel the idea of a Jewish homeland from the margins of political debate to the heart of international diplomacy. In 1917, Britain would issue a 67-word statement, the Balfour Declaration, that transformed Zionism from aspiration to geopolitical reality.

### The World at War

The outbreak of the First World War in 1914 plunged Europe into chaos. The Ottoman Empire, aligned with Germany and Austria-Hungary, suddenly found itself at war with Britain, France, and Russia. Palestine, once a distant provincial backwater, became a zone of strategic importance, a bridge between Asia and Africa, adjacent to the Suez Canal and vital to imperial communications.

For Britain, the war turned abstract interests in the Levant into pressing priorities. Protecting the Suez Canal, securing overland routes to India, and countering Ottoman influence became central to its strategy. At the same time, Britain began looking for ways to mobilise support from various communities — Arabs, Jews, and others — in a global conflict where alliances were currency.

**The Diplomatic Chessboard**

In this environment, Zionist leaders saw an opening. Chaim Weizmann, a chemist and committed Zionist based in Manchester, became the movement's most effective diplomat. Unlike Herzl, who had sought patronage through grand gestures, Weizmann excelled at quiet persuasion, cultivating personal relationships with key British officials and framing Zionist aspirations as aligned with British interests.

Weizmann's pitch was simple but shrewd: a Jewish homeland in Palestine, under British protection, would serve as a loyal outpost in a strategically vital region. It would not only offer refuge to persecuted Jews but also project British power across the Eastern Mediterranean.

**Britain's Strategic Calculations**

Britain's interest in supporting Zionism was never purely altruistic. It was shaped by three overlapping considerations:

1. **Imperial Strategy** – Control of Palestine would safeguard the approaches to the Suez Canal and secure a buffer against French or German ambitions in the region.

2. **Global Influence** – British leaders believed that public support for Zionism could bolster wartime alliances, particularly with Jewish communities in the United States

and Russia, where they hoped to sway opinion and secure financial backing for the war effort.

3. **Post-War Planning** – As Britain and France began negotiating the post-Ottoman map of the Middle East, a foothold in Palestine promised strategic advantage in an era of expanding imperial competition.

## The Arab Dimension

Britain's overtures to Zionist leaders came alongside simultaneous promises to Arab leaders. In the Hussein-McMahon correspondence (1915–1916), British officials encouraged Sharif Hussein of Mecca to lead an Arab revolt against the Ottomans, promising independence for Arab lands in return.

These parallel commitments — to both Jews and Arabs — were contradictory, though at the time Britain assumed it could manage the ambiguity. The later exposure of the Sykes-Picot Agreement (1916), secretly dividing Ottoman territories between Britain and France, only deepened the sense of betrayal felt by Arab leaders.

## The Balfour Declaration

On 2 November 1917, Britain issued the Balfour Declaration, named after Foreign Secretary Arthur James Balfour. Addressed to Lord Rothschild, a leader of the British Jewish community, it read:

*"His Majesty's Government view with favour the establishment in Palestine of a national home for the Jewish people, and will use their best endeavours to facilitate the achievement of this object, it being clearly understood that nothing shall be done which may prejudice the civil and religious rights of existing non-Jewish communities in Palestine, or the rights and political status enjoyed by Jews in any other country."*

This carefully crafted sentence was at once vague and momentous. It promised support for "a national home", deliberately avoiding the language of "statehood", while nodding to the rights of "non-Jewish communities", who, though unnamed, made up over 90 per cent of the population of Palestine.

### Immediate Reactions

Among Zionists, the declaration was greeted with euphoria. For the first time, a major world power had endorsed their project. Chaim Weizmann, who would later become Israel's first president, called it "the Magna Carta of Jewish history."

In Palestine, however, the reaction was starkly different. Arab leaders viewed the declaration as a betrayal, a sign that their lands were being promised to another people without their consent. The seeds of future resistance — and future violence — were sown in that moment.

### Ambiguity and Opportunity

The ambiguity of the Balfour Declaration was deliberate. For Britain, it allowed maximum flexibility in a fluid wartime situation. For Zionists, it provided a foothold in international law and a platform to accelerate immigration, fundraising, and institution-building.

But the tensions embedded in those 67 words — between a Jewish "national home" and the rights of "non-Jewish communities" — would haunt the region for decades. Britain had effectively set in motion a dual promise it could not reconcile: to facilitate Jewish settlement while preserving the rights of an indigenous population that had never been consulted.

### The War's End and a New Order

By the end of the First World War, the geopolitical map of the Middle East had been redrawn. The Ottoman Empire collapsed, and Britain assumed control of Palestine under a League of Nations mandate. What had begun as a small, contested migration project was now under the aegis of the world's dominant empire.

For Zionists, the combination of British sponsorship and a legal mandate provided unprecedented opportunities. For Palestinians, it marked the beginning of dispossession under the shadow of a foreign power.

The road to Balfour was paved with strategy, diplomacy, and opportunism — but also with profound miscalculations. Britain believed it could manage competing promises, that Arabs and Jews could be balanced in a single imperial equation. In reality, the stage had been set for a century of tension, mistrust, and violence.

# CHAPTER TWO

## Section 1: The Holocaust and the Urgency for Statehood

The Second World War ended not with triumph for Europe's Jews but with desolation. Six million had been murdered in ghettos, forests, and death camps across Nazi-occupied Europe. Communities that had existed for centuries — Vilnius, Warsaw, Salonika, Kraków — were erased almost overnight. Survivors emerged from the camps skeletal and traumatised, often to find their homes occupied or destroyed and their neighbours indifferent, if not openly hostile, to their return.

For the Zionist movement, the Holocaust, or *Shoah*, was a watershed. It validated Herzl's grim warning that antisemitism was not a temporary malady but a structural reality of the diaspora. The logic of Zionism, once debated within Jewish communities, now seemed incontrovertible: Jews needed a state, not tomorrow, not as a distant dream, but immediately, as a matter of survival.

### Displaced Persons and Statelessness

In 1945, Europe was littered with displaced persons (DP) camps. These makeshift facilities, established by Allied authorities, housed hundreds of thousands of Jewish survivors alongside millions of others uprooted by the war. Conditions were often grim: barracks hastily converted into dormitories, meagre rations, little medical care, and profound psychological scars.

For many survivors, the idea of returning "home" was impossible. Properties had been confiscated, families annihilated, and communities shattered. In Poland and Hungary, antisemitic violence flared even after the war, with pogroms such as Kielce in 1946 demonstrating that liberation had not brought safety.

The DP camps became fertile ground for Zionist organisers. Agents of the Jewish Agency and the Haganah, the main underground defence organisation in Palestine, arrived with literature, promises, and logistical support. They helped organise illegal immigration to Palestine, offering survivors a path out of limbo and into a collective project of renewal.

### The British White Paper and Restricted Immigration

But the road to Palestine was blocked. Britain, which had governed Palestine under a League of Nations mandate since 1920, maintained strict immigration limits under the 1939 White Paper. The policy, introduced to placate Arab opposition during the Arab Revolt (1936–39), capped Jewish immigration at 75,000 over five years and required Arab consent for further arrivals — consent that would never be granted.

In the aftermath of the Holocaust, this restriction seemed not only unjust but cruel. Ships carrying survivors, such as the *Exodus 1947*, which attempted to land 4,500 Jewish refugees in Palestine, were intercepted by the British Navy and forced back to Europe. Images of exhausted, stateless Jews being turned away from what they saw as their only refuge shocked global opinion and eroded Britain's moral authority.

For Zionist leaders, these episodes were propaganda gold. They illustrated, in stark and emotional terms, that there was no safety for Jews without sovereignty, and no sovereignty without a state in Palestine.

### American and Soviet Calculations

The post-war years also saw a dramatic shift in global power. Britain, exhausted and financially weakened by six years of war, was retreating from its imperial commitments. The United States and the Soviet Union emerged as the two dominant powers, each with its own reasons for taking an interest in the fate of Palestine.

President Harry Truman, moved by both humanitarian concern and domestic political considerations, pressed Britain to allow greater Jewish immigration. His appeals were shaped by lobbying from American Jewish organisations and by the broader geopolitical imperative of stabilising the Middle East.

The Soviet Union, meanwhile, saw support for a Jewish state as a way to accelerate Britain's retreat from the region and potentially gain influence over a socialist-oriented Jewish leadership in Palestine. This convergence of interests, rare in the early days of the Cold War, would prove decisive in the diplomatic battles to come.

### Zionist Strategy After 1945

Within the Yishuv, the Jewish community in Palestine, the trauma of the Holocaust hardened resolve. For leaders like David Ben-Gurion, head of the Jewish Agency, the lesson was clear: passive reliance on others had failed. The only path forward was to build a state, secure international recognition, and prepare for armed defence.

The Haganah expanded recruitment and training, while its more militant counterparts, the Irgun and the Lehi (also known as the Stern Gang), intensified their insurgency against British targets, bombing railways, police stations, and administrative buildings. To some, these groups were freedom fighters; to others, they were terrorists. But their message was unmistakable: Britain could no longer govern Palestine without cost.

### The Moral Imperative

For ordinary Jews, the moral imperative was visceral. The Holocaust had stripped away illusions about safety in the diaspora. For survivors, Palestine was not merely a destination; it was redemption, dignity, and the promise of collective strength in place of perpetual vulnerability.

Letters from survivors to relatives in Palestine capture this urgency:

*"We have nothing left here. No home, no family, no life. Only in Eretz Yisrael can we be whole again."*

This emotional urgency also reframed the Zionist narrative for the world. No longer was the movement a utopian experiment in nation-building. It was a humanitarian necessity, a response to the greatest atrocity in modern history. That argument, amplified through lobbying, media campaigns, and personal testimony, resonated deeply in the corridors of power from Washington to Moscow.

### Britain's Waning Grip

For Britain, the post-war situation in Palestine became untenable. The mandate had been difficult enough to administer in the interwar years; after 1945, it became a quagmire. British soldiers patrolled roads under constant threat of ambush, while international condemnation grew louder with every intercepted refugee ship and every photograph of children behind barbed wire in Cyprus detention camps.

Financial strain compounded the problem. Britain, heavily indebted to the United States, lacked the resources or political will to maintain an unpopular and increasingly violent colonial administration. By 1947, London had made its decision: the "Palestine problem" would be handed to the newly formed United Nations.

### A Movement Transformed

The Holocaust did not create Zionism, but it transformed it. What had been one solution among many — assimilation, socialism, Bundism — became, for many Jews, the only viable path. The horrors of the camps made sovereignty an existential imperative, while the inability or unwillingness of the international community to provide refuge sharpened the sense of urgency.

By the time Britain referred the issue to the United Nations, Zionism was no longer a marginal project. It was a disciplined, well-organised movement with an armed presence on the ground, a sophisticated diplomatic network abroad, and the moral weight of an unspeakable tragedy behind it.

The stage was set for the next phase of the struggle, one that would turn Palestine into the epicentre of competing national movements, irreconcilable narratives, and a conflict that would shape the modern Middle East.

## Section 2: The UN Partition Plan (1947)

By the summer of 1947, Britain had run out of options and patience. The mandate over Palestine, assumed in 1920 as a strategic prize of empire, had become a grinding liability. Violence from Jewish militias, resistance from Arab communities, and international condemnation over refugee ships intercepted at sea combined to make Palestine, in the words of one weary British official, "a poisoned chalice".

Unable to impose a solution acceptable to both Jews and Arabs, Britain announced it would hand the problem to the newly formed United Nations. What followed would reshape the modern Middle East and set the stage for a conflict that continues to this day.

### The Creation of UNSCOP

The UN established the United Nations Special Committee on Palestine (UNSCOP) in May 1947. Composed of representatives from eleven countries, including Canada, Sweden, India, Australia, and Czechoslovakia, the committee was tasked with investigating the situation on the ground and recommending a path forward.

UNSCOP members travelled extensively in Palestine, visiting cities, towns, and kibbutzim, and met with leaders from both Jewish and Arab communities. They also visited displaced persons camps in Europe, where the plight of Holocaust survivors made an indelible impression. Jewish leaders skilfully presented the narrative of a people in need of a homeland, highlighting agricultural achievements, thriving communities, and the moral claim born of unparalleled suffering.

Arab leaders, in contrast, largely boycotted the proceedings, believing that participation would legitimise a process they saw as inherently biased towards Zionist claims. Instead, they issued statements rejecting any plan that did not guarantee a unitary state with an Arab majority.

## The Partition Proposal

On 31 August 1947, UNSCOP issued its majority report, recommending the partition of Palestine into two states:

• A Jewish state, encompassing roughly 55% of the territory, including the fertile coastal plain, the Jezreel Valley, and much of the Negev Desert.

• An Arab state, comprising the hill country of the West Bank, the Gaza Strip, and the northern Galilee region.

• Jerusalem, with its profound religious significance, would be placed under international administration as a *corpus separatum*, a separate, neutral entity.

The proposal allocated a majority of the land to the Jewish state, despite Jews making up only one-third of the population and owning less than 7% of the land. Proponents justified this imbalance by pointing to expected waves of Jewish immigration and the need for viable territorial contiguity.

For Zionist leaders, the report was not perfect. Jerusalem outside their control was a bitter pill, but it was good enough. It provided international legitimacy, a legal foundation for statehood, and, critically, a green light for immigration and institutional consolidation.

**Lobbying and the Vote**

The run-up to the vote on the partition plan was one of the most intense lobbying campaigns in the early history of the United Nations. The Jewish Agency, under the leadership of Chaim Weizmann and Abba Hillel Silver, mobilised diaspora communities, leveraged personal relationships, and appealed to the moral weight of the Holocaust.

The United States, under President Harry Truman, lobbied aggressively for passage, influenced by both humanitarian concern and domestic political considerations. The Soviet Union, eager to weaken Britain's imperial grip in the region, also threw its support behind partition, an unusual moment of Cold War alignment.

On 29 November 1947, the UN General Assembly voted on Resolution 181. The results were:

- 33 in favour
- 13 against
- 10 abstentions

The jubilation in Jewish communities around the world was immediate and unrestrained. In Tel Aviv, crowds danced in the streets, waving flags and singing, convinced that statehood was now inevitable. Newspapers declared the dawn of a new era, and young men and women rushed to enlist in the Haganah to prepare for the coming conflict.

**Arab Rejection and the Seeds of War**

For the Arab population of Palestine, and for the surrounding Arab states, the vote was an unmitigated disaster. To them, partition was a foreign imposition, a violation of the principle of self-determination, and an act of dispossession sanctioned by the international community.

How, they asked, could a population that was still a minority be granted the majority of the land? How could their homes, farms, and cities be handed to another people by a vote of nations thousands of miles away? The Arab League issued a statement rejecting the plan outright, declaring that it would never accept the division of Palestine or the establishment of a Jewish state.

The rejection was not only political but emotional. Many Arabs saw partition as the culmination of decades of betrayal: by Britain, which had promised independence during the First World War; by the Balfour Declaration, which had privileged Jewish aspirations; and now by a global order that seemed indifferent to their claims.

## Escalation of Violence

The passage of Resolution 181 marked the point of no return. Almost immediately, violence erupted across the country. In Jerusalem, Jaffa, and Haifa, clashes between Jewish and Arab militias escalated into bombings, ambushes, and reprisals. Roads became dangerous, convoys were attacked, and markets turned into battlegrounds.

The Haganah, the organised military wing of the Yishuv, began to transition from defensive operations to strategic offensives, while more radical groups like the Irgun and Lehi carried out bombings and assassinations aimed at intimidating Arab communities and undermining British authority.

Arab militias, less centralised and less well-armed, responded with sporadic attacks, but coordination was limited, and local leaders often acted independently. The result was a spiral of violence that neither side could, or wished to, control.

## Britain's Retreat

Caught between escalating violence and international scrutiny, Britain accelerated its withdrawal. By early 1948, British forces were concentrating in coastal enclaves and key bases, leaving much of the countryside effectively ungoverned. Administrative functions crumbled, and the space between British retreat and the formal end of the mandate became a vacuum filled by militias, fear, and the growing inevitability of full-scale war.

### The Fragile Promise of Partition

For the Zionist movement, partition represented a historic victory: international recognition and a pathway to statehood. But leaders like David Ben-Gurion understood that the vote was only the beginning. Arab rejection meant that any attempt to implement the plan would be met with force. Preparations for war, including military training, arms smuggling, and strategic planning, accelerated in anticipation of what was to come.

For Palestinians, the partition plan became the symbol of betrayal and dispossession, a turning point that transformed political opposition into armed resistance. In towns and villages, families began to prepare for what they knew would follow: violence, uncertainty, and the fight for their homes.

By early 1948, the contours of the conflict were set — a Jewish community determined to turn international legitimacy into sovereignty, and an Arab population unwilling to accept what they saw as the theft of their land under the auspices of the global order. The fragile promise of Resolution 181 had, within weeks, become the prelude to war.

## Section 3: Civil War – November 1947 to May 1948

The vote for UN Resolution 181 on 29 November 1947 was met with dancing in the streets of Tel Aviv, and dread in the streets of Jaffa, Haifa, and Jerusalem. For Jews in Palestine, partition was a green light for statehood, the culmination of decades of organisation and sacrifice. For Arabs, it was a sentence of dispossession, passed without their consent by distant powers. Within hours of the announcement, violence erupted. By dawn, Palestine was sliding into civil war.

## The First Shots

On 30 November, Arab fighters ambushed two buses carrying Jewish passengers near Lydda. In retaliation, Haganah units attacked Arab villages suspected of harbouring the attackers. What followed was a grim pattern of tit-for-tat violence that would escalate steadily over the next six months.

Markets that had been shared for decades became zones of fear. Roads were dangerous, and public transport convoys required armed escorts. Bombings, shootings, and ambushes became daily events. Ordinary life disintegrated as trust collapsed and communities turned inward, preparing for the inevitability of war.

## The Haganah and the Jewish Militias

At the centre of the Yishuv's strategy was the Haganah, the main paramilitary organisation of the Jewish community. Founded in the 1920s as a defensive force, by 1947 the Haganah had evolved into a disciplined, semi-professional military with tens of thousands of trained fighters, an intelligence network, and access to arms smuggled from Europe.

Under the leadership of David Ben-Gurion, the Haganah began to shift from a purely defensive posture to an offensive strategy aimed at securing Jewish settlements, maintaining supply routes, and preparing for the expected invasion by Arab armies after the British withdrawal.

Alongside the Haganah were two more radical groups:

• **Irgun (Etzel)**, led by Menachem Begin, a nationalist militia willing to use terrorist tactics to achieve its goals.

• **Lehi (the Stern Gang)**, a smaller but even more militant faction, infamous for its assassinations and bombings.

These groups often operated independently, and sometimes in defiance of the Haganah, but their actions, particularly attacks on Arab civilians, helped sow fear and deepen the spiral of violence.

**Arab Response and Fragmentation**

On the Arab side, the response to partition was immediate and fierce but hampered by disunity. The Arab Higher Committee, led by Haj Amin al-Husseini, the exiled Grand Mufti of Jerusalem, called for a general strike and organised local militias, but coordination was limited and resources scarce.

Arab fighters, often local volunteers rather than trained soldiers, relied on small arms and hit-and-run tactics. Rural villages formed defence committees, while in urban centres like Jaffa and Jerusalem, irregular forces attempted to impose control.

By early 1948, Fawzi al-Qawuqji, a veteran of earlier Arab revolts, had arrived to lead the Arab Liberation Army (ALA), composed of volunteers from neighbouring Arab countries. But his forces, though symbolically important, were poorly equipped and lacked cohesion.

**The British Vacuum**

As violence escalated, Britain, weary of its mandate, began to disengage. Soldiers were ordered to avoid confrontation unless directly attacked. Police stations were abandoned, and administrative functions slowed to a crawl.

The result was a power vacuum. In areas with strong Jewish organisation, the Haganah and local committees stepped in to maintain order, enforce curfews, and distribute food. In Arab areas, authority was more fragmented, with local leaders struggling to coordinate under the pressure of raids and reprisals.

By early 1948, British rule existed largely on paper. The real power in much of Palestine had shifted to armed militias.

**Plan Dalet and Strategic Shifts**

By March 1948, as the British prepared to leave, the Jewish leadership concluded that a decisive military strategy was necessary to secure the territory allocated to the Jewish state under the UN plan, and, where possible, beyond it.

The result was Plan Dalet (Plan D), adopted by the Haganah in March. Its objectives included:

- Securing key roads and supply routes.

- Occupying Arab villages deemed strategically significant.

- Expelling, where necessary, hostile populations that could threaten Jewish control.

Plan Dalet has been the subject of fierce historical debate. Israeli historians such as Benny Morris have described it as a military necessity in the context of escalating war; others, like Ilan Pappé, have characterised it as a blueprint for systematic ethnic cleansing. What is clear is that by April 1948, Plan Dalet marked a shift from defensive operations to offensive campaigns aimed at consolidating control.

## Urban Battlefields

The cities became the most contested spaces in this phase of the war.

In Jerusalem, Arab fighters imposed a blockade on the city's 100,000 Jewish residents, cutting off food and water supplies. Haganah convoys, often under heavy fire, attempted to resupply the besieged neighbourhoods via the narrow road from Tel Aviv, a route that would become infamous as the "Burma Road."

In Haifa, violence spiralled in early 1948 as Arab snipers targeted Jewish neighbourhoods and the Haganah responded with mortar fire and coordinated assaults. By April, as British troops withdrew, Jewish forces launched Operation Bi'ur Hametz, seizing key positions and taking control of the city. Tens of thousands of Arab residents fled, many by boat, under a combination of fear, chaos, and sporadic violence.

**The Deir Yassin Massacre**

One event in this period would leave an indelible scar on Palestinian memory: the massacre at Deir Yassin.

On 9 April 1948, fighters from the Irgun and Lehi attacked the Arab village of Deir Yassin, near Jerusalem. The village had not been a significant military threat, but its strategic location made it a target. By the end of the operation, over 100 villagers, men, women, and children, were dead. Survivors recounted scenes of brutality; Jewish leaders condemned the attack, but the damage was done.

News of Deir Yassin spread rapidly, amplified by Arab media and word of mouth. For Palestinians, it was proof that the Zionist militias were not just fighting for territory but driving out the Arab population by force. For the Yishuv, it became a double-edged sword: militarily advantageous as Arab communities abandoned their homes, but diplomatically damaging as the world recoiled from the violence.

**Collapse of Arab Resistance**

By May 1948, the balance of power in the civil war had shifted decisively. The Haganah, now reorganised into the backbone of what would become the Israel Defence Forces (IDF), controlled most of the territory allocated to the Jewish state under the UN plan. Supply lines were secured, key cities such as Haifa and Tiberias were under Jewish control, and morale in the Yishuv was high.

Arab resistance, hampered by poor organisation, lack of resources, and limited external support, was collapsing. Villages were being depopulated, sometimes under fire, sometimes in fear of atrocities like Deir Yassin, and sometimes under direct orders from Arab commanders advising temporary evacuation.

**The Road to Statehood**

As the British prepared to end their mandate on 14 May 1948, the Yishuv stood ready to declare independence. Its military position was strong, its political institutions robust, and its leadership united behind David Ben-Gurion.

For Palestinians, the situation was increasingly desperate. Hundreds of thousands had already fled or been forced from their homes, and the prospect of war with neighbouring Arab states offered little hope of reversal. What had begun as a civil war between communities was about to become a regional conflict, one that would decide not only the borders of the new state but the fate of a people.

## Section 4: Declaration of the State of Israel (May 14, 1948)

By May 1948, the British Mandate in Palestine was in its final days. In Jerusalem, the Union Jack still fluttered above government buildings, but British rule was all but gone, its authority replaced by a fragile patchwork of militias, local committees, and chaos. In Tel Aviv, David Ben-Gurion and the leadership of the Jewish Agency were preparing for a moment they had spent decades imagining, organising, and, in recent years, fighting to secure.

### The Political Calculus

The decision to declare independence before the British withdrawal was complete was not inevitable. Some within the Yishuv urged caution, worried that a premature declaration would provoke an immediate and overwhelming response from neighbouring Arab states. Others argued that delay risked losing the initiative and, with it, the legitimacy conferred by the UN vote.

Ben-Gurion, ever the strategist, chose to seize the moment. He recognised that time favoured the Yishuv: Jewish forces controlled most of the territory allocated under the partition plan, morale was high after a series of military successes, and international sympathy, particularly in the United States and the Soviet Union, could be harnessed to secure early recognition.

**The Declaration**

On the afternoon of 14 May 1948, as the last British soldiers prepared to leave, members of the Jewish National Council gathered in a modest hall at the Tel Aviv Museum. At exactly 4.00 p.m., Ben-Gurion stood before the assembled leaders and read the *Declaration of the Establishment of the State of Israel*:

"The Land of Israel was the birthplace of the Jewish people. Here their spiritual, religious and political identity was shaped… After being forcibly exiled from their land, the people kept faith with it throughout their dispersion… Accordingly, we… hereby declare the establishment of a Jewish state in Eretz-Israel, to be known as the State of Israel."

The declaration was brief but deliberate, blending historical claim with modern political language. It invoked the biblical connection to the land, referenced the Holocaust as moral justification, and pledged that the new state would ensure equality "irrespective of religion, race or sex," while extending an invitation of peace to neighbouring Arab states.

Outside, in the streets of Tel Aviv, the announcement was met with unrestrained jubilation. Crowds gathered, singing, dancing, and waving improvised flags. In cafés and on rooftops, people embraced strangers, their joy tempered by the knowledge that war, larger and more brutal than anything yet seen, was only hours away.

**Immediate Recognition**

Within minutes of the declaration, the United States, under President Harry Truman, extended de facto recognition to the new state, a diplomatic coup that bolstered Israel's legitimacy and morale. The Soviet Union followed quickly with de jure recognition, signalling a rare moment of alignment between the two emerging superpowers.

For Ben-Gurion and the leadership, this was no small victory. Early recognition ensured access to critical political and economic support and signalled to the world that the Jewish state, once a dream, now existed as a legal and political fact.

## The Arab Invasion

If independence was a triumph, it was also an alarm bell. The day after the declaration, armies from Egypt, Jordan, Syria, Lebanon, and Iraq crossed into the former Mandate territory. What had been a civil war between Jewish and Arab communities became a full-scale regional conflict.

The balance of forces was complex. The Arab armies, though larger and better equipped in some respects, were poorly coordinated and often driven by competing agendas. Jordan's Arab Legion, trained and commanded by British officers, focused on securing the West Bank and East Jerusalem rather than destroying the nascent Jewish state. Egypt's army, less disciplined, advanced through the south towards Tel Aviv but quickly bogged down.

For the Yishuv, the war became an existential struggle. Outnumbered and outgunned, Jewish forces relied on superior organisation, high morale, and the cohesion of a society mobilised for total war. Every man, woman, and child in the Yishuv contributed — in the fields, in the factories, or on the front lines.

## Jerusalem Under Siege

Nowhere was the battle more desperate than in Jerusalem. The city, sacred to three religions, was encircled by Arab forces, and its Jewish population faced severe shortages of food, water, and medicine. Convoys attempting to break the blockade were ambushed and casualties mounted. The creation of the makeshift "Burma Road", a rough track through the hills, eventually provided a lifeline, but the city remained under siege for much of the war.

## A State in the Making

Even as fighting raged, the machinery of statehood began to take shape. Ministries were formed, the provisional government met daily, and the Haganah was transformed into the Israel Defence Forces (IDF), a unified military under central command.

Ben-Gurion's leadership in this period was decisive. He pushed through difficult decisions, often overriding opposition from within his own ranks, and laid the foundations of a state that would not only survive the war but emerge stronger and more cohesive.

## The Symbolism of 14 May

The declaration of independence remains one of the most significant moments in modern Jewish history — a moment of rebirth and return, of collective triumph against unimaginable odds. But for Palestinians, 14 May is remembered very differently. It was not a day of liberation but the beginning of the *Nakba*, the catastrophe that would see over 700,000 people expelled or fleeing from their homes.

This duality — one people's independence as another's dispossession — is the defining paradox of 1948, and the source of a wound that, decades later, remains unhealed.

# Section 5: The Nakba – Catastrophe and Dispossession

For Jews, the spring and summer of 1948 were the fulfilment of a collective dream, the establishment of a sovereign state after millennia of statelessness, persecution, and genocide. For Palestinians, it was *al-Nakba* — the catastrophe. Over 700,000 people, more than half the Arab population of Mandatory Palestine, were uprooted from their homes. Hundreds of villages were depopulated, many erased entirely. Cities that had been shared spaces — Jaffa, Haifa, Lydda, Acre — became sites of flight, fear, and irrevocable loss.

The *Nakba* is not just history; it is a living trauma, passed from generation to generation. It is the key to understanding the enduring bitterness of the conflict and why, even today, any discussion of peace or reconciliation inevitably returns to the events of 1948.

### The Waves of Displacement

The exodus of Palestinians occurred in several overlapping phases, beginning even before the official declaration of Israeli independence on 14 May 1948.

**December 1947 – March 1948:** In the aftermath of the UN partition vote, violence and uncertainty drove thousands of Palestinians from mixed cities and rural areas. Wealthier families often left first, assuming they would return once the violence subsided.

**April – June 1948:** With the launch of Plan Dalet (Plan D) by the Haganah, the conflict shifted decisively. Strategic offensives were launched to secure key roads, towns, and villages. In many cases, these operations led directly to the forced expulsion of Arab residents, either through direct military action or fear of attack.

**July – October 1948:** As the war escalated into full-scale fighting with Arab armies, further waves of displacement swept the country. Cities like Lydda (*al-Lydd*) and Ramle were emptied almost overnight during Operation Dani, with tens of thousands of civilians ordered to march eastward under the summer sun, many without food or water.

### Deir Yassin and the Politics of Fear

Among the events that catalysed mass flight, none was more significant than the massacre at Deir Yassin in April 1948. The attack by Irgun and Lehi forces on the village near Jerusalem left more than 100 Palestinians dead, many of them women and children.

News of the massacre spread rapidly, amplified by Arab leaders and the media. For Palestinians, it confirmed their worst fears: that Jewish militias were not only seizing territory but seeking to expel Arabs entirely. For many, the safest course of action was to flee before similar violence reached their villages.

The psychological impact of Deir Yassin cannot be overstated. In village after village, word-of-mouth accounts of atrocities — sometimes exaggerated, often accurate — spurred panic and accelerated the pace of the exodus.

## Plan Dalet: Strategy or Ethnic Cleansing?

Plan Dalet, adopted by the Haganah in March 1948, remains one of the most debated documents in Israeli and Palestinian historiography.

Supporters of the official Israeli narrative have long argued that Plan Dalet was a defensive strategy, an effort to secure territory allocated under the UN partition plan and to protect Jewish communities from Arab attack. Critics, most notably historian Ilan Pappé, have described it as a blueprint for ethnic cleansing, a coordinated effort to create a Jewish majority by forcibly removing Arab populations.

Archival evidence paints a more complex picture. While there was no single, explicit order for mass expulsion, operational directives frequently authorised the clearing of villages deemed hostile or strategically important. In practice, this often meant the depopulation, whether through force, intimidation, or fear, of large swathes of Palestinian territory.

## The Lydda and Ramle Expulsions

Nowhere was this reality starker than in the twin towns of Lydda (*al-Lydd*) and Ramle in July 1948. As part of Operation Dani, Israeli forces under the command of Yigal Allon and Yitzhak Rabin captured the towns, which sat astride key supply routes between Tel Aviv and Jerusalem.

In the aftermath, an estimated 50,000 to 70,000 residents were ordered to leave. Many were marched eastward towards the Jordanian lines in searing heat, with little water or food. Dozens, perhaps hundreds, died along the way. The towns were subsequently repopulated by Jewish immigrants, and their original Arab inhabitants were never allowed to return.

**Refugees and the Birth of the Camps**

By the end of 1948, more than 700,000 Palestinians were refugees, scattered across the West Bank, Gaza, Jordan, Lebanon, and Syria. Many believed their exile would be temporary — that the war would end, the political situation stabilise, and they would return to their homes. Few anticipated that their displacement would become permanent.

Refugee camps sprang up almost overnight, initially as makeshift tent cities on the margins of towns and villages. Over time, these camps, administered by the newly formed United Nations Relief and Works Agency (UNRWA), became semi-permanent settlements with basic infrastructure but few opportunities for work or mobility. Entire generations would grow up in these camps, their lives defined by poverty, statelessness, and the unfulfilled promise of return.

**The Denial of the Nakba**

Inside Israel, the *Nakba* was, for decades, a story that could not be told. The dominant narrative of the new state emphasised heroism, survival, and rebirth. Palestinian flight was framed as voluntary, the result of Arab leaders urging their people to evacuate temporarily while invading armies drove the Jews into the sea.

This narrative served a purpose: it absolved Israel of responsibility for the refugee crisis and provided moral cover for the new state. But it bore little resemblance to the complex reality documented in military archives, eyewitness testimonies, and international reports.

It was not until the rise of the so-called *New Historians* in the 1980s and 1990s scholars like Benny Morris, Avi Shlaim, and Ilan Pappé that a more nuanced, and often uncomfortable, picture emerged. Their research, based on declassified Israeli archives, revealed patterns of forced displacement, military pressure, and explicit decisions to prevent the return of refugees after the war.

## Memory and Inheritance

For Palestinians, the *Nakba* is not simply a historical event but a lived reality. Every family has a story of loss: a house left unlocked, a key carried into exile, a village name preserved in memory. The trauma of 1948 was transmitted across generations, shaping identity, politics, and resistance.

The "right of return", enshrined in UN Resolution 194, remains one of the most intractable issues in any discussion of peace. For many Israelis, the return of millions of refugees is seen as an existential threat to the Jewish character of the state. For Palestinians, abandoning the demand is tantamount to erasing their history.

## Parallel Narratives

The events of 1948 produced two competing national narratives that have never been reconciled:

• For Israelis, Independence Day is a celebration of courage and renewal, the miraculous rebirth of a people in their ancestral homeland.

• For Palestinians, Nakba Day is a day of mourning, a reminder of dispossession, injustice, and a world that looked away.

These narratives are not merely academic. They shape politics, education, and even the language of the conflict. In Israeli discourse,

"1948" marks the founding of the state; in Palestinian discourse, it marks the beginning of exile and occupation.

### International Response

The international response to the refugee crisis was muted. The world, exhausted by war and reluctant to confront the complexities of the conflict, offered humanitarian relief but little in the way of political solutions. The creation of UNRWA in 1949 provided basic services but did nothing to address the underlying issue of displacement or the right of return.

In Arab capitals, the plight of the refugees became a rallying cry, but solidarity rarely translated into meaningful support or durable solutions. In many host countries, Palestinians were marginalised, denied citizenship, and confined to the limbo of statelessness.

### A Permanent Wound

By the time the guns fell silent in 1949, the map of Palestine had been irrevocably altered. Israel controlled 78% of the former Mandate territory, far more than had been allocated under the UN partition plan, while Jordan controlled the West Bank and East Jerusalem, and Egypt administered Gaza.

For Israel, survival in the face of invasion was an undeniable achievement, cementing the legitimacy of the new state in the eyes of the world. For Palestinians, it was the beginning of a catastrophe that has never truly ended: exile, statelessness, and a conflict perpetuated by the unaddressed grievances of 1948.

The Nakba remains the original wound, the event that explains so much of what came after. Without reckoning with it, any discussion of peace, justice, or reconciliation is little more than an exercise in wishful thinking.

## Section 6: The New State and the Broken Nation

By the spring of 1949, the guns had fallen silent. Ceasefire agreements brokered by the United Nations froze the frontlines of the war and brought a tenuous end to the fighting. But the armistice did not bring peace, only a pause. What it left in its wake were two peoples living in parallel realities, each defined by the transformative and searing events of the previous year.

## A State Born in War

For the Jewish population of Israel, 1948 was both a miracle and a crucible. The war had cost more than 6,000 lives, roughly one per cent of the Yishuv, but it had also delivered what generations had dreamed of: sovereignty.

In the months following independence, the provisional government, led by David Ben-Gurion, moved quickly to consolidate the new state. Ministries were formalised, a parliament convened, and the Israel Defense Forces (IDF), forged from the Haganah and other militias, became a national army. The urgency of survival created a sense of unity and shared purpose that enabled extraordinary feats of state-building under conditions of scarcity and uncertainty.

The fledgling state also embarked on an ambitious programme of immigration and absorption. Between 1948 and 1951, more than 700,000 Jews arrived in Israel: Holocaust survivors from Europe, Jews expelled from Arab countries, and immigrants from Yemen, Iraq, and North Africa. These new arrivals doubled the population almost overnight, placing immense strain on housing, employment, and infrastructure, but also fulfilling the Zionist vision of a homeland for Jews everywhere.

## The Palestinians in Exile

For Palestinians, the same months were marked not by state-building but by dispossession. More than 700,000 refugees remained scattered across the region — in Gaza, the West Bank, Lebanon, Syria, and Jordan — their lives confined to tent cities that would soon become semi-permanent camps.

Many believed their exile would be temporary. The Arab states that had gone to war with Israel promised that victory and return were inevitable, but the reality was stark: Israel refused to allow refugees to return, seeing their mass repatriation as an existential threat to the demographic balance of the new state.

In 1949, the United Nations passed Resolution 194, affirming the right of refugees to return to their homes or receive compensation. Israel rejected the resolution, and Arab states, unwilling or unable to integrate the refugees, left them in a legal and political limbo. What was initially seen as a temporary displacement hardened into a permanent condition of statelessness, with profound political and psychological consequences.

**The Lines of 1949**

The armistice agreements left Israel in control of 78 per cent of the former British Mandate, far beyond the 55 per cent allocated under the UN partition plan. Jordan annexed the West Bank, including East Jerusalem, while Egypt took control of the Gaza Strip.

These lines, known as the Green Line, would remain the de facto borders until 1967. But they were never recognised as legitimate by Arab states, which continued to view Israel as a colonial implant imposed by Western powers. For Israel, the armistice lines were seen as temporary and insecure, a ceasefire boundary rather than a permanent frontier.

**Two Divergent Narratives**

The aftermath of 1948 cemented two competing narratives that continue to define the conflict.

For Israelis, the war of independence was a story of heroism, survival, and moral vindication: a tiny, embattled community defeating overwhelming odds to reclaim its ancestral homeland. The collective memory of vulnerability and victory became foundational to the young state's identity, shaping its politics, its military doctrine, and its sense of perpetual insecurity.

For Palestinians, 1948 was and remains the *Nakba* — the catastrophe. It was the year they lost their land, their homes, and, for many, their sense of agency over their own history. The trauma of expulsion and the daily reality of exile created a national identity forged in dispossession and resistance. The keys to abandoned houses, the names of lost villages, and the stories of flight became sacred heirlooms, passed from generation to generation.

## Britain's Departure, America's Arrival

The war also marked a decisive shift in the geopolitics of the region. Britain, exhausted and diminished, relinquished its role as the primary power in the Middle East. Into that vacuum stepped the United States, whose early recognition of Israel signalled a new phase in the relationship — one that would deepen over the coming decades as Cold War rivalries shaped global alignments.

The Soviet Union, which had initially supported partition and recognised the new state, quickly recalibrated its position, aligning more closely with Arab nationalist movements as the Cold War polarised the region.

## The Politics of Refuge

In the Arab world, the plight of the Palestinian refugees became both a humanitarian crisis and a potent political symbol. Arab regimes, humiliated by their failure to defeat the new state, used the refugee issue to deflect internal dissent and to legitimise their opposition to Israel. Yet for all the rhetoric of solidarity, practical support for refugees was limited. Most were denied citizenship, work permits, and basic rights in their host countries, confined to a permanent liminality that would shape Palestinian politics for decades.

## The Seeds of Future Conflict

The war of 1948 did not resolve the conflict; it transformed it. For Israel, survival came at the cost of deep insecurity. Surrounded by hostile neighbours and isolated in the region, the new state adopted a posture of vigilance and self-reliance that would define its foreign and security policies.

For Palestinians, the *Nakba* became the foundation of a politics of resistance, rooted in the belief that dispossession could only be reversed through struggle. Out of the refugee camps and the ashes of 1948 would emerge movements — first the Palestine Liberation Organization (PLO), later Hamas — dedicated to reclaiming the land lost in that year of catastrophe.

## A Broken Landscape

By the close of 1949, the map of Palestine had been irrevocably redrawn. Where once Arabs and Jews had lived, often uneasily but side by side, there now stood two fractured worlds: a new state struggling to build itself in the shadow of war, and a dispersed people clinging to the hope of return.

The armistice lines froze the conflict but did not resolve it. Instead, they hardened divisions, sowed mistrust, and set the stage for the cycles of violence, displacement, and negotiation that would follow.

The story of 1948 — of independence and catastrophe, of triumph and trauma — is not a closed chapter. It is the foundation on which everything else in the conflict rests, a shared past that neither side can escape and that continues to shape the possibilities and limits of the present.

## Pragmatism in Peril: Zionism and the Nazi Era

History rarely offers moments free from ambiguity. In the turbulent years between Hitler's rise to power in 1933 and the outbreak of World War II, the Zionist movement, still in its formative stages, faced an impossible dilemma: how to secure the survival of Europe's Jews while confronting a regime whose antisemitism would soon escalate into genocide.

Zionism, by the mid-1930s, was no longer a fringe idea. It had become a movement with organisational strength, international reach, and a growing foothold in Palestine. But the rise of fascism in Europe, and Nazism in particular, posed new and harrowing questions. For a people still stateless and facing escalating violence, the urgency of finding refuge outweighed almost everything else.

It was in this climate of desperation that Zionist leaders found themselves making choices that, decades later, would remain both deeply uncomfortable and fiercely contested.

The most infamous expression of this pragmatism was the Haavara Agreement of 1933, negotiated between representatives of the Zionist movement and officials of Nazi Germany. Under its terms, approximately 60,000 German Jews were permitted to emigrate to Palestine, transferring a portion of their assets in the form of German goods that would be sold upon arrival. For a movement desperate to populate the fledgling Yishuv, and for families desperate to escape, the agreement was a lifeline. For others, particularly those advocating for a global boycott of Nazi Germany, it was an unforgivable compromise, collaboration dressed up as pragmatism.

As Israeli historian Francis Nicosia notes in *The Third Reich and the Palestine Question*, the context of the agreement was brutally pragmatic. Hitler's regime in 1933 had not yet implemented the "Final Solution", and many Jewish leaders still hoped to pressure or negotiate their way towards emigration or relief. The Haavara deal offered the possibility of saving tens of thousands of lives at a time when borders were closing and antisemitism was rising across Europe.

Yet this same pragmatism provoked a furious backlash. The American Jewish Congress and other organisations condemned the agreement as undermining the boycott of German goods, a boycott they saw as the only viable form of international protest against the Nazi regime. In retrospect, critics argue, the deal fractured Jewish solidarity at a time when unity was desperately needed.

**The Ethical Dilemma**

The ethical fault lines of the Haavara Agreement remain a subject of historical debate. On one side, scholars such as Lenni Brenner, author of *Zionism in the Age of the Dictators*, have argued that this episode reflects a more insidious alignment between elements of Zionism and Nazi policy, claiming that both saw Europe as untenable for Jews and Palestine as the only viable solution. Brenner's work, however, has been heavily criticised for overstating ideological convergence and conflating survival-driven pragmatism with active collaboration.

More mainstream historians, including Nicosia and Israeli scholars such as Shlomo Aronson, place the agreement firmly in the realm of tragic necessity: a morally compromised decision made under unimaginable pressure, designed to save as many lives as possible within the limits imposed by a genocidal regime.

**Lessons in Power and Pragmatism**

Whether one views the Haavara Agreement as a moral failure or a grimly necessary compromise, it reveals key themes that resonate throughout the Zionist project:

• A relentless focus on pragmatism and survival.

• A willingness to make difficult, even morally fraught, decisions in the service of a greater strategic objective.

• A deep-seated understanding that, in the words of future Israeli leaders, "no one will save the Jews but the Jews themselves".

These lessons, forged in the crucible of crisis, informed the strategies of the Zionist leadership well beyond the war years, shaping the security-first ethos that would define the State of Israel after 1948.

## The Politics of Memory

Today, the history of the Haavara Agreement and other instances of limited Nazi-Zionist interaction remains a contested and weaponised subject. Holocaust denialists and anti-Zionist polemicists sometimes seize upon this history to delegitimise Zionism or to suggest ideological affinity where none meaningfully existed. Such distortions ignore the overwhelming context of desperation: a stateless and persecuted people trying to negotiate their survival with a regime intent on their destruction.

What this history demands instead is nuance, an acknowledgement that moral clarity is often elusive in moments of existential peril, and that the compromises made in those years were not made in comfort but under duress.

## Continuity and Discontinuity

Understanding this moment in history does not absolve later policies, nor does it suggest that Israel's subsequent trajectory was inevitable. But it does illuminate a continuity of mindset: a security doctrine grounded in survivalism, a belief that alliances, however uncomfortable or transactional, are justified if they advance the core imperative of Jewish safety and statehood.

# CHAPTER THREE

## Section 1: Six Days That Remade the Map (1967)

History rarely turns in a week, but in June 1967 it did. In six days, Israel moved from anxious containment to sweeping command of the land between the Jordan River and the Mediterranean, plus the high volcanic rim of the Golan. The transformation was military, geographic, psychological, and ultimately constitutional. It reset borders, identities, and the grammar of the conflict.

### The Road to War

The months before June were a chain of escalations. Syrian-Israeli artillery duels across the demilitarised zones fed a cycle of raids and reprisals. In May, Soviet intelligence falsely warned Egypt that Israel was massing to strike Syria. Whether a misreading or manipulation, the report proved catalytic. Egyptian President Gamal Abdel Nasser ordered UN peacekeepers (UNEF) out of Sinai. Secretary-General U Thant, lacking a legal mandate to resist, withdrew them, and then closed the Straits of Tiran, cutting Israel's maritime access to the Red Sea and Asia. Under international law, Israel framed the closure as a *casus belli*; domestically, it triggered dread of encirclement. Jordan entered a mutual defence pact with Egypt; Iraqi units moved west. Israeli reservists were mobilised for weeks, the economy idled, and radio commentators spoke, without irony, of existential peril.

### The Pre-emptive Strike

At dawn on 5 June 1967, Israel launched Operation Focus, a meticulously planned pre-emptive air offensive that decimated the Egyptian air force on the ground within hours, then rolled over Syrian and Jordanian air assets. Air supremacy reset the campaign. Israeli armour and infantry pushed across Sinai, reached the Suez

Canal, and encircled Egyptian units. In the east, battles raged for East Jerusalem and the West Bank; to the north, the Golan Heights fell after fierce fighting in steep terrain.

By 10 June, the map was unrecognisable. Israel held the Sinai Peninsula and Gaza Strip (taken from Egypt), the West Bank including East Jerusalem (from Jordan), and the Golan Heights (from Syria). It had tripled its territorial reach, acquired commanding high ground, and surrounded, now containing, Palestinian population centres.

## A Military Victory, a Symbolic Earthquake

Among Israelis, the lightning victory landed as a secular miracle. The capture of East Jerusalem — paratroopers at the Western Wall, the Old City's gates opened — united secular nationalism and religious yearning. "We are in Jerusalem," radioed commander Motta Gur. The phrase told a nation that history had bent toward it. For religious Zionists, biblical Judea and Samaria were no longer scripture but jurisdiction. For secular Israelis, the victory dissolved the underdog self-image and replaced it with confidence, and for some, destiny.

For Palestinians, the shock was different. In a week they moved from Jordanian and Egyptian rule to direct Israeli military control. Refugee flows from 1948 were joined by fresh displacement; tens of thousands fled the Jordan Valley and Latrun corridor. Some, like residents of the villages in the Latrun "no-man's land", saw homes levelled in the days after the war. The "temporary" became an ambient, undefined time frame.

## Law, Diplomacy, and the Ambiguity of 242

The UN Security Council adopted Resolution 242 that November. Its opening line declared the "inadmissibility of the acquisition of territory by war", then called for "withdrawal of Israeli armed forces from territories occupied in the recent conflict" and for the right of every state to live in peace within secure and recognised boundaries. The English text's omission of a definite article ("from the territories") and the French text's inclusion ("des territoires occupés") created a diplomatic ambiguity that successive Israeli, Arab, American, and European governments would exploit. The formula of "land for peace" was born; its precise exchange rate was left purposely vague.

### East Jerusalem: Annexation in Stages

Within weeks, Israel moved to alter Jerusalem's status. In late June 1967, it extended Israeli law, jurisdiction, and administration to East Jerusalem and expanded the municipal boundaries, annexing surrounding villages and open land. Holy sites were placed under formal protection, while Islamic *waqf* authorities retained day-to-day administration of the Haram al-Sharif/Temple Mount, an arrangement meant to steady a volatile equilibrium.

Internationally, the steps went unrecognised; domestically, they were foundational. New Jewish neighbourhoods — Ramat Eshkol, Gilo, Pisgat Ze'ev, Ramot — were built to ring and bind the city to the west. The language of "unified and eternal capital" entered Basic Laws and schoolbooks. For Palestinians, residency in their own city became conditional, revocable if they lived abroad too long or failed bureaucratic tests of "centre of life". Sovereignty, once a theological abstraction, took concrete form in roads, zoning, and police stations.

### From Victory to Governance

Israel's leaders described the occupation as temporary, pending negotiations. In practice, a governance architecture took shape immediately. Military commanders issued orders that overrode existing Jordanian and Egyptian law wherever deemed necessary for "public order" or "security". Land registries were frozen or revised; travel permits, curfews, and closures were instituted as required. The Defence Ministry assumed control of bridges, borders, and population registries. The word "provisional" did heavy lifting while institutions settled in.

At the same time, a debate opened inside Israel that would shape the next half-century. One camp, echoing a pragmatic Ben-Gurionist realism, argued for trading most of the territories for peace — preferably with Jordan and Egypt — retaining only limited adjustments for "security". Another, energised by the experience of Jerusalem and Hebron, insisted that relinquishing Judea and Samaria would betray history and God. The state tried to straddle both, proclaiming readiness for peace on favourable terms while taking steps that made relinquishment ever harder.

### The Settlement Seed

The first settlers after 1967 did not look like a movement; they looked like returnees. Kfar Etzion, a bloc south of Jerusalem destroyed in 1948, was re-established. Religious students moved into the Hebron area, first as a yeshiva in a hotel, then as a neighbourhood. The government, tentative in public, quietly helped with land, security, and services. What began as memorials became municipalities.

Within a decade, ideology caught up with geography. *Gush Emunim*, the "Bloc of the Faithful", formed in the mid-1970s, preaching that Jewish sovereignty over the West Bank was a divine imperative and a national necessity. Settlements were recast from security buffers to fulfilment; "facts on the ground" became a policy, not a metaphor. Ministries budgeted for roads and utilities; the army guarded and escorted; courts wrestled with the line between "military necessity" and civilian colonisation. The project of permanence had begun.

### Strategic Depth, Strategic Hubris

If the Six-Day War generated euphoria, it also bred overconfidence. The belief that air power and initiative could always offset strategic warning would be tested and broken six years later in the Yom Kippur War. But in 1967's immediate afterglow, the concept of strategic depth took hold: the Jordan Valley as an eastern wall, the Golan as a northern rampart, Sinai as a southern cushion. Security arguments fused with settlement logic; what protected Israel must be populated by Israelis.

**The Palestinian Condition, Reset**

For Palestinians, June 1967 was less a chapter than a system. The military government controlled movement, land, and livelihoods; municipal leaders navigated a tightrope to keep services running. The promise of 1948's refugees returning to cities now under Israeli control — Jaffa, Lydda, Haifa — evaporated; a new generation encountered checkpoints instead. The vocabulary of daily life shifted to permits, closures, work passes, and later IDs and magnetic cards. "Temporary" acquired the texture of routine.

In six days, the conflict changed register. What had been, since 1949, a dispute across armistice lines became, from 1967, a relationship of ruler and ruled. The victory delivered security and symbolism for Israel; it delivered a durable, bureaucratised subordination for Palestinians. From this hinge point, the chapter's remaining sections trace how "temporary" rule was converted — law by law, road by road, outpost by outpost — into an apparatus of permanence.

**Section 2: From 'Temporary' Control to a System of Rule**

In the immediate aftermath of June 1967, Israeli leaders insisted that their hold on the newly captured territories — the West Bank, Gaza Strip, Golan Heights, and Sinai Peninsula — was temporary. The territories, they argued, were bargaining chips to be traded for peace, a pragmatic application of the "land for peace" formula implicit in UN Resolution 242.

But while the rhetoric was of transience, the reality on the ground told a different story. Almost from the first days of occupation, Israel established a system of governance designed not just to maintain order but to shape, regulate, and ultimately control the lives of millions of Palestinians. Over time, what had begun as "provisional" became institutionalised, forming a complex web of laws, permits, and administrative mechanisms that made the occupation self-perpetuating.

**Military Government and Legal Supremacy**

Immediately after the war, Israel imposed a military government over the West Bank and Gaza. Under the Fourth Geneva Convention, an occupying power is permitted to administer occupied territory temporarily, maintaining existing laws unless absolutely necessary for security. In practice, Israeli commanders issued military orders that superseded Jordanian and Egyptian laws wherever convenient.

These orders touched every aspect of daily life:
• Land use and ownership
• Movement and residency
• Trade and labour
• Political assembly and association

Military law placed ultimate authority in the hands of the regional commander, whose decrees carried the force of law but could be amended or revoked at will. Civilian Palestinians had no vote, no representation, and no meaningful recourse.

**Land: The Heart of Control**

Land became the central axis of the occupation. Israeli legal and bureaucratic ingenuity produced a set of doctrines that allowed for systematic expropriation while maintaining the appearance of legality.

Key mechanisms included:

• "Absentee Property" Laws – lands owned by Palestinians who had fled during the war were declared abandoned and seized by the state.

• "State Land" Declarations – large swathes of the West Bank were reclassified as state land under Ottoman-era laws that permitted such designation if land was not under continuous cultivation.

• Military Seizures – land was taken "temporarily" for security purposes, often to build infrastructure, military bases, or roads that would later serve settlements.

• Nature Reserves and Closed Zones – designations that restricted Palestinian use while leaving room for future Israeli development.

By the mid-1970s, these policies had paved the way for the first settlements, initially justified as security outposts but increasingly permanent.

### The Civil Administration

In 1981, Israel established the Civil Administration, nominally a civilian agency but in practice an arm of the military government. The Civil Administration became the nerve centre of occupation bureaucracy, issuing permits for everything from travel and construction to importing spare parts for agricultural machinery.

This system, layered and opaque, created a structure of dependency. Palestinians seeking permission to build, farm, or even leave their villages had to navigate an administrative maze, reinforcing the sense of subordination while providing Israel with granular control over the occupied population.

### The Permit Regime

At the core of this control was the permit regime, a constantly evolving system of identity cards, checkpoints, and movement restrictions. Palestinians needed permits to:

• Travel between Gaza, the West Bank, and East Jerusalem.

• Work in Israel or in settlements.

• Access medical care in Israeli hospitals.

• Export agricultural goods or import basic supplies.

This regime was justified in the name of security, but its effect was profoundly political: it fragmented Palestinian society into zones of varying mobility and rights, undermining collective organisation while deepening economic dependency on Israel.

## Fragmentation and Micro-Geographies

One of the most consequential features of the occupation was its ability to fragment Palestinian space. What had once been a relatively contiguous social and economic geography was broken into a patchwork of enclaves, bypass roads, and restricted areas.

• In Gaza, control over entry and exit points made the enclave increasingly isolated.

• In the West Bank, the proliferation of settlements, military zones, and restricted roads carved the territory into isolated cantons, each subject to different rules and levels of control.

• In East Jerusalem, residency rights were conditional, and zoning restrictions made Palestinian construction nearly impossible while facilitating Israeli expansion.

This fragmentation, physical, administrative, and psychological, ensured that no unified Palestinian polity could emerge within the occupied territories.

## Economics of Dependence

Economically, the occupation created a system of dependence that benefited Israel. By the 1970s, tens of thousands of Palestinians were working in Israel as cheap labour, building homes, harvesting crops, and working in factories. Wages were low, protections minimal, and opportunities for independent Palestinian economic development were systematically curtailed.

This arrangement provided Israel with a flexible, low-cost workforce while tying the livelihoods of Palestinian families to the stability of the occupation. When uprisings or strikes occurred, work permits could be revoked, tightening economic pressure almost overnight.

### Security and Administration: A Blurring of Lines

From the outset, security and administration were inseparable. The intelligence apparatus embedded itself in the fabric of occupation governance, from the recruitment of informants to surveillance of community leaders. The military courts processed tens of thousands of Palestinians each year, often for minor infractions or acts of resistance such as graffiti, leaflets, or attendance at unauthorised meetings.

This blurring of lines between civilian life and security control meant that resistance, however small, was easily criminalised, reinforcing the sense that the occupation was not just about land or territory but about managing and containing a population.

### The Illusion of Temporariness

Throughout the early years, Israeli leaders maintained that the occupation was temporary, pending negotiations. But on the ground, every new road, settlement, and administrative layer suggested otherwise. The Allon Plan, an internal Israeli proposal drafted just after the 1967 war, envisioned permanent control over the Jordan Valley and key highlands for security purposes, while leaving densely populated Palestinian areas under some form of autonomy or Jordanian rule.

Though never formally adopted, the Allon Plan became a de facto blueprint: build where strategic, hold where necessary, and keep options open. Temporary governance slowly became permanent architecture.

### Palestinian Responses

For Palestinians, the first decade after 1967 was a period of adjustment and quiet resistance. Many hoped that the international community would enforce the withdrawal promised in Resolution

242; others adapted to the new reality, working in Israel during the day and returning to their villages at night.

But beneath the surface, resentment grew. Small acts of defiance, protests, strikes, and underground organising hinted at a larger shift to come. By the late 1970s and early 1980s, the sense that occupation was no longer temporary but entrenched was widespread, setting the stage for the First Intifada in 1987.

## Section 3: The Settler Movement and an Ideology of Permanence

If the first years of Israel's post-1967 occupation were marked by uncertainty and ambivalence, the 1970s and 1980s brought clarity and determination. What had begun as a provisional military administration steadily evolved into a project of territorial entrenchment, driven by two intertwined forces: strategic security thinking and a burgeoning ideological movement convinced that the territories were not bargaining chips but divine inheritance.

### The Early Outposts

The first settlements after 1967 were tentative, cautious, and framed as pragmatic. In Kfar Etzion, south of Jerusalem, survivors of a kibbutz destroyed in the 1948 war returned to re-establish their community. In Hebron, a small group of religious students checked into the Park Hotel during Passover in 1968, declaring their intention to restore a Jewish presence in one of Judaism's holiest cities.

The government, wary of domestic and international backlash, hesitated at first but ultimately facilitated these efforts. Land was allocated quietly, military escorts were provided, and infrastructure followed. These early settlements were justified as security buffers, nodes of presence along strategic corridors that, in the language of officials, would "enhance defensive depth" without precluding eventual territorial compromise.

## The Birth of Gush Emunim

The war of 1967 had done more than redraw maps; it had redrawn the political imagination. For a generation of religious Zionists, the capture of the West Bank, or as they preferred, Judea and Samaria, was nothing less than providential. The dream of redemption, once abstract, was now tangible in the hills of Hebron, Shiloh, and Nablus.

In 1974, in the aftermath of the Yom Kippur War, a group of activists founded Gush Emunim ("Bloc of the Faithful"). They rejected the notion that the territories were negotiable and embraced an ideology that fused religious messianism with nationalist realism: the land belonged to the Jewish people by divine right, and the state had a duty to settle it.

Gush Emunim activists were disciplined, organised, and unrelenting. They established outposts, often in defiance of government policy, daring authorities to evict them. More often than not, the state relented, retroactively legalising the encampments and providing support in the form of electricity, water, and security that signalled tacit approval.

## State Sponsorship and "Facts on the Ground"

While early settlement efforts had been piecemeal, the late 1970s saw the state embrace a policy of active encouragement. Under Prime Minister Menachem Begin and his Likud government, which came to power in 1977, settlements became a central pillar of national policy.

Budgets were allocated for roads, housing, and subsidies; the army provided security details; and government ministries coordinated planning and expansion. The phrase "creating facts on the ground", a bureaucratic euphemism for irreversible territorial change, became a guiding principle.

By the early 1980s, hundreds of new settlements dotted the West Bank, from the Jordan Valley to the highlands near Ramallah. Some were small, ideologically driven enclaves; others, like Ma'ale Adumim east of Jerusalem or Ariel in the northern West Bank, were planned as suburban cities designed to attract secular Israelis with affordable housing, good schools, and short commutes to Tel Aviv or Jerusalem.

**Legal Alchemy**

The expansion of settlements required legal innovation. Israeli courts, particularly the High Court of Justice, played a pivotal role in shaping and legitimising the process.

In 1979, the Elon Moreh case forced the government to halt the seizure of private Palestinian land for purely civilian settlements. But rather than slowing the settlement project, the decision spurred a shift in tactics. Instead of taking private land, the state began designating vast areas as "state land" based on interpretations of Ottoman-era laws that allowed uncultivated land to be claimed by the state.

This legal sleight of hand enabled the expropriation of more than 40% of the West Bank by the early 2000s, providing a legal veneer for settlement growth while insulating the process from international criticism.

**Settlements as Ideological Frontiers**

The settlement enterprise was never monolithic. For some, particularly in Gush Emunim and its successors, settlement was a religious imperative, a means of fulfilling a divine commandment and hastening redemption. For others, particularly secular Israelis, the appeal was more practical: cheap housing, economic incentives, and quality of life.

But regardless of motivation, the effect was the same — a steady deepening of Israeli presence across the West Bank, supported by state infrastructure and protected by the military. Settlements became facts, their expansion creating a political geography that made withdrawal increasingly costly and politically fraught.

**Hebron and the Politics of Presence**

No city better encapsulates the ideological dimension of settlement than Hebron. The site of the Tomb of the Patriarchs holds profound religious significance for Jews, Christians, and Muslims alike. For settlers, a Jewish presence in Hebron was non-negotiable, a matter of historical justice and religious destiny.

The result has been decades of tension, violence, and division. The city today is a microcosm of the occupation: fortified checkpoints, segregated streets, and a heavily militarised enclave of a few hundred settlers living amidst tens of thousands of Palestinians under tight restrictions. Hebron illustrates how settlement policy is not only about land but also about symbolism and permanence.

**The Politics of Incentives**

By the 1980s, settlement had become institutionalised in Israeli politics. Incentive structures, such as tax breaks, subsidised mortgages, and infrastructure investment, encouraged families to move to the West Bank. Entire suburban blocs were planned with an eye toward normalisation, transforming the image of settlements from isolated hilltop outposts to thriving commuter towns indistinguishable from communities inside the Green Line.

This normalisation had profound political consequences. It blurred the line between Israel proper and the occupied territories, making the idea of territorial compromise increasingly abstract and politically toxic. By the time peace negotiations began in earnest in the 1990s, the settler population had grown to more than 200,000, a demographic reality that could not easily be reversed.

**Violence and Protection**

As settlements expanded, so too did violence. Clashes between settlers and Palestinians became frequent, often sparked by disputes over land or access to resources. The Israeli military, tasked with protecting settlers, found itself increasingly enmeshed in daily policing of Palestinian communities.

This dynamic blurred the lines between security and ideology. Soldiers guarded settlers not only as civilians but as extensions of a state project to solidify territorial claims. For Palestinians, the presence of armed settlers, often accompanied by violence and harassment, reinforced the sense that the occupation was not provisional but permanent.

**An Ideology of Permanence**

By the late 1980s, the occupation had undergone a quiet but profound transformation. What had been presented as a temporary measure pending negotiations was now underpinned by an ideology of permanence. The settlement enterprise had created a reality in which the West Bank was crisscrossed by Israeli roads, dotted with fortified towns, and integrated into the economic and administrative systems of the state.

This was not accidental. It was the product of deliberate policy choices, driven by a coalition of ideological conviction and pragmatic statecraft. The map of the West Bank was being rewritten, one settlement, one road, one outpost at a time, creating a geography that would shape every future negotiation, every diplomatic initiative, and every effort to imagine a different future.

## Section 4: Security as a Doctrine and an Industry

If settlement reshaped the map of the territories, security reshaped their daily reality. What began as a military occupation framed in provisional terms evolved into a complex system of control, where the language of "security" justified almost everything: land seizures, movement restrictions, collective punishment, surveillance, and lethal force. Over time, security ceased to be merely a policy; it became a doctrine, a worldview, and eventually an industry, one that would export its technologies and tactics around the world.

## The Architecture of Control

By the late 1970s, as settlement expanded and Palestinian resistance grew, Israel refined the machinery of occupation. The West Bank and Gaza were divided into zones of graduated control, enforced through a dense network of:

• Checkpoints, fixed and mobile, regulating every aspect of movement between villages, cities, and borders.

• Curfews, imposed frequently, sometimes for days or weeks, to suppress unrest.

• Permits, required for work, travel, medical treatment, or even visiting family members in other towns.

This apparatus was not static. Each round of conflict — the First Intifada in 1987, the Second Intifada in 2000, wars in Gaza, and lone-wolf attacks — produced new layers of regulation and surveillance. The occupation became a living system, constantly adapting and expanding in response to events, but always reinforcing the same hierarchy: one population with rights and mobility, another confined and regulated.

## The Separation Barrier

The Second Intifada (2000–2005), marked by suicide bombings in buses and cafés, was a turning point. In 2002, Israel began constructing what it called a security fence; Palestinians called it the apartheid wall — a concrete and wire barrier that snakes for more than 700 kilometres through the West Bank.

In official narratives, the barrier was a defensive necessity, credited with sharply reducing attacks inside Israel. In reality, its route rarely followed the Green Line; instead, it looped deep into the West Bank, incorporating major settlement blocs on the Israeli side and cutting Palestinian towns and villages into isolated cantons.

The barrier redefined geography and time. Commutes that once took minutes stretched into hours; farmers required special permits to access their fields; students navigated checkpoints just to attend school. Beyond its physical presence, the wall functioned as a psychological marker, reinforcing the sense of division and permanence.

### Surveillance and the Data State

As the occupation matured, it became increasingly technological. Israel pioneered the integration of surveillance tools into daily governance:

• Databases that tracked every Palestinian's ID, biometric information, family ties, and movement history.

• Cameras and drones monitoring checkpoints, streets, and borders.

• Predictive algorithms used to flag suspect patterns of behaviour.

These technologies created a system of total visibility, where every aspect of Palestinian life could be monitored, analysed, and acted upon. For many Palestinians, resistance — even passive forms such as protest or boycott — came with the expectation of swift, often disproportionate, retaliation.

### The Export of Security

By the 1990s, Israel had turned its expertise in occupation into a global commodity. Arms fairs in Europe, Asia, and Latin America showcased surveillance drones, facial recognition software, and crowd-control weapons, all marketed as battle-tested in the West Bank and Gaza.

Israeli defence firms, often in collaboration with the state, developed and exported technologies that would shape policing and security worldwide from US border enforcement to counterinsurgency operations in Afghanistan and Iraq. Training programmes brought foreign security officials to Israel to study crowd control, urban warfare, and intelligence-gathering techniques honed under the occupation.

This export economy blurred the line between military necessity and commercial opportunity. What had begun as a doctrine of survival became an industry, embedding the occupation not only in the politics of the region but in the global economy of security.

**Dual Legal Regimes**

Security also structured law. In the territories, two systems of justice operated side by side:

• Israeli civil law for settlers, with full rights and access to Israeli courts.

•Military law for Palestinians, with military courts, administrative detention, and rules that allowed indefinite imprisonment without charge or trial.

This dual legal regime institutionalised inequality, transforming the language of security into a legal architecture that normalised exceptionalism. Security concerns justified everything — house demolitions, night raids, and restrictions on assembly — while insulating the system from meaningful oversight.

**Economics of Control**

The occupation was also an economic machine. Checkpoints and closures created dependency; permits to work in Israel became both a lifeline and a lever of control. Palestinian labour flowed into Israeli agriculture, construction, and industry, providing cheap and often unprotected manpower.

At the same time, a small but lucrative economy grew around the occupation itself: contracts for construction companies, service providers, and technology firms supplying everything from surveillance towers to electronic gates. The occupation was not cost-free, but it was self-sustaining, and for some sectors, profitable.

**Security as Worldview**

Over time, security ceased to be a narrow response to specific threats and became a worldview — a lens through which every Palestinian act was read as potential hostility, and every policy justified as a defensive necessity.

This mindset was deeply internalised, shaping politics and society alike. In Israeli media and public discourse, the occupation was rarely described as an occupation; it was a security challenge, an enduring conflict that required management, not resolution. The language of security turned political questions into technical problems, solvable only through more technology, more surveillance, and more control.

**The Human Cost**

For Palestinians, the human cost of this system was measured not only in deaths and arrests but in the erosion of normal life. Checkpoints meant missed funerals, births unattended, and jobs lost. The constant threat of raids and detention fostered a pervasive sense of insecurity. Children grew up in a world where soldiers and guns were everyday sights, where movement was conditional, and where the future was always provisional.

For Israelis too, the security doctrine carried costs. It fostered a society accustomed to control, surveillance, and militarisation; where dissent could be framed as weakness, and where the occupation, once framed as temporary, became invisible — normalised as a permanent condition.

**A System Entrenched**

By the early 2000s, the occupation had been transformed into a self-reinforcing system: settlements justified more security; more security justified more control; and more control created conditions that sustained settlement expansion. What had begun in 1967 as a temporary military presence had become a deeply entrenched structure of governance — one that blurred the lines between war and peace, between security and ideology, and between necessity and choice.

## Section 5: Shocks and Consolidations

The story of Israel's occupation after 1967 is not linear; it is a cycle of shocks and consolidations. Each crisis, each war, intifada, or diplomatic breakthrough, did not loosen the structures of control but rather tightened them, embedding the occupation more deeply in the political and geographic fabric of the land.

### The Yom Kippur War (1973): The Lesson of Vulnerability

In October 1973, six years after the triumph of the Six-Day War, Israel was jolted by the Yom Kippur War. On the holiest day of the Jewish calendar, Egyptian and Syrian forces launched a coordinated surprise attack, crossing the Suez Canal in the south and reclaiming parts of the Golan Heights in the north.

For three harrowing days, the survival of the state appeared uncertain. Israeli forces, caught unprepared, suffered heavy casualties before counterattacking and eventually pushing back the invading armies. The war ended with a ceasefire, but the psychological damage lingered.

The lesson many Israelis took from 1973 was clear: strategic depth was not a luxury, it was a necessity. The territories captured in 1967 were no longer bargaining chips but defensive walls. In political discourse, this sense of vulnerability merged with an emerging belief that holding the West Bank, Gaza, and the Golan Heights was essential for survival.

## The Begin Revolution and Accelerated Settlement

In 1977, Menachem Begin's Likud Party came to power, ending three decades of Labour dominance. Begin's government aligned itself closely with the settler movement, seeing in it both ideological resonance and a loyal constituency.

Settlements expanded at an unprecedented pace. Roads were paved, subsidies provided, and strategic blocs, such as Ma'ale Adumim near Jerusalem, were planned not as temporary outposts but as permanent suburbs. The state had moved beyond tacit acceptance of settlements; it had embraced them as a national project.

## Camp David and Peace with Egypt

Ironically, it was under Begin that Israel signed its first peace treaty with an Arab state. The Camp David Accords of 1978, brokered by US President Jimmy Carter, led to Israel's full withdrawal from the Sinai Peninsula in exchange for peace with Egypt.

While the accords demonstrated that territorial compromise could bring peace, they also had unintended consequences. The withdrawal from Sinai was used by the settler movement to argue that the West Bank must never be ceded. Sinai, they claimed, was peripheral; Judea and Samaria were the biblical heartland. For Palestinians, Camp David deepened disillusionment: their rights were discussed but never guaranteed, their fate postponed to an indefinite future.

## Lebanon 1982: Exporting the Conflict

In 1982, Israel invaded Lebanon, launching what was officially called *Operation Peace for Galilee*. The stated goal was to drive the Palestine Liberation Organization (PLO) away from northern Israel, where cross-border attacks had intensified.

The operation quickly escalated into a full-scale war. Israeli forces advanced to Beirut, laying siege to the city for months. In the chaos that followed the PLO's evacuation, allied Christian militias massacred hundreds, perhaps thousands, of Palestinians in the Sabra and Shatila refugee camps, while Israeli forces, in control of the area, stood by.

The war marked a turning point. It exposed the limits of Israel's military power and eroded the sense of moral clarity that had surrounded its earlier conflicts. Domestically, it fuelled dissent, with mass protests in Tel Aviv demanding accountability. Yet strategically, the occupation of the West Bank and Gaza deepened. Attention shifted outward, but the machinery of control at home grew ever more entrenched.

### The First Intifada (1987–1993): Uprising from Below

By the late 1980s, two decades of occupation had created a combustible mix: economic dependency, political disenfranchisement, and the visible permanence of settlements. On 9 December 1987, a traffic accident in Gaza, an Israeli truck colliding with a car carrying Palestinian workers, ignited a spontaneous uprising.

The First Intifada spread rapidly from Gaza to the West Bank. It was a grassroots movement: teenagers throwing stones at armoured vehicles; merchants closing shops in protest; women organising underground schools during curfews. The uprising was largely unarmed but met with heavy force — beatings, arrests, and live ammunition.

Internationally, the Intifada shattered the illusion that the occupation was stable or manageable. Televised images of children facing soldiers with rifles shifted global opinion, creating pressure for a political resolution and elevating the PLO, led by Yasser Arafat, as the recognised representative of the Palestinian people.

## Oslo and the Architecture of Division

The Oslo Accords of 1993 were born of this pressure and of a sense of fatigue on both sides. Negotiated in secret and signed on the White House lawn, Oslo promised a phased process: limited Palestinian self-rule in parts of the West Bank and Gaza, Israeli withdrawal from major population centres, and a path towards final-status negotiations within five years.

For a brief moment, optimism flourished. Checkpoints were eased, joint patrols were established, and economic cooperation was touted as the foundation for peace. But the optimism was short-lived.

Oslo's flaws were structural. The West Bank was carved into Areas A, B, and C:

• Area A (about 18%) — full Palestinian civil and security control, primarily urban centres.

• Area B (about 22%) — Palestinian civil control with joint Israeli security oversight.

• Area C (about 60%) — full Israeli control, encompassing most settlements and key strategic lands.

This fragmentation institutionalised the occupation. Instead of a pathway to statehood, Oslo created a patchwork of enclaves, while settlements expanded more rapidly than before, fuelled by government subsidies and shifting political currents inside Israel.

## The Second Intifada (2000–2005): The Age of Fear

By 2000, frustration with Oslo's failures boiled over. The Second Intifada, sparked by Ariel Sharon's visit to the Temple Mount/Haram al-Sharif, was far more violent than the first. Suicide bombings ripped through buses, cafés, and markets, while Israeli airstrikes and incursions devastated Palestinian towns and refugee camps.

Israel responded with overwhelming force: targeted assassinations, mass arrests, and the reoccupation of major West Bank cities during *Operation Defensive Shield* in 2002. The separation barrier, begun that same year, became the physical embodiment of this era — a structure of concrete and steel, built in the name of security but mapped to the contours of settlement expansion.

The Second Intifada reshaped both societies. For Palestinians, it deepened fragmentation and despair; for Israelis, it entrenched a security-first worldview and a scepticism towards negotiations, paving the way for the rightward drift in Israeli politics that continues today.

### Gaza Disengagement and West Bank Entrenchment

In 2005, Prime Minister Ariel Sharon executed a unilateral withdrawal from Gaza, evacuating 8,000 settlers and dismantling 21 settlements. The move was framed as a step towards reducing friction and preserving Israel's Jewish majority.

But while Israel withdrew its troops and settlers from Gaza, it retained control over the enclave's borders, airspace, and maritime access. Gaza became a sealed territory, effectively under siege, while in the West Bank, settlement expansion accelerated. The disengagement thus reinforced the bifurcation of the territories: Gaza isolated and blockaded, the West Bank increasingly integrated into Israel's administrative and infrastructural systems.

### Consolidation Through Crisis

Each shock, whether war, uprising, or withdrawal, left the occupation not weakened but strengthened. The Yom Kippur War justified strategic depth; the First Intifada justified tighter security; Oslo's failure legitimised settlement expansion; the Second Intifada entrenched the separation barrier and the surveillance state; Gaza's disengagement cemented the illusion that the occupation could be managed indefinitely without resolution.

By the early 2010s, what had begun in 1967 as a temporary military occupation had hardened into a system of permanent control: a dual legal regime, fragmented geographies, and an economy of dependence, all reinforced by the politics of fear and the language of security.

## Section 6: From Provisional to Permanent

The occupation of the West Bank, Gaza, and East Jerusalem was not meant to last. In the immediate aftermath of the Six-Day War, Israeli leaders spoke in terms of leverage and diplomacy: land to be exchanged for peace, territory to be held until Arab states were ready to negotiate. But over the decades, that language of provisionality gave way to the reality of entrenchment.

Today, more than half a century later, what was temporary has become permanent, not by declaration but by accumulation. Roads, laws, settlements, and walls have turned a military occupation into a complex, institutionalised system of control that resists both internal reform and external pressure.

### The Settlement Archipelago

The most visible sign of this permanence is the network of settlements that now covers the West Bank. From isolated hilltop outposts to fully developed towns with shopping malls and industrial zones, these communities are home to over 700,000 Israelis, connected by a lattice of bypass roads, security fences, and checkpoints.

What began as scattered, strategic nodes has evolved into an archipelago of permanence. Settlements have carved the territory into disconnected cantons, rendering any contiguous Palestinian state almost impossible without large-scale evacuation, a political move no Israeli government has shown the will or capacity to undertake.

The geography of the occupation is deliberate: major settlement blocs sit atop key highlands and water aquifers. Roads bypass Palestinian towns, integrating settlers into Israel proper while isolating Palestinian communities from one another. Maps that once promised a two-state solution now look like a jigsaw puzzle of fragmentation and constraint.

**A Dual Legal System**

Legal duality is another marker of permanence. In the West Bank, two parallel legal regimes operate side by side:• Israeli civil law applies to settlers, granting them full rights, legal protections, and access to Israeli courts.• Military law governs Palestinians, subjecting them to military orders, tribunals, and administrative detention that can last months or years without charge.

This dual system, often described as "one state, two systems", institutionalises inequality. It normalises the exceptional, embedding it in bureaucratic procedure and everyday practice. International law regards the territories as occupied, while Israeli law treats settlements as legitimate extensions of the state. The result is a legal grey zone that functions seamlessly in practice while remaining unresolved in principle.

**Economy and Dependency**

Economically, the occupation has created a relationship of asymmetrical dependency. The Palestinian economy, constrained by movement restrictions, land confiscations, and limited access to resources, is tethered to Israel. Thousands of Palestinians work in construction, agriculture, and low-wage sectors inside Israel or in industrial zones tied to settlements, often without labour protections or collective bargaining rights.

International donors have sought to mitigate this dependency, channelling billions into the Palestinian Authority and development projects. But these efforts often stabilise the status quo rather than disrupt it, creating what some analysts describe as a "donor-enabled occupation" — a system in which external aid subsidises the costs of control without altering its fundamentals.

### Politics of Paralysis

Inside Israel, the occupation has been normalised. Generations have grown up with checkpoints and settlements as ordinary features of the landscape. Political discourse that once spoke of "land for peace" has shifted toward management rather than resolution: the belief that the conflict can be contained, if not solved, through technology, military superiority, and economic incentives.

For Palestinians, the paralysis takes a different form. The failure of the Oslo process, the fragmentation of the West Bank and Gaza, and the internal divisions between Fatah and Hamas have left a leadership vacuum. Popular resistance exists but struggles to coalesce into a unified strategy. The sense of dispossession that began in 1948 has been compounded by the structural realities of a 56-year-old occupation that shows no sign of retreat.

### International Condemnation, Minimal Consequence

Internationally, the occupation is widely condemned. UN resolutions, European Union statements, and reports by human rights organisations regularly declare the illegality of settlements, the violation of Palestinian rights, and the urgent need for a negotiated solution.

Yet condemnation rarely translates into meaningful consequences. U.S. military aid to Israel remains robust; European trade and research partnerships continue; diplomatic pressure is episodic and inconsistent. The occupation, once viewed as a temporary response to war, has become a structural feature of the regional order, maintained not only by Israeli policy but by the inertia of global politics.

Sean Hogan

## The Security-Settlement Feedback Loop

At the heart of the occupation's permanence is a self-reinforcing feedback loop:

• Settlements expand, requiring greater military protection.

• Increased military presence leads to tighter controls over Palestinian movement and land use.

• Palestinian resistance, whether violent or non-violent, is framed as a security threat, justifying further control.

• New security measures, in turn, facilitate further expansion.

This cycle has been remarkably resilient, surviving wars, uprisings, and diplomatic initiatives. Each shock — the First Intifada, the Second Intifada, Gaza's disengagement, even international boycotts — has been met with adjustments that deepen rather than dismantle the architecture of occupation.

## The Normalisation of the Exceptional

Perhaps the most striking feature of the post-1967 trajectory is the normalisation of the exceptional. What was once described as temporary military rule has become an accepted reality, both within Israel and internationally. The language of occupation has faded from much of Israeli political discourse, replaced by euphemisms such as "disputed territories", "Judea and Samaria", and "security zones", which obscure the legal and moral dimensions of control.

For Palestinians, this normalisation is experienced not as abstraction but as the texture of daily life: permits, checkpoints, surveillance, and the quiet, relentless encroachment of settlements on land that was once theirs.

## A System Resistant to Change

The occupation endures because it is adaptive. It absorbs shocks, adjusts to new realities, and continually reinvents its mechanisms of control. It has survived waves of international diplomacy, from the Camp David Accords to Oslo and beyond; it has outlasted uprisings

88

and wars; it has withstood shifts in global politics, from the end of the Cold War to the rise of populist movements across the West.

This resilience is not accidental. It is the product of incrementalism, small continuous actions that, over decades, have transformed a temporary military presence into an entrenched system that feels immovable.

### From Occupation to Annexation

In recent years, the line between occupation and annexation has blurred. Legislative proposals in the Knesset to formally annex parts of the West Bank have gained traction, while de facto annexation has proceeded through administrative integration: applying Israeli law to settlers, extending infrastructure networks, and folding security coordination into state planning.

For Palestinians, the message is clear: the "temporary" occupation has become a permanent reality, one that shapes every aspect of their lives while offering no clear horizon for change.

### The Politics of Permanence

The occupation today is less a policy choice than a political condition, sustained by ideology, inertia, and the absence of viable alternatives. It is a system that manages, contains, and profits from the status quo while rendering transformative change almost unthinkable.

This permanence does not mean stability. It is a brittle equilibrium, sustained by force and fear, vulnerable to shocks such as regional upheavals, demographic shifts, or changes in international attitudes. But for now, it endures a structure built one decision at a time, one settlement at a time, over more than five decades.

# CHAPTER FOUR:
# The Power Network
# Lobbying, Intelligence, Media, Money

## Section 1: AIPAC and the Pro-Israel Lobby Architecture

To understand the resilience of Israeli policy and the depth of U.S. support, military, financial, and diplomatic, one must first understand AIPAC: the American Israel Public Affairs Committee, and the web of affiliated organisations, donors, and networks that surround it. For decades, AIPAC has been the central node in the pro-Israel lobbying ecosystem in Washington, a system built on discipline, access, and an acute understanding of American politics.

### The Origins of a Powerhouse

AIPAC traces its roots to the early 1950s, founded by Isaiah L. Kenen, a former journalist and publicist for the Israeli government. In the aftermath of Israel's creation, its leaders understood that the survival of the young state would depend not only on regional strength but on securing the support of its most important ally: the United States.

Kenen's genius lay in understanding the machinery of Congress. He built relationships quietly, across party lines, positioning AIPAC not as a foreign agent but as a domestic advocacy organisation. By the 1970s, AIPAC had grown into a formidable presence in Washington, with a reputation for discipline, discretion, and effectiveness.

### Methods and Mechanics

AIPAC operates with a clarity of purpose that is the envy of other lobbies. Its mission is simple: to maintain and deepen the U.S.–Israel relationship, ensuring that Israel remains a bipartisan priority on Capitol Hill. Its methods are sophisticated but not mysterious.

- **Relationship-building**: AIPAC cultivates personal ties with members of Congress and their staff, providing briefings, trips to Israel, and access to high-level officials.
- **Policy advocacy**: It drafts talking points, letters, and bills, shaping the language of legislation and debate.
- **Campaign financing**: While AIPAC itself does not directly donate to candidates, it coordinates networks of donors and political action committees (PACs) that channel millions of dollars into campaigns each election cycle.
- **Rapid response**: When criticism of Israel surfaces, whether over settlements, military actions, or human rights issues, AIPAC mobilises instantly, ensuring that key allies on the Hill deliver rebuttals and that dissenting voices face political consequences.

This disciplined, bipartisan strategy ensured that, for decades, support for Israel was a political given in Washington, not a partisan issue but an article of faith.

### Bipartisanship and the Evangelical Alliance

AIPAC's strength has always rested on its ability to straddle the partisan divide. It cultivated close ties with Democratic stalwarts like Lyndon Johnson and Hubert Humphrey, even as it built alliances with Republicans from Ronald Reagan to George W. Bush.

The rise of the Christian evangelical movement in the 1980s added a powerful new dimension. Evangelical leaders, viewing Israel through a biblical lens, brought not only grassroots enthusiasm but also political muscle, particularly within the Republican Party. This alliance deepened during the Trump administration, which delivered policies long championed by the pro-Israel right: the recognition of Jerusalem as Israel's capital, the relocation of the U.S. embassy, and the recognition of Israeli sovereignty over the Golan Heights.

### The AIPAC Network

To speak of AIPAC alone is to understate the breadth of the pro-Israel network. Alongside AIPAC are dozens of affiliated and aligned organisations:

- Political Action Committees (PACs) that aggregate donations to candidates supportive of Israeli policy.
- Think tanks like the Washington Institute for Near East Policy (WINEP), which provide research and policy analysis aligned with Israeli security interests.
- Legal advocacy groups, such as the Anti-Defamation League (ADL) and the American Jewish Committee (AJC), which often engage in issues related to antisemitism and campus discourse.
- Media and communications outfits that amplify key narratives and mobilise rapid response during crises.

This ecosystem operates with remarkable coordination, ensuring that support for Israel remains deeply embedded in the American political system.

### Discipline and Deterrence

AIPAC's influence is not solely about access and persuasion; it is also about discipline and deterrence. Legislators who deviate from the consensus often find themselves facing well-funded primary challengers. Campaign donations can surge for opponents, while supportive ads and messaging bolster allies.

This dynamic has been particularly visible in recent election cycles. In 2022 and 2024, AIPAC-backed super PACs spent heavily in Democratic primaries, targeting progressive candidates critical of Israel. The message was unmistakable: criticism of Israeli policy carries a political cost.

## Challenges to the Status Quo

Yet, beneath the surface of apparent continuity, the ground is shifting. The war in Gaza, the images of civilian devastation, and the rise of a younger, more progressive generation of voters have begun to erode the bipartisan consensus that AIPAC has cultivated for decades.

- Within the Democratic Party, polling shows a widening gap between the party base, particularly younger voters, voters of colour, and progressives, and its leadership.
- The Republican Party, meanwhile, has moved sharply toward unconditional support for Israel, driven by the evangelical alliance and the influence of Trump-era politics.

This divergence has not yet translated into a collapse of support on Capitol Hill. Aid packages continue to pass with overwhelming majorities, but the tenor of debate is changing. Criticism that was once confined to the margins now echoes in committee hearings, op-eds, and even presidential primaries.

## AIPAC in the Post-2023 Era

The events of 7 October 2023 and the subsequent Israeli military operations in Gaza have been a stress test for AIPAC's model. In the immediate aftermath, there was a surge of solidarity: resolutions condemning Hamas, pledges of additional aid, and bipartisan affirmations of support for Israel's right to defend itself.

But as images of mass civilian casualties, starvation, and destruction mounted, the political cost of unconditional support began to rise. Protests erupted on college campuses, in city streets, and even within congressional offices. The language of accountability, war crimes, proportionality, and international law, began to creep into debates once defined by uncritical support.

AIPAC has responded with characteristic aggression, ramping up spending, doubling down on lobbying efforts, and framing criticism of Israeli policy as antisemitism. But the terrain has shifted. What was once a fortress of consensus is now a contested space, with cracks widening under the weight of public opinion.

**Looking Ahead**

AIPAC remains one of the most powerful lobbies in Washington. Its ability to mobilise funds, influence legislation, and shape narratives is unmatched. But it faces challenges unprecedented in its history:

- The generational shift in attitudes toward Israel among younger Americans.
- The rise of alternative organisations, like J Street, that advocate for a two-state solution and more conditional U.S. support.
- The growing disconnect between the political establishment and public opinion, particularly in the wake of humanitarian crises in Gaza.

Whether AIPAC can adapt, maintaining bipartisan influence while navigating a more polarised environment, will shape not only U.S. policy toward Israel but also the trajectory of the conflict itself.

## Section 2: Counterweights and Coalition Politics

For decades, support for Israel in Washington was a near-immutable constant. But politics, like nature, abhors a vacuum. Over the past two decades, and accelerating since the wars in Gaza from 2023 onward, a network of counterweights has begun to take shape, challenging the narrative monopoly once held by AIPAC and its allies.

This is not to suggest that pro-Israel lobbying power has waned to irrelevance; it has not. But the environment in which it operates is more contested, more polarised, and more visible than at any time in the modern era. The shift is not just in the United States but also in Europe, Latin America, Africa, and the Global South: a recalibration of alliances, advocacy, and political courage.

**The Rise of Progressive Advocacy**

The first major counterweight to AIPAC emerged not from foreign governments or grassroots activism abroad, but from within the Jewish-American community itself.

In 2008, a group of American Jews, frustrated by what they saw as AIPAC's reflexive defence of Israeli policies regardless of their impact on peace prospects, founded J Street. Billing itself as *"pro-Israel, pro-peace"*, J Street positioned itself as an alternative voice, supportive of Israel's right to exist but sharply critical of settlement expansion and the Netanyahu government's hardline policies.

J Street's strategy was to mirror AIPAC's organisational discipline but to advance a different message: that unconditional U.S. support for Israel, particularly for policies entrenching occupation, was harmful to both Israelis and Palestinians. While never matching AIPAC's financial muscle or access, J Street succeeded in giving political cover to members of Congress, particularly Democrats, who were uneasy with the status quo but wary of crossing AIPAC openly.

**Grassroots Mobilisation and the Progressive Base**

If J Street provided the institutional scaffolding for dissent within the Democratic Party, the real shift has come from grassroots activism.

The wars in Gaza, especially the humanitarian devastation broadcast in real time on social media, catalysed a generational realignment. Younger Americans, particularly those on college campuses and in activist spaces, increasingly see the Palestinian struggle through the lens of social justice, anti-colonialism, and human rights. Hashtags like #FreePalestine, once fringe in mainstream political discourse, have entered the language of progressive movements alongside climate justice, racial equality, and gender rights.

This activism has not been confined to the streets. Progressive members of Congress, the so-called *"Squad"*, have amplified these voices in hearings and debates, calling for conditions on U.S. aid and accountability for violations of international law. In turn, these members have faced well-funded primary challenges backed by AIPAC-affiliated PACs, highlighting the growing tension between the party base and its establishment leadership.

**The Evangelical Factor**

On the other side of the political spectrum, the alliance between Israel and the American evangelical movement has only deepened. Evangelicals see Israel not only as a strategic ally but as a theological partner, central to eschatological beliefs about prophecy and redemption.

This alliance ensures that even as cracks appear in bipartisan support, the Republican Party remains firmly aligned with Israel, often to the right of Israel's own governments. Figures like former Vice President Mike Pence and Florida Governor Ron DeSantis have built entire foreign-policy platforms around unconditional support for Israel, framing criticism of the state as tantamount to antisemitism or even heresy.

This dynamic creates a political paradox. As support for Israel becomes more polarised, with Democrats divided and Republicans doubling down, U.S. policy risks being shaped less by strategic calculation and more by partisan tribalism.

**Emerging Global Counterweights**

Outside the United States, the conversation has shifted even more dramatically.

- In Europe, while governments in Berlin, London, and Paris have remained staunchly supportive of Israel's security needs, public opinion has shifted sharply. Protests in European capitals, often drawing hundreds of thousands, have pushed parliaments to debate arms sales, military cooperation, and trade relationships.

- In the Global South, Israel's alignment with Western powers and its actions in Gaza have eroded the quiet relationships it once cultivated. Countries like South Africa have taken leadership roles in international forums, most notably bringing the genocide case against Israel before the International Court of Justice in The Hague.

- In Latin America, governments from Chile to Colombia have recalled ambassadors, suspended trade talks, or issued blistering condemnations of Israeli policy, reflecting both domestic pressure and long-standing solidarities with the Palestinian cause.

These shifts reflect a broader trend: the erosion of the moral high ground Israel once claimed in the wake of the Holocaust. While antisemitism remains a potent and dangerous force globally, it is increasingly recognised as distinct from criticism of Israeli state policy, a distinction that pro-Israel advocacy groups have struggled to erase.

### Digital Media and the Collapse of Narrative Control

One of the most significant factors in this shift has been the rise of digital media. For decades, narratives about the conflict were filtered through mainstream outlets, newspapers, television networks, and official spokespeople. But the ubiquity of smartphones and social platforms has changed the information battlefield.

In Gaza, videos of bombings, funerals, and desperate families are uploaded within minutes, reaching millions without editorial mediation. Citizen journalism has pierced the veil of official narratives, making it harder to control perception or downplay humanitarian crises.

For Israel and its allies, this has created a new and unpredictable front: narrative decentralisation. Traditional lobbying and public relations campaigns are less effective in an environment where raw images of suffering compete with official talking points in real time.

## Coalitions of Conscience

The backlash to Israeli policy is no longer confined to Palestinian advocacy groups or Arab American communities. Intersectional coalitions have formed, linking the Palestinian cause to other movements for justice: Black Lives Matter, Indigenous rights campaigns, and climate activism.

This intersectionality has amplified the reach of Palestinian advocacy, framing the issue not as a distant geopolitical conflict but as part of a global struggle against oppression, militarisation, and inequality. For many younger activists, *"Free Palestine"* is not a foreign policy slogan; it is an ethical imperative.

## The Changing Democratic Landscape

Nowhere is the tension more apparent than within the Democratic Party. Polls show that younger Democrats are far more critical of Israel than their parents' generation, with some surveys indicating majority support for conditioning or reducing U.S. military aid. Yet at the leadership level, figures like President Biden and Senate Majority Leader Chuck Schumer have maintained strong support for Israel, often citing strategic ties and shared values.

This disconnect has created political volatility. Progressive candidates face aggressive opposition from pro-Israel groups in primaries, while incumbents risk alienating younger voters by maintaining unconditional support. The result is a party increasingly split between its base and its establishment, with implications that extend far beyond foreign policy.

**Pressure, Backlash, and the Future**

As counterweights grow stronger, so too does the backlash. Anti-BDS legislation has proliferated across U.S. states, often with bipartisan support, raising profound questions about free speech and the limits of dissent. On college campuses, students and faculty face intimidation, doxxing, and professional repercussions for expressing pro-Palestinian views.

Yet these tactics, effective in the short term, have long-term costs. They reinforce perceptions of overreach and censorship, galvanising opposition rather than silencing it.

The battle for public opinion, once fought quietly in committee rooms and donor dinners, is now public, visible, and global. And while AIPAC and its allies retain formidable institutional power, the narrative battlefield is no longer theirs to control.

# Section 3: Mossad, Intelligence, and the Darker Corners of Power

## Introduction – Myth and Reality

Few intelligence agencies command the same mix of fear, admiration, and suspicion as Israel's Mossad. Since its founding in 1949, Mossad has cultivated and earned a reputation for precision, audacity, and reach far beyond the country's small size.

To supporters, it is the sharp edge of Israel's survival instinct: small teams, high stakes, global reach, and operational brilliance. To critics, it is a shadowy force operating with near-total deniability, blurring the line between security and extrajudicial action.

What makes Mossad so unique in the global imagination is not just its operational record but its mythos. Popular culture, from novels and Hollywood films to the pages of *Time* and *Newsweek*, has elevated the agency to near-mystical status, an omnipresent, omniscient player in every major geopolitical drama. The truth, as with most intelligence organisations, is both more impressive and more prosaic: a small, tightly run service with strategic priorities, a limited budget, and a remarkable ability to leverage intelligence into political capital.

## A Brief History of Mossad

Mossad, formally *HaMossad leModi'in uleTafkidim Meyuhadim* ("The Institute for Intelligence and Special Operations"), was founded in December 1949, one year after the creation of the State of Israel. Its early mandate was simple: to coordinate intelligence gathering abroad, complementing the domestic security agency (Shin Bet) and military intelligence (Aman).

Its first years were characterised by improvisation. With limited resources, Mossad relied on global Jewish networks, sympathetic foreign operatives, and clandestine relationships with allies such as France to secure weapons, technology, and intelligence during the volatile early years of statehood.

By the 1950s, Mossad had evolved from a scrappy start-up into a disciplined, professional service. Under legendary directors like Isser Harel, it developed a reputation for daring and precision, particularly in operations targeting existential threats to the young state.

## Early Operations and Foundational Myths

Several early operations cemented Mossad's reputation:

• **The Capture of Adolf Eichmann (1960):** Perhaps its most famous mission, a Mossad team tracked down Adolf Eichmann, a key architect of the Holocaust, living under an assumed name in Buenos Aires. Eichmann was abducted, flown to Israel, and tried in Jerusalem in a landmark case that seared the Holocaust into Israeli and global consciousness.

• **Covert Arms Procurement:** In the years following independence, Mossad played a critical role in sourcing arms from

Europe and bypassing embargoes to secure the weaponry that ensured Israel's survival during early conflicts.

• **Penetration of Arab States:** Throughout the 1950s and 1960s, Mossad ran extensive human intelligence networks across Egypt, Syria, Lebanon, and Jordan, often using deep-cover operatives fluent in Arabic and integrated into local societies.

These formative missions established Mossad's reputation as an agency that could punch far above its weight, relying on meticulous planning, operational discipline, and boldness.

### Doctrine: Small, Agile, Deniable

Unlike the CIA or MI6, Mossad was never about size. It operated, and still operates, on the principle that quality matters more than quantity. The service maintains only a few thousand operatives, but their agility, cultural fluency, and integration with Israel's strategic needs make the agency unusually effective.

Mossad's core priorities have historically revolved around:

• Preventing existential threats, particularly weapons of mass destruction programmes in hostile states.

• Disrupting terrorism directed against Israeli or Jewish targets worldwide.

• Gathering political and military intelligence to inform Israeli policy and military planning.

• Maintaining deniable influence in foreign capitals to shape perceptions and policy.

This strategic discipline explains both its successes and its mystique.

### Successes and Controversies

Mossad's operational record reads like the script of a geopolitical thriller, but it is also marked by controversy and failure.

**Successes:**

• **Wrath of God (1972–1980):** In the wake of the Munich Olympics massacre, in which 11 Israeli athletes were killed by Black September, Mossad launched a global campaign of targeted assassinations against those linked to the attack. The operations were lethal and, in many cases, spectacularly precise.

• **Operation Entebbe (1976):** Mossad's intelligence enabled the daring rescue of more than 100 hostages from an Air France jet hijacked to Uganda. The raid became a defining moment in Israel's national story, reinforcing the perception of a state that could and would act anywhere to protect its citizens.

• **Iran and Covert Sabotage:** In the decades that followed, Mossad honed its reputation for surgical operations, including assassinations of nuclear scientists in Iran, cyber operations such as Stuxnet (in collaboration with the United States), and sabotage campaigns designed to slow Tehran's nuclear ambitions.

**Controversies and Failures:**

• **The Lillehammer Affair (1973):** In Norway, a Mossad team mistakenly assassinated an innocent Moroccan waiter, believing him to be a senior Palestinian operative. The botched operation led to arrests, diplomatic embarrassment, and criticism of Mossad's methods.

• **Diplomatic Strains:** Operations in friendly countries, from forging passports in New Zealand to the 2010 assassination of Mahmoud al-Mabhouh in Dubai, have periodically strained alliances, highlighting the risks inherent in operating globally with minimal oversight.

**Influence and Strategic Value**

Mossad's value has never been measured solely in operations but in the strategic intelligence it provides. During the Cold War, Israel's intelligence-sharing arrangements with the United States and European powers gave it leverage far beyond its size. In return for access to American technology and political support, Israel provided high-quality, actionable intelligence on Soviet arms transfers, Arab military capabilities, and emerging terrorist networks.

This intelligence-for-influence exchange remains a pillar of the US–Israel relationship. In the post-9/11 world, as counterterrorism became a global priority, Mossad's expertise in tracking non-state actors and pre-empting attacks became an invaluable commodity.

**Myth, Reality, and the Public Imagination**

What sets Mossad apart in the global imagination is not only what it does but what people believe it does. The agency has carefully cultivated an aura of omniscience and reach, an image that deters adversaries and amplifies its influence without requiring proof.

In reality, Mossad, like all intelligence agencies, operates within constraints: human error, incomplete information, and the political oversight (however minimal) of the Israeli state. But the myth of the all-seeing, all-powerful Mossad serves as a force multiplier, making its small size and limited resources seem irrelevant.

**Epstein, Maxwell, and the Allegations**

Few narratives have captured the darker suspicions surrounding Israel's intelligence apparatus like the complex web of Jeffrey Epstein, Ghislaine Maxwell, and Robert Maxwell. The story is intoxicating: a disgraced billionaire financier with ties to global elites, a British socialite daughter of a publishing tycoon with documented connections to Israel, and whispers, never fully substantiated, of espionage, *kompromat*, and blackmail.

To write honestly about these connections is to tread carefully, separating what is verifiable from what is alleged, and noting where gaps in evidence leave space for speculation but not for certainty.

### Robert Maxwell – The Patriarch

The starting point is Robert Maxwell, the Czech-born British media baron who built a publishing empire and died mysteriously in 1991, falling (or jumping) from his yacht, the *Lady Ghislaine*.

### What is known:

• Maxwell had deep, documented ties to Israel. He maintained relationships at the highest levels of Israeli politics and intelligence. He was instrumental in the distribution of the PROMIS software, later linked to espionage scandals, and he used his media influence to shape narratives favourable to Israel.

• Upon his death, the Israeli government afforded him a state-level funeral in Jerusalem. Six current and former heads of Israeli intelligence attended, along with Prime Ministers Yitzhak Shamir and Shimon Peres. That attendance was not ceremonial; it was an acknowledgment of a man who had served the state in ways the public might never fully know.

### What remains unclear:

• While numerous intelligence officials and journalists have suggested Maxwell worked as a long-time asset or collaborator of Mossad, the operational details remain opaque, and much of the speculation is built on inference rather than declassified evidence.

### Ghislaine Maxwell and the Epstein Connection

Ghislaine Maxwell, Robert's daughter, inherited his elite networks and used them to establish a close, decades-long relationship with Jeffrey Epstein.

The documented facts about Epstein:

• He cultivated relationships with influential figures worldwide, from Wall Street bankers to scientists, politicians, and royals.

• He maintained properties in New York, Palm Beach, New Mexico, and the U.S. Virgin Islands, some of which were equipped with extensive surveillance systems.

• He was convicted in 2008 for soliciting prostitution from a minor and arrested again in 2019 on federal charges of sex trafficking of minors. He died in jail under disputed circumstances.

Ghislaine Maxwell, for her part, was convicted in 2021 of multiple federal charges related to Epstein's abuse network.

**The Intelligence Allegations**

The most explosive and least substantiated claims concern links between Epstein's operation and intelligence agencies, including Mossad.

Points often cited by researchers and journalists include:

• Epstein and Maxwell's proximity to Israeli officials and well-connected operatives in finance and media.

• The surveillance infrastructure in Epstein's properties, which some argue suggests a *kompromat* operation targeting influential figures.

• Testimony from individuals in law enforcement and intelligence, often off-the-record, describing Epstein as a "protected" figure for years.

The evidentiary gaps include:

• There is no declassified documentation directly tying Epstein to Mossad or any intelligence service.

• Publicly available records, including court filings, deposition transcripts, and financial disclosures, show a man with immense wealth, murky sources of income, and extraordinary access, but no conclusive operational link to an intelligence agency.

Investigative journalists such as Vicky Ward and Dylan Howard have explored these threads, and whistleblowers have provided anecdotal claims, but the hard evidence remains elusive. To present speculation as fact would collapse the distinction between credible inquiry and conspiracy theory, a distinction this manuscript will maintain.

## Why the Allegations Persist

The persistence of these theories is not surprising. They are sustained by several factors:

• **Pattern and precedent:** Mossad has a documented history of running human intelligence and *kompromat* operations globally.

• **Opacity:** Epstein's financial empire was labyrinthine, his relationships unusually elite, and the circumstances of his 2019 death suspicious to many.

• **Mistrust of institutions:** The failure of law enforcement and political figures to act decisively, despite years of credible allegations, created a vacuum into which speculation poured.

These dynamics create a fertile environment for theories of intelligence involvement, some plausible and others entirely unsubstantiated.

## Documented Influence Operations

Where the record is clearer is in the coordination of influence and narrative by Israeli intelligence and allied networks in the West. Mossad, like the CIA or MI6, maintains a presence in the information space:

• Funding or cultivating relationships with think tanks and lobby groups.

• Coordinating messaging during diplomatic crises, such as wars in Gaza or campaigns against Iran's nuclear programme.

• Conducting *hasbara* campaigns designed to shape foreign media narratives and mobilise diaspora communities in support of Israeli policies.

This machinery of influence, while less sensational than the Epstein saga, is more consequential. It is not covert *kompromat* but overt soft power, and it has been a key pillar of Israel's diplomatic leverage for decades.

**The Importance of Precision**

It is tempting to fold every unexplained detail, every unexplained wealth transfer, and every suspicious connection into a grand narrative of intelligence conspiracy. But to do so risks undermining the credibility of legitimate inquiry.

A rigorous account must do three things:

1. Distinguish fact from inference.
2. Acknowledge the limits of public evidence.
3. Recognise the difference between plausible hypothesis and proven history.

The reality, as it stands, is that Robert Maxwell's service to Israel is well-documented. Ghislaine Maxwell's role in Epstein's network is proven, but Epstein's direct operational ties to any intelligence agency, including Mossad, remain unproven.

**Narrative Power and Public Perception**

Regardless of what is ultimately proven, the perception of intelligence involvement has been devastating. It has deepened cynicism about elite impunity, reinforced suspicions of covert influence operations, and fed into broader narratives about the entanglement of intelligence, finance, and politics.

This matters because perception shapes legitimacy. In the same way that Mossad's mythos amplifies its operational reach, the Epstein-Maxwell saga has amplified global scepticism toward Israeli lobbying and intelligence activity, particularly among younger and more digitally native audiences.

**Narrative Management and Hasbara**

If Mossad represents the hard edge of Israeli power, *hasbara*, literally "explanation" in Hebrew, represents the soft edge: a strategic communications framework designed to shape global narratives, build sympathy for Israel, and counter criticism. For decades, this narrative management has been as important as any military or intelligence operation.

## The Origins of Hasbara

From the moment of Israel's founding in 1948, its leaders understood that survival would depend not just on military strength but on the ability to win and maintain international legitimacy. The young state, surrounded by hostile neighbours and dependent on Western support, invested heavily in messaging, emphasising its democratic values, its role as a refuge for Holocaust survivors, and its alignment with Western liberalism.

By the 1967 war, *hasbara* had matured into a disciplined, coordinated effort. Ministries, diaspora organisations, and sympathetic media channels worked in sync to present Israel as a beleaguered but moral actor, an underdog fighting for survival in a hostile region. The imagery of paratroopers at the Western Wall, broadcast globally, cemented this image.

## The Global Hasbara Network

In the decades that followed, *hasbara* evolved into a global ecosystem:

• Government agencies, including the Ministry of Foreign Affairs, the Prime Minister's Office, and intelligence services, coordinated talking points and rapid response.

• Diaspora organisations, from AIPAC in Washington to the Board of Deputies in London, mobilised local advocacy and lobbying.

• Media relationships were cultivated, providing sympathetic journalists with exclusive access and shaping coverage in major outlets.

• Digital operations emerged as the internet age dawned, with Israel investing in social media engagement, deploying both overt and covert campaigns to influence discourse.

This machinery ensured that for decades, Israel was able to dominate the narrative in Western capitals, framing itself as a democratic bulwark against extremism and casting Palestinian resistance, whether armed or non-violent, as terrorism.

### Information Warfare in the Digital Age

The rise of social media in the 2010s disrupted this model. Platforms like Twitter, Facebook, and TikTok gave Palestinians, particularly in Gaza and the West Bank, a direct line to global audiences. Smartphone footage of bombings, funerals, and checkpoints bypassed traditional gatekeepers, presenting raw, unmediated images that often contradicted official Israeli narratives.

The 2023–2025 Gaza war accelerated this shift. In an environment where every airstrike was documented in real time, the language of "precision strikes" and "human shields" rang hollow against footage of bombed apartment blocks, starving children, and mass graves. *Hasbara*, once a powerful tool of narrative control, struggled to keep pace.

### Lawfare and the Battle for Legitimacy

In parallel with narrative management, Israel, often in coordination with pro-Israel legal groups abroad, embraced lawfare, the strategic use of legal systems to advance policy goals:

• **Anti-BDS Legislation:** Across U.S. states, laws were passed penalising companies and individuals that boycotted Israel or Israeli products. Civil libertarians challenged these laws as violations of free speech, but they underscored the extent to which pro-Israel advocacy had embedded itself within American legislative frameworks.

• **Litigation and intimidation:** Advocacy groups funded legal actions against activists, academics, and NGOs critical of Israel, framing criticism as antisemitic or supportive of terrorism.

• **International institutions:** Israel lobbied aggressively against investigations by the International Criminal Court (ICC) and United Nations bodies, often with support from Washington.

For years, these tactics were effective. But as public opinion shifted, particularly in Europe and the Global South, the effectiveness of lawfare began to erode, giving way to calls for sanctions, embargoes, and even war crimes prosecutions.

### The Erosion of the Narrative

By 2025, the cracks in Israel's narrative control were undeniable. The images from Gaza, amplified globally, reframed the conflict not as a battle against terrorism but as a humanitarian catastrophe. Statements by Israeli ministers, calling for the "erasure" of towns, describing Palestinians as "human animals" and even suggesting nuclear options, were translated, subtitled, and disseminated worldwide within hours, often without context or mitigation.

Where once such rhetoric would have been dismissed or ignored, it now circulated instantly, becoming evidence in the court of global opinion and, increasingly, in formal legal forums. The International Court of Justice (ICJ) and the International Criminal Court (ICC) cited such statements in preliminary findings and investigative frameworks, highlighting the way words had consequences beyond domestic politics.

### Mossad, Influence, and Perception

Mossad's role in this shifting landscape is complex. The agency remains one of the world's most capable intelligence organisations, but its aura of invincibility has been eroded by transparency and digital scrutiny. Operations that once slipped quietly into history now face near-instant documentation and forensic analysis by journalists, activists, and open-source investigators.

The Epstein-Maxwell saga amplified this erosion. Even absent conclusive proof of intelligence links, the association of Israeli networks with scandal, impunity, and exploitation fuelled suspicion and cynicism. The very perception of intelligence involvement became corrosive to Israel's broader narrative of moral clarity.

**From Dominance to Defensiveness**

By the middle of the decade, the tone of *hasbara* had shifted from confident to defensive. Where once Israel projected an image of moral certainty, it now finds itself on the back foot, responding to accusations of war crimes, genocide, and systemic dehumanisation.

Efforts to equate criticism of Israel with antisemitism still resonate in some political and media circles, particularly in the United States and parts of Europe, but they ring increasingly hollow in a world where digital evidence tells a different story.

This defensive posture is more than a communications problem; it is a strategic liability. Legitimacy, once a source of strength, is now contested in every arena: legal, diplomatic, cultural, and informational.

**The Global Perception Shift**

Perhaps the most profound change is not in the machinery of influence itself but in global perception. In the 1970s and 1980s, Israel was widely seen, in the West at least, as a beleaguered democracy, an outpost of liberal values in a hostile region. By 2025, that image has been overtaken by a different narrative: Israel as an occupier, a state wielding overwhelming force against a largely defenceless population, sustained by Western complicity.

This perception shift has had tangible effects:

• Diplomatic isolation in forums such as the UN General Assembly, where votes condemning Israeli actions now draw overwhelming support.

• Legal jeopardy, with proceedings in The Hague challenging not only specific operations but the structure of the occupation itself.

• Grassroots mobilisation, from university campuses to labour unions, driving divestment campaigns and public protests on an unprecedented scale.

## Conclusion: Influence and Its Limits

For decades, Israel, through Mossad, through AIPAC, and through the diffuse machinery of lobbying and narrative management, maintained an extraordinary hold over how its story was told. But power built on perception is vulnerable to transparency.

The digital age, the rise of open-source investigation, and the sheer scale of human suffering in Gaza have combined to erode that hold. What remains is a reputation crisis: a state still militarily dominant, still backed by powerful allies, but increasingly isolated in the arena that matters most for legitimacy: global public opinion.

# CHAPTER FIVE:
# Gaza and the Collapse of Legitimacy
# (2023–2025)

## Section 1 – A Timeline of Destruction

The Gaza war that erupted on 7 October 2023 was not the first conflict between Israel and Hamas. There had been four major Gaza wars since 2008, each brutal in its own way, each leaving the enclave more devastated than before. But what began that October morning marked a rupture: an unprecedented attack, an unrestrained military response, and a humanitarian catastrophe that would fundamentally reshape the global conversation on Israel, Palestine, and Zionism itself.

### 7 October 2023 – The Breach

At dawn on 7 October, Hamas launched Operation Al-Aqsa Flood, breaching the heavily fortified barrier around Gaza with explosives and bulldozers. Thousands of rockets rained down on Israeli towns and cities, overwhelming Iron Dome batteries. Militants streamed into southern Israel on foot, on motorbikes, and by paragliders.

In kibbutzim and border communities such as Be'eri, Kfar Aza, and Nir Oz, massacres unfolded. By the end of the day, 1,200 Israelis were dead, including civilians attending the Nova music festival. Hundreds more were injured, and over 200 hostages, from infants to the elderly, were taken back into Gaza. The scale and savagery of the attack stunned Israel and the world.

Israel's vaunted security apparatus, including Mossad and the IDF, appeared blindsided. The breach of what was considered an impenetrable perimeter shattered public confidence and triggered a national crisis.

## 8–15 October 2023 – The Immediate Response

Within hours, Israel declared a state of war and mobilised 360,000 reservists, the largest mobilisation in decades. Prime Minister Benjamin Netanyahu vowed "mighty vengeance," framing the war as an existential battle against barbarism.

Gaza, already under a 16-year blockade, was placed under a "total siege": no electricity, no water, no food, no fuel. Bombing campaigns began almost immediately, targeting what the IDF described as command centres, weapons caches, and tunnel networks. In reality, the strikes also decimated residential towers, markets, schools, and mosques.

By mid-October, Gaza's health ministry reported over 4,000 Palestinians killed, many of them women and children. Entire neighbourhoods were reduced to rubble. Communications blackouts, imposed intermittently, made independent verification difficult, but satellite imagery confirmed widespread devastation.

## Late October–November 2023 – The Ground Invasion

On 27 October, the IDF launched its ground invasion, advancing from the north into Gaza City. The stated goal was to destroy Hamas's military capabilities and dismantle its tunnel network, dubbed the "Gaza Metro."

Urban combat was fierce, with Hamas fighters using tunnels and dense urban terrain to their advantage. Israel responded with overwhelming firepower: artillery, airstrikes, and drone strikes levelled entire city blocks to secure narrow territorial gains.

By the end of November, casualty figures had climbed to over 15,000 Palestinians dead and 1.7 million displaced, more than 70% of Gaza's population. Aid agencies warned of a spiralling humanitarian crisis: hospitals overwhelmed, morgues overflowing, and clean water running out.

## December 2023 – Hospitals Under Siege

In early December, images of bombed hospitals shocked global audiences. The Al-Shifa Medical Complex, Gaza's largest hospital, became the focal point of the war as Israeli forces claimed it was being used as a Hamas command centre.

The IDF raided the facility, releasing videos purporting to show weapons and tunnels. Independent journalists and humanitarian observers questioned the evidence, highlighting the scale of civilian suffering. By Christmas, Gaza's healthcare system had collapsed. Doctors performed amputations without anaesthesia; neonatal units ran on dwindling generator fuel; the World Health Organization warned of an "unprecedented health disaster."

## January–March 2024 – The War Deepens

By early 2024, the war showed no sign of ending. Israeli forces expanded their operations southward, ordering civilians to evacuate repeatedly, from north to central Gaza, then to Khan Younis, and finally to Rafah, the last remaining refuge near the Egyptian border. Each time, areas designated as "safe zones" were bombed within days.

By March, over 30,000 Palestinians had been killed, according to Gaza's health authorities, with UN monitors and independent analysts confirming high civilian casualty rates. Entire families were wiped out in single strikes.

Humanitarian agencies described conditions in apocalyptic terms:

• Starvation: food supplies were critically low; children were photographed eating grass and animal feed.

• Disease: overcrowding and contaminated water triggered outbreaks of cholera and respiratory infections.

• Education: every school in Gaza was either destroyed or converted into a shelter.

### April–June 2024 – International Outcry

As images of mass graves, skeletal children, and bombed UN facilities circulated globally, the international narrative shifted decisively. Protests erupted in cities from London to New York, Cape Town to Jakarta. On university campuses, encampments demanding divestment from Israel sprang up across the United States, Canada, and Europe.

At the United Nations, emergency sessions were convened almost weekly. The United States vetoed multiple Security Council resolutions calling for an immediate ceasefire, isolating itself diplomatically. In The Hague, South Africa filed a case at the International Court of Justice accusing Israel of genocide, a move supported by dozens of states across the Global South.

### Mid–Late 2024 – Political Fallout and Stalemate

By mid-2024, the war had ground into a brutal stalemate. Northern Gaza was largely depopulated; the south, overcrowded and starving. Israel claimed to have destroyed much of Hamas's infrastructure but failed to secure a decisive victory or rescue most hostages.

Inside Israel, political pressure mounted. Families of hostages demanded a ceasefire and prisoner exchange, clashing with hardline ministers who called for the war to continue "until total victory." Netanyahu, facing plummeting approval ratings and corruption trials, doubled down, framing the war as an existential struggle and rejecting international calls for restraint.

### Early 2025 – Collapse of Gaza

By early 2025, Gaza was unrecognisable. Satellite imagery showed entire districts erased. The United Nations described conditions as "beyond catastrophic." Famine was declared in northern Gaza, with UNRWA reporting children dying daily from hunger and dehydration.

Despite mounting evidence of mass civilian deaths and war crimes, major Western powers continued to supply weapons and diplomatic cover. The United States approved emergency arms transfers; the UK and Germany resisted domestic calls to suspend exports; France wavered but stopped short of sanctions.

At the same time, the humanitarian crisis deepened the political isolation of Israel globally. Latin American governments cut diplomatic ties; South Africa, Brazil, and Turkey led calls for arms embargoes; and even traditional allies in Europe began to distance themselves rhetorically, if not materially.

**Spring–Summer 2025 – The World Watches**

By mid-2025, Gaza had become the most documented humanitarian disaster of the century. Every atrocity, every bombing, every plea for aid was broadcast globally, unfiltered, in real time.

This unprecedented transparency eroded the narrative of moral clarity Israel had long cultivated. Statements by Israeli ministers referring to Palestinians as "human animals," calls for the "erasure" of Gaza, and suggestions of nuclear options circulated widely, cited in legal filings and international debates.

For much of the world, Gaza became the moment where the myth of Israel as a besieged democracy collapsed, replaced by an image of an occupying power wielding unrestrained force against a defenceless population.

## Section 2 – Civilian Toll and the Siege Economy

The statistics alone are staggering. By the summer of 2025, more than 45,000 Palestinians were dead, according to Gaza's health authorities, a figure broadly corroborated by United Nations monitors and independent analysts. Over 70% of the dead were women and children. Nearly two million people, over 85% of Gaza's population, were displaced, forced into tents, makeshift shelters, or the ruins of their homes.

But the raw numbers only hint at the scale of Gaza's collapse. Beneath the data lies a story of starvation, despair, and systemic destruction, a deliberate dismantling of the fabric of life in one of the most densely populated places on earth.

### Starvation as a Weapon

When Defence Minister Yoav Gallant announced a "complete siege" on 9 October 2023, "no electricity, no food, no fuel, no water," it was framed as a tactical measure to weaken Hamas. But as the siege dragged on, it became clear that the policy had indiscriminate humanitarian consequences.

By December 2023, food pipelines had collapsed. The World Food Programme (WFP) warned of "imminent famine." By March 2024, UNICEF was reporting that children in northern Gaza were eating grass and animal feed to survive.

Satellite images captured the extent of agricultural destruction: fields bulldozed, greenhouses flattened, and fishing fleets sunk or confiscated. Starvation was no longer a by-product of war; it had become a strategic instrument of pressure in violation of international humanitarian law prohibiting the use of food as a weapon.

### The Collapse of Healthcare

The healthcare system, fragile even before the war, collapsed under the strain of relentless bombing and siege.

• Hospitals bombed: from Al-Shifa in Gaza City to Nasser Hospital in Khan Younis, medical facilities were targeted, often justified by Israeli officials as strikes on Hamas command centres.

• Doctors under fire: the World Health Organization (WHO) documented dozens of attacks on ambulances and medical convoys, despite advance notification to Israeli authorities of their coordinates.

• Medicine shortages: insulin, antibiotics, anaesthetics all ran out within weeks. Surgeons performed amputations without painkillers. Neonatal units failed as generators ran out of fuel, leading to the deaths of premature infants.

By mid-2024, the WHO declared Gaza's health system "non-functional." Cholera outbreaks swept through crowded displacement camps, compounding the death toll.

### Infrastructure Erased

The scale of physical destruction is without precedent in Gaza's modern history.

• Homes: UN satellite imagery estimates that over 60% of all housing units were damaged or destroyed by mid-2024. Entire districts of Gaza City, Khan Younis, and Rafah were flattened.

• Water and sanitation: desalination plants and pumping stations were destroyed early in the war, leaving millions reliant on contaminated water sources.

• Electricity: the Gaza power plant shut down within days of the siege. By late 2023, the entire strip had been plunged into darkness.

• Education: every school in Gaza, including those run by UNRWA, was either damaged, destroyed, or converted into shelters for displaced families.

This destruction was not random. Analysts noted a pattern of systematic targeting of civilian infrastructure, creating conditions that UN agencies and humanitarian groups described as "engineered uninhabitability."

### The Siege Economy

Gaza had long been described as an "open-air prison," with a tightly controlled economy dependent on Israel for everything from food imports to building materials. The 2023–2025 war turned that prison into an economic graveyard.

• Employment collapsed: by early 2024, unemployment in Gaza had reached over 80%. Factories, farms, and workshops were destroyed. Fishing, once a key source of income, was banned.

• Currency and trade: with banks destroyed and cash scarce, barter economies emerged in displacement camps, where food, clean water, and basic medicines became the only real currency.

• Humanitarian dependence: the United Nations Relief and Works Agency (UNRWA) became the de facto lifeline for the population, distributing dwindling rations in unsafe conditions. Aid convoys were regularly delayed or blocked, often targeted in airstrikes despite coordination with Israeli authorities.

This collapse was not an accident of war. It was the predictable outcome of policies that deliberately restricted civilian access to resources.

**Children in the Crosshairs**

Perhaps the most searing indictment of the war is its impact on children. By late 2024, Save the Children estimated that over 17,000 children had been killed. Those who survived faced unimaginable trauma:

• Witnessing the deaths of parents, siblings, or entire families.

• Living in tents or on the streets, with no access to education or consistent food.

• Suffering untreated injuries and psychological scars that will last generations.

UNICEF officials described Gaza as "the most dangerous place in the world to be a child." The phrase, repeated across headlines, became a shorthand for the war's moral collapse.

**The Dehumanisation Narrative**

The humanitarian disaster was worsened by the language of dehumanisation emanating from Israeli officials throughout the war. Phrases such as "human animals" and calls to "erase" Gaza were broadcast globally, feeding perceptions that the suffering was not collateral but intentional.

This rhetoric had real-world consequences. In legal forums, including proceedings before the International Court of Justice (ICJ), such statements were cited as evidence of genocidal intent. In the court of global opinion, they erased the last remnants of Israel's moral high ground.

### The Global Humanitarian Response

International aid organisations mounted heroic efforts to deliver assistance, often at extraordinary personal risk. Convoys were bombed, warehouses destroyed, and aid workers killed. By early 2025, the death toll among humanitarian personnel had surpassed 200, the highest for any modern conflict zone.

Despite the overwhelming need, aid remained inadequate and sporadic. The combination of bureaucratic restrictions, security threats, and political calculations created a Kafkaesque system in which trucks sat idle while people starved.

International outrage grew louder, but material relief did not follow at the scale required. For many in Gaza, the lesson was bitter and clear: the world was watching, but it was not acting.

### The Economic Aftermath

By mid-2025, Gaza's economy had not just collapsed. It had been obliterated. Reconstruction, experts warned, would take decades, and only if the blockade were lifted. Without that, Gaza risked becoming a permanent humanitarian ghetto, dependent on external aid, stripped of agency, and locked in a cycle of destruction and dependency.

### A Moral and Legal Reckoning

The deliberate nature of Gaza's collapse, the starvation, the destruction of civilian infrastructure, and the forced displacement transformed the conflict in the eyes of the world. What had once been framed as a war of self-defence came to be seen as a collective punishment of an entire population, in violation of the Geneva Conventions and the basic principles of international humanitarian law.

This shift is the pivot point, the moment where the narrative of victimhood and survival gave way to one of domination and cruelty, setting the stage for a global reckoning with Zionism's trajectory in the 21st century.

## Section 3 – Law, War Crimes, and Genocide Claims

The Gaza war of 2023–2025 unfolded in a world where international law, once the domain of diplomats and scholars, had become a public battleground. Every strike, every siege, and every ministerial statement was documented, dissected, and debated not only in courtrooms but on social media feeds across the globe.

By mid-2024, what had begun as a "war of self-defence" in the rhetoric of Israeli officials had become, in the eyes of much of the world, a case study in violations of international humanitarian law, raising the gravest charge of all: genocide.

### The Framework of International Humanitarian Law

At the core of the legal debate are the Geneva Conventions and Customary International Humanitarian Law (IHL), which govern the conduct of war. Three principles are particularly relevant to Gaza:

1. **Distinction**: parties must distinguish between combatants and civilians, targeting only the former.
2. **Proportionality**: even when striking legitimate military targets, the incidental civilian harm must not be excessive relative to the anticipated military advantage.
3. **Precaution**: feasible steps must be taken to minimise harm to civilians, including advance warnings and safe corridors.

Israel has long argued that Hamas's tactics, embedding fighters and tunnels in dense urban areas, complicate compliance with IHL. But as casualty numbers climbed, neighbourhoods were flattened, and evidence of systematic deprivation mounted, these defences rang increasingly hollow outside Israel and its closest allies.

### The International Court of Justice – South Africa v. Israel

On 29 December 2023, South Africa filed a case against Israel at the International Court of Justice (ICJ), accusing it of violating the 1948 Genocide Convention. The filing was exhaustive, citing satellite images, casualty statistics, and crucially, statements by Israeli officials that appeared to advocate the destruction of Gaza and its population.

Among the most cited were:

• Defence Minister Yoav Gallant's reference to Palestinians as "human animals."

• Minister Amichai Eliyahu's suggestion of considering "nuclear options" for Gaza.

• Finance Minister Bezalel Smotrich's call for the town of Huwara to be "wiped out."

In January 2024, the ICJ issued provisional measures, ordering Israel to prevent acts of genocide, facilitate humanitarian aid, and report regularly to the court. While the ruling stopped short of demanding a ceasefire, it marked a seismic shift: for the first time in its history, Israel was formally accused of genocide by a state party to the convention.

### The International Criminal Court

Parallel to the ICJ proceedings, the International Criminal Court (ICC) accelerated its own investigations. The ICC had opened a file on the situation in Palestine in 2021, covering alleged crimes in Gaza, the West Bank, and East Jerusalem. The events of 2023–2025 turbocharged that inquiry.

By mid-2024, ICC prosecutor Karim Khan had issued statements indicating that evidence of war crimes and crimes against humanity, including intentional targeting of civilians, collective punishment, and the use of starvation as a weapon, was under active review. Arrest warrants were later sought for senior Israeli officials, including members of the war cabinet, alongside Hamas leaders accused of war crimes for the atrocities of 7 October.

The response from Israel and the United States was swift and hostile. Netanyahu dismissed the ICC as "politically motivated," while U.S. lawmakers threatened sanctions against court officials. But the symbolism of the moment, Israeli leaders named alongside those of other states accused of grave crimes, was inescapable.

**Evidence and Documentation**

Unlike past conflicts, the Gaza war unfolded in a world saturated with open-source intelligence (OSINT).

• Satellite imagery documented the progressive destruction of Gaza's urban fabric, correlating with casualty surges.

• Geolocated video evidence, verified by independent researchers, showed strikes on hospitals, ambulances, and refugee shelters.

• Testimonies from aid workers and survivors, collected by organisations like Human Rights Watch, Amnesty International, and Médecins Sans Frontières, provided consistent accounts of indiscriminate bombardment and systematic deprivation.

This flood of documentation created a real-time evidentiary archive, making denial and obfuscation far more difficult than in previous wars.

**The Genocide Debate**

The question of whether the events in Gaza constitute genocide is not merely legal but deeply political. The Genocide Convention defines the crime as acts "committed with intent to destroy, in whole or in part, a national, ethnical, racial, or religious group."

Proponents of the genocide framing point to:

• The sheer scale of destruction and civilian deaths.

• The targeting of essential infrastructure, including food systems, water supplies, and hospitals, necessary for survival.

• The dehumanising rhetoric from senior officials, broadcast globally and cited in formal legal submissions.

Critics of the genocide label argue that:

• Israel's stated objective was the destruction of Hamas, not the Palestinian people as a whole.

• Civilian casualties, while catastrophic, were a function of the battlefield environment, not of genocidal intent.

• The use of the term risks politicising and diluting a legal concept with a high evidentiary threshold.

Whatever the eventual legal determination, the charge itself has been transformative, reframing Israel's image from embattled democracy to pariah state in many parts of the world.

**Western Governments and the Legal Tightrope**

For Israel's Western allies, particularly the United States, the United Kingdom, and Germany, the legal cases posed a profound dilemma.

Public opinion, especially among younger generations, demanded accountability. Legal scholars and human rights organisations called for arms embargoes and sanctions. Yet governments, citing alliance obligations and security concerns, resisted.

In Washington, military aid continued to flow even as images of mass civilian deaths dominated headlines. In Berlin, leaders invoked Germany's historical responsibility toward Israel, a position increasingly challenged by legal scholars arguing that that responsibility includes preventing genocide, not enabling it.

### The UN and Diplomatic Isolation

At the United Nations, the Gaza war triggered an unprecedented level of diplomatic isolation for Israel and, by extension, its key backers.

• Security Council: multiple resolutions calling for ceasefires or humanitarian corridors were vetoed by the United States, often leaving Washington standing alone or with a single partner such as the United Kingdom.

• General Assembly: resolutions condemning the war passed by overwhelming margins, with support from the Global South, much of Europe, and even some traditional allies.

• Human Rights Council: investigative mechanisms were expanded, and special rapporteurs openly described the situation as "a case of apartheid escalating toward genocidal violence."

This isolation did not immediately translate into policy change, but it marked a profound shift in global discourse, one that Israel's hasbara apparatus struggled to contain.

### The Erosion of Legal Exceptionalism

For decades, Israel had navigated international law with relative impunity, shielded by U.S. vetoes and diplomatic cover. The Gaza war exposed the limits of that protection.

The combination of real-time documentation, grassroots mobilisation, and formal legal action created a feedback loop that eroded the perception of Israeli exceptionalism. The old arguments, that Israel is held to a double standard and that criticism is antisemitic, found diminishing traction in a world where images of dead children, bombed hospitals, and starving families circulated hourly.

**The Legacy of Accountability**

Whether or not the ICJ ultimately rules that Israel committed genocide, and whether the ICC succeeds in enforcing arrest warrants, the legal and political impact is already profound:

• Normalised scrutiny: Israeli actions are now routinely analysed through the lens of war crimes and crimes against humanity, not merely "collateral damage."

• Diplomatic costs: countries once unwilling to challenge Israel now do so openly, citing legal obligations and public opinion.

• Future constraints: the threat of future prosecutions hangs over Israeli political and military leaders, altering the calculus for future operations.

## Section 4 – The Global Shift

The Gaza war of 2023–2025 did more than devastate a territory; it reshaped the global political landscape. What had long been framed, especially in the West, as a conflict between a democratic state and terrorist adversaries morphed, almost in real time, into a narrative of power, oppression, and unrestrained violence.

For decades, Israel had managed to maintain a delicate balance, defending itself militarily while preserving an image of moral restraint. But in an era of digital transparency, that narrative collapsed under the weight of images and evidence too stark to ignore.

**The United States: A House Divided**

Nowhere was the shift more profound or more politically fraught than in the United States, Israel's closest ally and largest military benefactor.

**The Political Establishment**

At the outset, the Biden administration offered unequivocal support. In the days after 7 October, President Biden described Israel as fighting for its survival, and Congress passed emergency military aid packages with overwhelming bipartisan support. Statements condemning Hamas and reaffirming Israel's "right to self-defence" dominated the airwaves.

But as the war dragged on, and images of mass civilian casualties dominated the news cycle, the tone began to shift, not in the White House or Congress, but in the streets and across campuses.

**Grassroots Mobilisation**

By November 2023, protests erupted across U.S. cities: New York, Chicago, Los Angeles, and Washington. College campuses became the epicentre of dissent, with students staging sit-ins, walkouts, and mass rallies demanding a ceasefire and an end to unconditional U.S. support for Israel.

Social media amplified their message, bypassing traditional media filters and allowing activists to share unfiltered accounts from Gaza in real time. For the first time, a generation raised on Black Lives Matter and climate justice saw Palestine through the same intersectional lens of systemic injustice.

**A Generational Divide**

Polling captured the shift: by early 2024, nearly 70% of Americans under 30 believed the U.S. should condition or reduce aid to Israel, compared to less than 30% of those over 65. Among Democrats, the split was stark. Progressive lawmakers, "The Squad" and their allies, openly criticised the administration, while centrist and establishment figures doubled down on traditional talking points about Israel's security and America's strategic partnership.

By 2025, the political cost of unquestioned support for Israel had become clear. Candidates in safe Democratic districts faced primaries driven by younger, activist voters demanding accountability. The era of bipartisan silence on Palestinian suffering was over.

## Europe: From Quiet Support to Open Criticism

In Europe, the shift was slower but no less significant.

• **United Kingdom**: Initially, London mirrored Washington's position, offering strong rhetorical support for Israel with minimal attention to civilian casualties. By early 2024, as marches filled the streets of London, Manchester, and Glasgow, public pressure forced Parliament to hold debates on arms sales and trade agreements. The government stopped short of suspending weapons exports but signalled growing unease.

• **France and Germany**: Both countries, historically staunch supporters of Israel, found themselves navigating rising domestic anger. In Germany, where historical memory of the Holocaust has shaped foreign policy, criticism of Israel had long been politically taboo. By 2025, even mainstream politicians began calling for reviews of arms exports and for stronger humanitarian interventions.

• **Ireland, Spain, and Scandinavia**: Smaller European states moved faster. Dublin, Madrid, Oslo, and Stockholm openly condemned Israeli actions, recognised the State of Palestine in symbolic parliamentary votes, and called for sanctions.

## The Global South: A Resurgence of Solidarity

If the West struggled with nuance and inertia, the Global South spoke with clarity and conviction.

• **South Africa**: Leading the charge, Pretoria filed its genocide case against Israel at the International Court of Justice, galvanising a coalition of states across Africa, Asia, and Latin America. The case was not only legal but symbolic, a nation that had dismantled apartheid confronting what it openly called "a system of apartheid and extermination" in Gaza.

• **Brazil and Latin America**: In Brasília, President Lula da Silva recalled his ambassador to Israel and denounced the war as "indefensible." Colombia, Chile, and Bolivia followed suit, suspending diplomatic ties or summoning Israeli ambassadors for reprimand.

• **Asia and Africa**: From Malaysia to Kenya, protests surged, governments issued condemnations, and in some cases, bilateral agreements with Israel were suspended or frozen.

This groundswell of opposition reframed the conflict not as a regional issue but as a global struggle for justice, resonating especially in post-colonial societies familiar with the language of dispossession and occupation.

### The United Nations: Isolation and Paralysis

At the United Nations, the Gaza war triggered one of the sharpest episodes of diplomatic isolation Israel, and the United States, had ever experienced.

• **Security Council**: Resolution after resolution calling for ceasefires or humanitarian pauses were vetoed by Washington, often leaving the U.S. standing alone or with a solitary partner, such as the UK.

• **General Assembly**: In contrast, resolutions condemning Israeli actions passed with overwhelming majorities, underscoring the growing global consensus that the war represented a moral and legal catastrophe.

• **Human Rights Council**: Special rapporteurs used the language of apartheid and genocide openly, signalling a shift from cautious criticism to direct moral and legal indictment.

### Media Transformation: The End of Narrative Control

For decades, Israel and its allies had been able to shape the narrative in Western media, framing its military actions as defensive and measured. The Gaza war exposed the limits of that control.

Digital platforms, from TikTok to X (formerly Twitter), became real-time archives of atrocity: live-streamed airstrikes, the cries of trapped civilians, and the desperate pleas of aid workers. Hashtags like #CeasefireNow and #GazaGenocide trended globally for weeks at a time.

Even mainstream outlets, traditionally cautious, began adopting a more critical tone. By mid-2024, terms like "collective punishment," "war crimes," and "apartheid" were no longer confined to activist spaces; they appeared in headlines of major papers from *The Guardian* to *The New York Times*.

### Grassroots Mobilisation: The Streets Speak

The sheer scale of grassroots mobilisation was unprecedented.

• **Europe**: Millions marched in London, Paris, Berlin, and Madrid.

• **United States**: Encampments spread across more than 150 college campuses, reminiscent of the anti-Vietnam War protests of the 1960s.

• **Global South**: From Jakarta to Johannesburg, solidarity rallies drew massive crowds, often dwarfing official political responses.

This activism was not limited to demonstrations. Labour unions, professional associations, and even corporate employees began pressing for divestment from Israeli firms or companies profiting from the war. The Boycott, Divestment, and Sanctions (BDS) movement, long marginalised, found new momentum and legitimacy.

### The Collapse of Hasbara

Israel's sophisticated global communications machine, hasbara, faltered under the weight of raw, irrefutable evidence. Clips of ministers referring to Palestinians as "human animals" were subtitled and shared worldwide. Aerial footage of bombed hospitals and aid convoys turned carefully crafted talking points into hollow phrases.

The traditional framing of Israel as a democracy under siege gave way to a new narrative: a militarised state waging a campaign of collective punishment against a trapped civilian population. The myth of moral exceptionalism, cultivated over decades, collapsed.

### Political Fallout

The political costs were immediate and profound.

• In Washington, younger Democrats openly challenged party leadership, forcing debates on conditioning aid to Israel.

• In London and Berlin, public anger translated into sharp drops in approval ratings for governments seen as complicit.

• In the Global South, the war accelerated strategic realignments, with many states deepening ties with China and Russia, both of whom positioned themselves as champions of Palestinian rights.

The net result was a world where Israel, though still militarily dominant and diplomatically protected in key Western capitals, faced unprecedented isolation.

### A Global Inflection Point

By 2025, the Gaza war had become a **global inflection point**. It marked the collapse of the old order — where Israel's narrative went largely unchallenged — and the birth of a new era in which legitimacy could no longer be secured by lobbying, alliances, or narrative control alone.

The war did not just kill tens of thousands in Gaza; it **killed the illusion** that Israel could act with impunity, that its actions would be accepted as defensive by default, and that the machinery of hasbara could always shape perception to its advantage.

## Section 5 – Leadership, Rhetoric, and Dehumanisation

Wars are fought with bombs and bullets, but they are also fought with words. In the Gaza war of 2023–2025, the language of Israeli leaders, unguarded, unrepentant, and often openly dehumanising, became one of the conflict's defining features.

In an era of digital transparency, every statement made by an Israeli minister, every soundbite from the Knesset floor, was clipped, subtitled, and broadcast globally within hours. The result was a rhetorical collapse that transformed Israel's image from embattled democracy to aggressor, from victim to perpetrator.

### Netanyahu and the Politics of Survival

At the centre of it all stood Benjamin Netanyahu, Israel's longest-serving prime minister, clinging to power in the midst of crisis. For Netanyahu, the war was both an existential struggle and a political lifeline.

Facing corruption trials and unprecedented domestic protests before October 7, the Hamas attack gave him an opportunity to reassert control. His rhetoric hardened almost immediately:

- "We are fighting human animals, and we will act accordingly."
- "Every Hamas member is a dead man."
- "Gaza will never threaten us again."

To his base, these words projected strength and resolve; to much of the world, they signalled a willingness to collectively punish an entire population.

### Gallant and the Total Siege

Defence Minister Yoav Gallant became the face of the "total siege" policy announced on 9 October 2023. His remarks, declaring that Israel would cut off electricity, food, fuel, and water to Gaza because "they are human animals," reverberated globally.

The phrase "human animals" was repeated endlessly, quoted in international headlines, cited in legal briefs, and referenced in UN debates. It crystallised the perception that Israel's leadership viewed Palestinians not as civilians trapped in a warzone but as a subhuman enemy to be eradicated.

### Eliyahu and the Nuclear Option

Perhaps the most incendiary rhetoric came from Amichai Eliyahu, Israel's Heritage Minister, who in November 2023 suggested that a nuclear strike on Gaza was "one of the possibilities." Though quickly walked back by other officials and met with temporary suspension from cabinet meetings, the damage was irreversible.

For global audiences, the image of a senior Israeli minister casually discussing nuclear options against a civilian population reinforced the sense of unrestrained violence and moral collapse. For legal experts building genocide cases, it provided another data point in demonstrating intent.

### Smotrich and the Language of Erasure

Finance Minister Bezalel Smotrich, a leading figure of Israel's far-right, had already drawn global condemnation earlier in 2023 when he said the Palestinian town of Huwara "should be wiped out." During the Gaza war, his rhetoric only intensified:

• Calls for the "erasure" of Gaza.

• Public statements questioning the very existence of the Palestinian people.

This language, once confined to the fringes, was now coming from the highest levels of government, broadcast live, archived online, and replayed in courtrooms and newsrooms worldwide.

### Amplification and Translation

The digital environment ensured that no statement remained domestic. Within minutes of a minister speaking in Hebrew, translations appeared online, often with accompanying video clips and subtitles. Platforms like TikTok, Instagram, and X (formerly Twitter) spread these soundbites virally, ensuring they reached millions across multiple languages and regions.

For decades, Israeli officials could rely on layers of context, careful framing in Western media, and the benefit of diplomatic nuance. By 2023, those buffers were gone. Words spoken in the heat of war were now global, immediate, and indelible.

### Impact on Legal Proceedings

In The Hague, at both the International Court of Justice (ICJ) and the International Criminal Court (ICC), these statements became central to legal arguments. South Africa's genocide filing at the ICJ quoted Gallant, Smotrich, and Eliyahu extensively, framing their rhetoric as evidence of genocidal intent.

Legal scholars pointed out that intent, the hardest element to prove in genocide cases, is often inferred from public statements by leaders. The language of erasure, extermination, and dehumanisation provided a rich evidentiary record for prosecutors and judges.

### The Domestic Audience

Inside Israel, this rhetoric resonated differently. In the wake of the October 7 massacres, a traumatised public demanded vengeance and security. Hardline language played well to a population in shock, fearful of further attacks, and distrustful of international criticism.

But even domestically, cracks began to show by 2024. Families of hostages began to question the government's strategy, arguing that maximalist war aims were putting their loved ones at risk. Civil society groups, while small and often marginalised, warned that the language of annihilation was corroding Israel's moral core.

### Global Reaction: Outrage and Isolation

Outside Israel, the reaction was visceral.

• In Europe, even traditionally pro-Israel leaders struggled to defend such rhetoric in the face of mounting public anger.

• In the Global South, it was seen as confirmation of long-standing accusations of apartheid and colonial violence.

• In legal and diplomatic forums, the language was treated not as hyperbole but as evidence, shaping resolutions, legal filings, and media coverage.

By mid-2024, Israel's diplomatic isolation was unprecedented. The narrative of self-defence had been eclipsed by a narrative of unchecked aggression, fuelled in no small part by the words of its own leaders.

## The Dehumanisation Effect

Dehumanising rhetoric is not abstract; it has tangible consequences. Scholars of genocide and mass violence have long documented the role of language in facilitating atrocities, from Rwanda to Bosnia, from Nazi Germany to Myanmar.

When leaders describe a population as animals, as vermin, or as an existential threat, it lowers the threshold for violence. It signals to soldiers, policymakers, and the public that extraordinary measures are not only permissible but necessary.

In Gaza, where civilians had nowhere to flee and no safe zones to shelter in, this rhetoric translated into a licence for destruction.

## From Rhetoric to Reckoning

By 2025, the cumulative effect of this language was undeniable. It had:

• Hardened global perceptions of Israel as an occupying power indifferent to civilian life.

• Strengthened legal cases at the ICJ and ICC.

• Accelerated diplomatic isolation, even among allies long reluctant to criticise.

- Fractured support within Israel itself, as the gap widened between hardline rhetoric and the realities of a protracted, unwinnable war.

Words, once seen as ancillary to the battlefield, had become a battlefield of their own, one where Israel, for the first time in its modern history, was losing.

## Section 6 – Silence, Complicity, and the Cost of Inaction

As Gaza descended into devastation, the world watched. Satellite images captured flattened neighbourhoods, journalists documented starving children, and humanitarian agencies issued desperate warnings. Yet, despite this unprecedented visibility, political leaders in Washington, London, Berlin, and beyond offered little more than words, and often not even that.

This silence, or worse, the active facilitation of Israel's military campaign through arms sales and diplomatic cover, became one of the enduring scandals of the 2023–2025 Gaza war. For millions around the globe, it crystallised the sense that the so-called guardians of the international order had abandoned their principles.

### The United States: The Enabler

No country bears more responsibility for enabling Israel's actions than the United States. From the first hours after October 7, the Biden administration positioned itself as Israel's unwavering ally.

- **Military Aid:** By November 2023, the U.S. had approved $14 billion in emergency military assistance, on top of the $3.8 billion provided annually under existing agreements.

- **Diplomatic Shield:** At the United Nations Security Council, Washington vetoed every resolution calling for a ceasefire, humanitarian pauses, or independent investigations, often standing isolated against overwhelming global consensus.

• **Arms Transfers:** Even as reports of mass civilian casualties mounted, the U.S. expedited shipments of precision-guided munitions, artillery shells, and small arms, citing Israel's right to self-defence.

Inside the White House, officials argued that support was necessary to preserve leverage over Israel, that by staying close, Washington could moderate Netanyahu's war aims. The reality, as events on the ground made clear, was that this leverage was illusory. The bombs kept falling, the siege tightened, and Gaza starved.

**Europe: Moral Paralysis**

Across Europe, governments oscillated between rhetorical concern and practical inaction.

• **United Kingdom:** Prime Minister Rishi Sunak's government mirrored Washington, offering full-throated support for Israel while ignoring calls to suspend arms exports. Public anger was immense, and protests drew hundreds of thousands to the streets of London.

• **Germany:** Haunted by its historical guilt over the Holocaust, Berlin provided unconditional support for Israel, even as evidence of atrocities mounted. By mid-2024, cracks appeared, and legal scholars warned that Germany's historical responsibility included preventing genocide, not enabling it.

• **France:** Initially supportive, Paris grew more cautious as images of civilian suffering dominated headlines. President Emmanuel Macron called for humanitarian corridors and a ceasefire but stopped short of imposing any material consequences.

• **Ireland, Spain, and Scandinavia:** Smaller European states, less bound by historical or strategic ties, took bolder stances, recognising Palestinian statehood, suspending arms export licences, and calling for international investigations.

This divergence revealed a continent split between the inertia of old alliances and the urgency of a new moral calculus.

### The Global South: Moral Clarity

While Western capitals equivocated, the Global South responded with moral clarity.

• **South Africa:** Pretoria's decision to take Israel to the International Court of Justice was both legal and symbolic, a former apartheid state challenging what it openly called "apartheid and genocide" in Gaza.

• **Brazil and Latin America:** President Lula da Silva condemned the war as "indefensible," recalled his ambassador, and suspended trade talks. Colombia, Chile, and Bolivia followed suit, severing or downgrading diplomatic ties.

• **Asia and Africa:** From Indonesia to Kenya, governments issued sharp condemnations, while civil society groups mobilised to demand sanctions and boycotts.

For much of the Global South, the war was not an abstract conflict but a vivid reminder of the colonial hierarchies that still define international politics: one set of rules for powerful states and their allies, another for the rest of the world.

### The UN: Paralysis and Outrage

The United Nations became the stage on which this global divide played out.

• **Security Council:** Time and again, resolutions calling for ceasefires were vetoed by the United States. Each veto deepened global anger and reinforced the perception that international law was optional for those with the power to ignore it.

• **General Assembly:** In contrast, resolutions condemning Israel's actions passed with overwhelming support, moral victories that underscored Israel's growing isolation but carried no binding force.

• **Humanitarian Agencies:** UNRWA, WHO, and OCHA became lifelines for Gaza's population and targets of disinformation campaigns designed to delegitimise their work. By early 2025, dozens of UN staff had been killed in strikes, prompting unprecedented statements of outrage from UN leadership.

**Economic and Strategic Interests**

Beneath the rhetoric of support and silence lay hard economic and strategic interests.

• **Defence Industries:** U.S., British, and German arms manufacturers profited from the conflict, securing lucrative contracts for munitions and systems replenishment.

• **Energy and Security:** Regional alliances, including the Abraham Accords, tied Western support for Israel to broader strategic goals in the Middle East, countering Iran, stabilising energy markets, and maintaining military access.

• **Domestic Politics:** In Washington, fear of alienating pro-Israel donors and evangelical voters reinforced the administration's inaction. In Berlin, historical guilt constrained any criticism beyond carefully worded statements.

These dynamics made bold action, sanctions, arms embargoes, or meaningful diplomatic pressure politically unthinkable, even as public outrage grew.

**Public Outrage, Political Inertia**

By mid-2024, the gap between public opinion and political action had become stark. Polls showed majorities in many countries supporting an immediate ceasefire and investigations into war crimes. In the United States, support for conditioning military aid grew month by month, particularly among younger voters.

Yet policy barely shifted. In Washington, billions in aid continued to flow. In London and Berlin, weapons shipments proceeded as planned. The dissonance between public morality and political expediency created a legitimacy crisis that extended far beyond Israel, eroding trust in the very institutions meant to uphold international law.

### Complicity and the Cost of Silence

The cost of this silence is measured not only in lives lost but in the corrosion of global norms. By failing to act decisively, Western powers signalled that international law is negotiable, that principles like proportionality, distinction, and the protection of civilians apply only when convenient.

This complicity has long-term consequences:

• It emboldens other states, from Myanmar to Russia, to act with similar disregard for civilian life.

• It fuels cynicism and resentment in the Global South, accelerating geopolitical realignments away from Western influence.

• It deepens the sense, particularly among younger generations, that the post-war international order is irreparably broken.

### A Moral Reckoning Deferred

History will judge the Gaza war not only by its immediate toll but by the failures of those who could have intervened and did not.

For decades, Israel's Western allies argued that their support was rooted in shared values: democracy, rule of law, human rights. In Gaza, those values collapsed under the weight of strategic calculation and political cowardice.

By 2025, the silence of leaders in Washington, London, and Berlin had become its own scandal, one that would haunt foreign policy debates for years to come, and one that ensured the collapse of legitimacy extended not just to Israel but to those who stood by.

# PART II: The Fracture

# CHAPTER SIX:
# Resistance, Terror, and the Politics of Labels

## Section 1 – Introduction: Language as a Battlefield

In every conflict, language is as powerful as bullets and bombs. It defines the terms of engagement, determines who is seen as the aggressor and who as the victim, and shapes how history remembers events long after the dust settles. In the case of the Israeli-Palestinian conflict, words have always been weapons, wielded not just in Tel Aviv and Ramallah but in Washington, London, Brussels, and at the United Nations.

For more than seven decades, the struggle over language has been as decisive as the battles on the ground. To call someone a "terrorist" is to strip their cause of legitimacy, to cast them beyond the bounds of political negotiation. To call someone a "freedom fighter" or a "resistance fighter" is to frame them as a participant in a just struggle, even if their methods are violent. These labels — "terrorist," "militant," "freedom fighter," "martyr," "occupier," "coloniser" — are not neutral descriptors. They are political constructs, loaded with history, emotion, and strategic intent.

### The Power of Framing

Consider the events of 7 October 2023. To Israel and its Western allies, the Hamas attack was "unprovoked barbarism," the equivalent of "Israel's 9/11." The word "terrorist" dominated headlines, speeches, and briefings from Washington to Berlin. But in much of the Global South, the attack was understood differently: as the violent outburst of a population subjected to decades of dispossession, blockade, and occupation.

Neither framing tells the full story, but both reveal how language shapes reality. Israel has long understood this dynamic, investing heavily in what it calls hasbara, the systematic effort to explain, justify, and legitimise its actions in global discourse. Every missile strike is a "precision attack." Every mass bombing is a "surgical operation." Every child killed is "collateral damage," every destroyed hospital a "Hamas command centre."

Language sanitises violence. It takes images of rubble and bodies and reframes them as the unfortunate, inevitable by-products of a defensive war. For decades, this narrative worked, at least in the West.

**The Politics of "Terrorism"**

The label of "terrorism" has been particularly powerful. After the Munich Olympics in 1972, where members of Black September killed eleven Israeli athletes, the image of the Palestinian fighter as a terrorist crystallised in global consciousness. The decades that followed — hijackings, bombings, and assassinations — reinforced that frame, erasing the context of dispossession and occupation in favour of a simpler binary: civilised democracy versus barbaric violence.

This framing gained new potency after September 11, 2001. The United States' "War on Terror" blurred distinctions between al-Qaeda, the Taliban, Hezbollah, and Hamas. In Washington and London, the same word, terrorist, applied to anyone who resisted Western-backed policies, regardless of history or context.

For Palestinians, this was devastating. It meant that even non-violent activism — boycotts, divestment campaigns, appeals to international law — could be dismissed as inherently illegitimate, part of a broader architecture of "terror."

**The Counter-Narrative**

But language is not static. The Gaza war of 2023–2025 shattered many of these assumptions. As Israeli bombs levelled neighbourhoods and aid groups described "engineered starvation," the word "terrorism" began to sound less like a definitive label and more like a political tactic.

In the Global South, leaders like South Africa's Cyril Ramaphosa, Brazil's Lula da Silva, and Malaysia's Anwar Ibrahim refused to parrot Western talking points. Instead, they reframed the conversation: Israel was not defending itself, it was perpetuating a system of apartheid and colonial domination.

This shift reflects a deeper truth: language reflects power. For decades, Israel and its allies controlled the narrative because they controlled the channels of power — Western media, diplomacy, and international institutions. But in the age of digital transparency, that monopoly has fractured. A teenager in Khan Younis with a smartphone can now bypass the BBC or CNN and show the world what is happening, unfiltered and unmediated.

**Language as Strategy**

It is no coincidence that the Israeli government has poured resources into lobbying, public relations, and what it openly calls "strategic communications." For years, Israeli embassies around the world have worked with PR firms and digital strategists to police language: to insist that the occupied West Bank be called "disputed territories," that settlements are "neighbourhoods," and that military incursions are "operations."

The success of this strategy is undeniable. In Western discourse, the term "occupation" virtually disappeared from mainstream media coverage between the 1990s and the early 2010s, replaced by vague references to a "conflict" between "two sides." But the Gaza war broke this spell. When hospitals were bombed, when children starved in front of cameras, when ministers spoke of "human animals" and "erasure," the euphemisms collapsed under the weight of reality.

### The Global Reckoning

By 2025, language itself had become a battlefield. In Washington, State Department officials insisted on describing Gaza as a "war zone," implying a conflict between two armies, even as satellite images showed the reality of one of the world's most advanced militaries targeting a defenceless, besieged population. In South Africa, parliamentarians used a different lexicon: apartheid, ethnic cleansing, genocide.

This battle over language was not academic. It carried real-world consequences:

- In courts, where the use of terms like "genocide" or "collective punishment" shaped legal arguments and judicial outcomes.
- In diplomacy, where governments faced domestic pressure to use or avoid certain words.
- In public discourse, where shifting language reflected shifting perceptions, especially among younger generations.

### Framing and Power

Control over language has always been a form of power. Colonial Britain called the Easter Rising of 1916 a "rebellion" led by "terrorists," while Irish republicans called it the first step toward liberation. In South Africa, the ANC's armed struggle against apartheid was branded as terrorism by the apartheid regime and by Western allies, until it was not, and Nelson Mandela was recast from a terrorist to a global icon of freedom.

The same dynamics are at play in Israel and Palestine. For decades, Israel successfully branded Palestinian resistance as terrorism, while its own violence was couched in the language of defence and security. But as the Gaza war unfolded in full view of the world, that monopoly cracked, revealing the contested, constructed nature of these labels.

**The Stakes of the Debate**

This is not just semantics. The words we use shape policy and perception. If Palestinians are terrorists, there is no need for negotiation, no room for empathy, no recognition of legitimate grievance. If they are an occupied people resisting a colonial power, the moral and political calculus shifts entirely.

The battle over language is, in many ways, the battle over the conflict itself: whose story is told, whose suffering is acknowledged, whose violence is condemned, and whose is excused.

## Section 2 – The Rise of the PLO: Resistance in the Early Years

The Palestine Liberation Organisation (PLO) was born of dispossession, a response to the catastrophe of 1948, known in Arabic as the Nakba ("catastrophe"), when over 750,000 Palestinians were expelled or fled from their homes during the creation of the State of Israel. For the hundreds of thousands forced into refugee camps in Gaza, Lebanon, Jordan, and Syria, the trauma of dispossession fused with a single, unifying demand: the right of return.

By the early 1960s, this desire for organised resistance had crystallised into the PLO, not as a coherent political or military body at first, but as an umbrella organisation for a fractured and dispossessed people, seeking voice and recognition in a hostile regional and global environment.

**The Seeds of Resistance**

In the decade after the Nakba, Palestinian communities were defined by displacement and statelessness. Camps run by the newly established UNRWA (United Nations Relief and Works Agency) became semi-permanent fixtures in places like Khan Younis, Nahr al-Bared, and Jerash.

In these camps, generations of young men grew up surrounded by stories of lost homes and villages, with no political horizon in sight. Arab regimes spoke of liberation but often acted in their own interests, using the Palestinian cause as a tool in regional rivalries.

This vacuum created the conditions for self-organisation. Early guerrilla groups, most notably Fatah, co-founded by a young engineer named Yasser Arafat, began to coalesce. Their message was simple and uncompromising: only armed struggle could reclaim the homeland.

### The Birth of the PLO

The PLO was officially founded in 1964 at the first Palestinian National Congress in Jerusalem, under the auspices of the Arab League. Initially, it was less a grassroots movement than a creation of Arab governments, particularly Egypt under Gamal Abdel Nasser, who sought to harness and manage Palestinian nationalism.

The organisation's early charter was uncompromising:

- Palestine, defined as the entire territory of the British Mandate, was the homeland of the Palestinian people.
- Armed struggle was the only path to liberation.
- Zionism was a colonial project with no legitimacy in the Arab world.

This early phase of the PLO reflected the anti-colonial currents sweeping across the developing world in the 1960s, from Algeria to Vietnam. The Palestinian struggle was framed not as a narrow territorial dispute but as part of a global liberation movement against imperialism and settler colonialism.

### The Rise of Fatah and Arafat

While the PLO began as a relatively top-down body, its transformation into a mass movement came with the ascendancy of

Fatah. Founded in the late 1950s by Arafat and a group of Palestinian exiles working in Kuwait, Fatah was pragmatic, fiercely independent, and committed to armed resistance outside the control of Arab regimes.

Arafat's strategy was simple but effective:

- Launch guerrilla raids across the Jordan River into Israeli territory to demonstrate that Palestinians were not passive victims.
- Build networks of support among the refugee population.
- Use bold, symbolic actions to place the Palestinian cause at the centre of regional and global politics.

By the late 1960s, Fatah had eclipsed other factions and seized control of the PLO. Under Arafat's leadership, the organisation became the undisputed voice of the Palestinian people, militant, defiant, and increasingly sophisticated in its ability to leverage both violence and diplomacy.

### The Impact of the Six-Day War (1967)

The 1967 Arab-Israeli War was a turning point. In just six days, Israel defeated the combined armies of Egypt, Jordan, and Syria, seizing the West Bank, East Jerusalem, Gaza, the Golan Heights, and the Sinai Peninsula. For Palestinians, the war was a second dispossession, doubling the number of people under occupation and dashing any remaining illusions that Arab states would liberate Palestine for them.

For the PLO and Fatah, the lesson was clear: Palestinians would have to fight for themselves. Recruitment surged. Training camps in Jordan and Lebanon filled with young men eager to join the resistance. The movement also gained international visibility, as the global media began to cover Palestinian guerrilla operations, often sensationalising their daring but deadly tactics.

## Guerrilla Warfare and Global Perception

In the late 1960s and early 1970s, the PLO adopted a strategy of guerrilla warfare and high-profile operations designed to internationalise the Palestinian struggle. These included:

- Cross-border raids into Israel.
- Sabotage operations targeting infrastructure.
- Skyjackings of commercial airliners to draw global attention.

The most infamous of these was the 1972 Munich Olympics attack, when members of the Black September faction of the PLO killed eleven Israeli athletes. The operation and the bloody German rescue attempt that followed horrified the world and cemented the label of "terrorist" in Western discourse.

For Palestinians, these actions were framed as acts of war by a dispossessed people with no other means to be heard. For much of the West, they were evidence of barbarity, erasing the context of occupation and dispossession.

## The Role of the Cold War

The PLO's rise unfolded against the backdrop of the Cold War, which shaped both opportunities and constraints.

- The Soviet Union and its allies provided arms, training, and political support, framing the Palestinian struggle as part of a global fight against imperialism.
- The United States, increasingly aligned with Israel after 1967, adopted the Israeli narrative wholesale, branding the PLO a terrorist organisation and blocking its attempts to gain legitimacy in international forums.

This binary framing — liberation versus terror, anti-imperialism versus democracy — hardened the battle lines and narrowed the space for diplomacy. It also set the stage for decades of narrative warfare that would play out in every major escalation of the conflict.

## The PLO as a Symbol

By the mid-1970s, the PLO had become more than a resistance organisation; it was a symbol of statelessness and struggle. Refugee camps in Jordan, Lebanon, and Syria became hubs of political and cultural life, with schools, clinics, and training centres operating under the PLO's umbrella.

At the same time, the organisation's armed activities and the retaliatory strikes they provoked exacted a heavy price on Palestinian civilians, particularly in host countries like Jordan and Lebanon. This tension between armed struggle and political pragmatism would define the PLO's trajectory for decades.

## International Recognition and the UN

The turning point in the PLO's international legitimacy came in 1974, when Yasser Arafat addressed the United Nations General Assembly, famously declaring:

"I come bearing an olive branch and a freedom fighter's gun. Do not let the olive branch fall from my hand."

The speech electrified the chamber and symbolised the duality of the Palestinian struggle, seeking recognition and negotiation while refusing to renounce armed resistance. That same year, the UN granted the PLO observer status, a symbolic but significant victory that marked its emergence as the legitimate representative of the Palestinian people.

## The Evolution of Resistance

By the end of the 1970s, the PLO had transitioned from a loosely organised militant movement to a complex political and diplomatic actor. It maintained armed operations but also began to engage in international diplomacy, seeking recognition, allies, and pathways towards a political settlement.

But the fundamental tension remained: to much of the West, the PLO was still a terrorist organisation; to much of the Global South, it was a legitimate liberation movement, part of a shared history of anti-colonial resistance.

## Section 3 – From Resistance to "Terrorism": The Global Narrative Shift

The transformation of the Palestinian struggle in global consciousness, from an anti-colonial resistance movement to a "terrorist threat," was neither inevitable nor organic. It was the result of strategic framing, geopolitical shifts, and a global information war that Israel mastered with remarkable precision from the late 1960s onward.

This shift, crystallised in the aftermath of high-profile attacks like Munich in 1972, reshaped the conflict. It redefined Palestinians in the Western imagination, stripping their cause of legitimacy and reducing their struggle for self-determination to a single, powerful word: terrorism.

### The Early Narrative: Liberation and Anti-Colonialism

In the 1960s, the Palestinian cause was widely seen, especially in the Global South, through the lens of anti-colonial struggle. From Algeria's FLN to the Viet Cong, liberation movements were challenging imperial powers and redrawing the map of the post-war world.

In newly independent African and Asian nations, Palestinians were embraced as fellow travellers in a shared battle against oppression and displacement. At the Bandung Conference and later at the Non-Aligned Movement, Palestinian representatives were welcomed as legitimate actors in a global fight for self-determination.

The PLO capitalised on this context, building alliances and cultivating a narrative of resistance that resonated in Havana, Dar es Salaam, and Delhi. In Latin America, revolutionary groups like the

Sandinistas and the Tupamaros cited Palestine as a model for their own struggles.

But this framing never took hold in the West. There, the ground was already shifting.

## The Power of Munich

The Munich Olympics attack in 1972 was a defining moment in the global narrative. Carried out by Black September, a faction of the PLO, the operation targeted Israeli athletes at the height of the Games, demanding the release of Palestinian prisoners. Eleven Israelis were killed, as were five of the attackers, during a botched German rescue attempt broadcast live to millions.

The images were seared into the global consciousness: masked men, trembling hostages, the Olympic rings as backdrop. Whatever the political motivations, the optics were catastrophic.

In Washington, London, and much of Western Europe, Munich cemented a frame that would endure for decades: Palestinians were no longer freedom fighters, they were terrorists. The underlying causes of the conflict — dispossession, occupation, the refugee crisis — disappeared from headlines, replaced by a single, emotionally charged narrative of barbarism and violence.

## The Western Media Landscape

The global media environment of the 1970s amplified this shift. In the age of television, images travelled fast, and Israel understood the power of controlling them. Spokespeople framed every Palestinian operation, however targeted or symbolic, as an attack on "innocent civilians," while Israeli military actions were couched in the language of "retaliation" and "self-defence."

This asymmetry in language created a lasting imbalance:

- Palestinian violence was terrorism.
- Israeli violence was security.
- Palestinian armed groups were illegitimate.

- Israeli occupation forces were defenders of democracy.

The shift in perception was so complete that by the late 1970s, even moderate Palestinian leaders, those seeking diplomatic channels, found themselves branded as extremists if they refused to renounce armed struggle outright.

### The Role of U.S. Foreign Policy

The United States played a decisive role in cementing the "terrorist" label. After the Six-Day War in 1967, Washington's strategic alignment with Israel deepened, driven by Cold War calculations and domestic political considerations. By the time of Munich, Israel was firmly cast as a frontline ally against Soviet influence in the Middle East.

In this framing, the PLO, which had ties to Moscow and received support from Eastern Bloc states, was more than a nationalist movement: it was an arm of the global communist threat.

This alignment was formalised in the 1970s and 1980s, as successive U.S. administrations, from Nixon to Reagan, adopted policies that:

- Designated the PLO as a terrorist organisation.
- Criminalised any contact with Palestinian representatives.
- Provided Israel with diplomatic cover at the UN and military support on the ground.

### The Sabra and Shatila Paradox

The irony and the hypocrisy of this narrative became apparent during events like the 1982 Lebanon War, when Israel invaded southern Lebanon to crush PLO bases. That campaign culminated in the Sabra and Shatila massacres, where Lebanese Phalangist militias, under the watch of Israeli forces, slaughtered over 3,000 Palestinian civilians in refugee camps.

Television crews documented the aftermath: streets littered with bodies, families executed in their homes, infants dead in their

153

mothers' arms. The world recoiled, but in Washington and much of the Western press, the narrative barely shifted. The PLO remained "terrorists," while Israeli officials deflected responsibility, framing the massacres as the work of rogue militias.

This episode revealed a painful truth: narrative control is power. In the West, Israel still held it.

## The Politics of Delegitimisation

Throughout the 1970s and 1980s, the battle for narrative legitimacy was relentless. The PLO sought recognition at the UN and among Western governments, but Israel and its allies countered with well-funded lobbying and media campaigns that painted any form of resistance, political, armed, or otherwise, as inherently illegitimate.

Even when Arafat made overtures toward diplomacy, including public acceptance of a two-state solution in the late 1980s, Western governments were slow to engage. The language of "terrorism" had become so entrenched that it foreclosed serious dialogue for years.

## The Oslo Moment

The signing of the Oslo Accords in the 1990s marked a partial shift. With Arafat shaking hands with Yitzhak Rabin on the White House lawn, the PLO gained a degree of international legitimacy it had long been denied. For a brief moment, Palestinians were reframed, not as terrorists but as partners in a fragile peace process.

Yet even during the hopeful years of Oslo, the old narratives persisted. Every suicide bombing by fringe factions was amplified in Western media, reinforcing the image of Palestinian violence as irrational and barbaric. Israeli settlement expansion, land confiscation, and the daily violence of occupation rarely received equivalent scrutiny.

By the early 2000s, the collapse of Oslo and the outbreak of the Second Intifada allowed Israel to reassert its dominant narrative:

that Palestinian violence was evidence not of resistance to occupation, but of incurable extremism.

### The Rise of the "Terror State" Narrative

By the time of September 11, 2001, the groundwork for a seamless narrative fusion was already in place. The "War on Terror" that followed blurred every distinction between Palestinian nationalism, Islamist militancy, and global jihadism. Hamas, Hezbollah, and al-Qaeda were spoken of in the same breath, as interchangeable manifestations of the same threat.

This conflation was deliberate and devastating. It allowed Israel to position itself as the frontline state in a global war against terror, a partner in a Western struggle that transcended the specifics of the Israeli–Palestinian conflict.

Palestinian resistance, in all its forms, was subsumed under a single, all-encompassing label: terrorism. In Washington, London, and Brussels, this language became policy, shaping aid, diplomacy, and military coordination for the next two decades.

### The Cost of the Narrative

This global shift in language and perception had profound consequences:

- It delegitimised Palestinian aspirations for self-determination, even when expressed through peaceful or diplomatic channels.
- It emboldened Israeli impunity, allowing repeated cycles of violence in Gaza and the West Bank with minimal international accountability.
- It flattened the complexity of the conflict into a binary morality tale: democracy versus terror, civilisation versus barbarism.

By the time Gaza descended into catastrophe in 2023, this narrative had begun to fracture, but its long shadow still shaped the political and media landscape, making it easier for Western governments to rationalise their silence and complicity in the face of overwhelming evidence of atrocity.

## Section 4 – Oslo and the Politics of Compromise

The early 1990s brought what many believed was a new dawn for the Israeli–Palestinian conflict. After decades of violence, displacement, and failed diplomacy, the Oslo Accords, signed in 1993 and 1995, seemed to promise a path toward peace and statehood. For the first time, the Palestine Liberation Organisation (PLO) and the State of Israel formally recognised one another, and the prospect of a two-state solution appeared, however faintly, within reach.

But the hope of Oslo, like so many other moments in the tortured history of this conflict, proved illusory. What began as a fragile experiment in compromise collapsed into disillusionment and violence, leaving Palestinians more divided, Israel more entrenched in its occupation, and the world grappling with the bitter lessons of a peace process that, in hindsight, may have been designed to fail.

### The Road to Oslo

The first Intifada, which erupted in 1987, was a turning point. Unlike the armed campaigns of the 1960s and 70s, the Intifada was a largely grassroots uprising, led by students, workers, and community leaders, marked by protests, boycotts, and civil disobedience. The images of young Palestinians confronting heavily armed Israeli soldiers with stones, slingshots, and graffiti reshaped global perceptions of the occupation.

By the early 1990s, several dynamics converged:

- The end of the Cold War weakened the PLO's traditional alliances and funding sources.
- The Gulf War in 1991, and the PLO's controversial support for Saddam Hussein, left it isolated in the Arab world.

- The Madrid Peace Conference in 1991 laid the groundwork for direct dialogue, bringing Israeli and Palestinian negotiators together for the first time.

Against this backdrop, secret negotiations began in Oslo, Norway, where Israeli academics and Palestinian officials worked quietly on what would become the Declaration of Principles.

## The Oslo Accords

Signed on the White House lawn in September 1993, the Oslo I Accord marked the first time that Israel and the PLO formally recognised each other. Yasser Arafat, in a letter to Israeli Prime Minister Yitzhak Rabin, renounced "terrorism and other acts of violence," while Rabin acknowledged the PLO as the legitimate representative of the Palestinian people.

The agreement envisioned a phased process:

- Mutual recognition between the two sides.
- Limited Palestinian self-rule in parts of Gaza and the West Bank under a newly created Palestinian Authority (PA).
- Final status negotiations within five years to resolve core issues: Jerusalem, refugees, settlements, borders, and security.

Two years later, Oslo II expanded the PA's administrative control over parts of the West Bank, dividing the territory into Areas A, B, and C, a complex patchwork that left ultimate control, particularly over borders, security, and resources, in Israeli hands.

## The Promise and the Reality

In the immediate aftermath of Oslo, there was genuine optimism. International donors pledged billions of dollars to support Palestinian institution-building. New checkpoints were established to facilitate the movement of people and goods. For many Palestinians, especially those in Gaza and Ramallah, there was a sense that life might finally begin to normalise.

But beneath the surface, Oslo was built on deep asymmetries:

- Israel remained the occupying power, controlling borders, airspace, and resources.

- Settlements in the West Bank expanded rapidly during the 1990s, in direct violation of the spirit, if not the letter, of the accords.

- The Palestinian Authority was granted limited autonomy, often described by critics as a form of subcontracted occupation: policing its own people while Israel maintained ultimate authority.

By the mid-1990s, frustration was boiling over. Checkpoints multiplied, settlement construction surged, and the economic benefits of peace failed to materialise for most Palestinians.

**Internal Palestinian Divisions**

Oslo also deepened internal Palestinian divisions. While the PLO leadership in Tunis embraced the accords, factions like Hamas and Islamic Jihad rejected them outright, arguing that the process legitimised occupation without delivering sovereignty.

For Hamas, Oslo became a rallying cry, proof, they argued, that the old guard of the PLO had compromised the core principles of resistance. This dynamic sowed the seeds for the factionalism that would explode in the years to come, particularly in Gaza after 2007.

**The Assassination of Rabin**

In Israel, Oslo was equally polarising. The far right denounced Rabin as a traitor, accusing him of endangering Israel's security. This rhetoric reached a fever pitch in November 1995, when Rabin was assassinated by a right-wing extremist at a peace rally in Tel Aviv.

Rabin's death marked the beginning of the end for Oslo. His successor, Shimon Peres, lacked Rabin's authority, and the political momentum for compromise waned. The election of Benjamin

Netanyahu in 1996, on a platform of security and opposition to Oslo, accelerated the process of retrenchment.

## The Second Intifada and the Collapse of Oslo

By the early 2000s, Oslo was effectively dead. The failure of the Camp David Summit in 2000, combined with Ariel Sharon's provocative visit to the Temple Mount/Al-Haram al-Sharif, ignited the Second Intifada, a far bloodier and more militarised uprising than the first.

Suicide bombings in Tel Aviv, Haifa, and Jerusalem hardened Israeli public opinion. Israel responded with overwhelming force: re-occupying West Bank cities, expanding settlements, and constructing the separation barrier that physically divided communities and further fragmented Palestinian territories.

For many Palestinians, the collapse of Oslo was not a surprise. The promised statehood had never materialised, the occupation had deepened, and the Palestinian Authority, increasingly seen as corrupt and ineffective, had lost much of its legitimacy.

## The Oslo Legacy

Oslo's legacy is bitter and contested.

- For supporters, it was a missed opportunity, a framework that might have worked if extremists on both sides had not undermined it.

- For critics, especially among Palestinians, Oslo was a trap: a process designed to manage occupation rather than end it, trading the rhetoric of liberation for the reality of deeper control.

Even today, the geography of Oslo, the fragmented map of Areas A, B, and C, the checkpoints, the restricted roads, defines Palestinian life in the West Bank. In Gaza, where Oslo's promises collapsed under the weight of blockade and war, the accords are remembered as a cruel mirage.

### A Moment of Illusion

Looking back from the vantage point of 2025, Oslo appears less as a roadmap to peace and more as a moment of illusion, a brief period when language shifted, when the world spoke of reconciliation and coexistence, but when the underlying structures of occupation remained untouched.

The politics of compromise gave way, in time, to the politics of despair, and in that despair, new actors, particularly Hamas, would rise to prominence, reshaping the conflict in ways that Oslo's architects never anticipated.

## Section 5 – The Rise of Hamas: Religion, Resistance, and Politics

The emergence of Hamas in the late 1980s reshaped the dynamics of the Palestinian struggle, injecting a powerful new force into a movement that, until then, had been dominated by the secular nationalism of the PLO and Fatah. Born during the turbulence of the First Intifada, Hamas, an acronym for Harakat al-Muqawama al-Islamiyya, or the Islamic Resistance Movement, fused religious ideology, grassroots organisation, and armed resistance into a potent formula that would, over time, challenge the PLO's monopoly over Palestinian politics.

### Origins in the First Intifada

The First Intifada, which erupted in December 1987, was a largely spontaneous uprising against decades of occupation, land seizures, and daily humiliations in the West Bank and Gaza. While the PLO and its factions had orchestrated armed raids and guerrilla actions abroad, they had struggled to mobilise a coherent resistance within the occupied territories themselves.

Hamas emerged in this context, founded by Sheikh Ahmed Yassin, a charismatic preacher affiliated with the Muslim Brotherhood, along with other activists in Gaza. Unlike the PLO, whose leadership operated from exile in Tunis, Hamas was rooted in the streets and mosques of Gaza, giving it a level of immediacy and authenticity that resonated deeply with ordinary Palestinians.

**Religion and Resistance**

Hamas presented itself as a religious alternative to the PLO's secular nationalism, framing the struggle against Israel not just as a national liberation movement but as a divine mandate. Its founding charter of 1988 spoke in absolutist terms:

- Palestine was Islamic land, and its liberation was a religious duty.
- Negotiation and compromise were rejected outright.
- Armed resistance, muqawama, was the only legitimate path to freedom.

This framing distinguished Hamas from its rivals and allowed it to appeal to communities disillusioned with the corruption and perceived failures of the PLO. Religion became both an ideological foundation and a mobilising tool, giving the movement moral clarity and resilience.

**The Social Infrastructure**

What set Hamas apart from other resistance groups was its dual identity: it was both a militant organisation and a provider of social services.

In Gaza, where poverty and unemployment were endemic even before the blockade, Hamas built a parallel infrastructure that provided:

- Schools and religious education programmes.
- Clinics and medical care for the poor.
- Charitable networks that distributed food and financial support to families in need.

This grassroots legitimacy allowed Hamas to build deep reservoirs of support, especially in the refugee camps where the

Palestinian Authority and international NGOs were often seen as distant or corrupt.

### The Role of the Israeli Occupation

Ironically, Israel's policies during the 1980s and early 1990s indirectly facilitated the rise of Hamas. Seeing Hamas and the Muslim Brotherhood as a counterweight to the secular and nationalist PLO, Israeli authorities allowed Islamic charities and mosques associated with the Brotherhood to operate relatively freely in Gaza.

This strategy, rooted in the logic of divide and rule, backfired spectacularly. By the time the Oslo Accords were signed in 1993, Hamas had already established itself as a formidable political and social force, and one deeply opposed to the compromises made by Arafat and the PLO.

### Opposition to Oslo

For Hamas, the Oslo Accords were nothing short of a betrayal. The organisation denounced Arafat for "selling out" the Palestinian cause in exchange for limited autonomy and international recognition, while the occupation, and the settlement project, deepened.

This opposition resonated with many Palestinians, particularly in Gaza, where economic conditions worsened even as promises of peace and prosperity failed to materialise. By positioning itself as the uncompromising voice of resistance, Hamas gained ground while the Palestinian Authority, increasingly mired in allegations of corruption and authoritarianism, saw its credibility erode.

### The Militarisation of Resistance

By the mid-1990s, Hamas had developed its military wing, the Izz al-Din al-Qassam Brigades, named after a Syrian-Palestinian resistance leader from the 1930s. Initially focused on small-scale attacks and ambushes, the Brigades expanded their capabilities during the Second Intifada (2000–2005), employing tactics such as:

- Suicide bombings in Israeli cities, which killed hundreds of civilians and fuelled international condemnation.
- Improvised rocket attacks from Gaza, primitive at first but increasingly sophisticated over time.
- Cross-border raids targeting military outposts and settlements.

These tactics entrenched Hamas in the global narrative as a terrorist organisation, particularly after the 9/11 attacks, when the Bush administration folded Hamas into its broader "war on terror."

### The 2006 Elections and Political Legitimacy

The surprising victory of Hamas in the 2006 Palestinian legislative elections was a watershed moment. Running on a platform of anti-corruption and resistance, Hamas won a decisive majority, defeating Fatah in what international observers recognised as a free and fair election.

The reaction from the United States, Israel, and much of the international community was immediate:

- Hamas was boycotted and sanctioned.
- Western funding to the Palestinian Authority was suspended unless Hamas renounced violence and recognised Israel.
- The refusal to engage with a democratically elected government deepened Palestinian divisions and undermined international credibility.

The outcome was predictable. By 2007, the rivalry between Hamas and Fatah erupted into violence, culminating in Hamas seizing control of Gaza, while the Palestinian Authority maintained limited control over parts of the West Bank. From that point on, the Palestinian polity was split, geographically, politically, and ideologically.

## The Gaza Blockade

Following the Hamas takeover, Israel imposed a comprehensive blockade on Gaza, controlling its borders, airspace, and maritime access. The blockade, justified as a security measure, had devastating humanitarian and economic consequences:

- Unemployment soared above 40 per cent.
- Access to food, medicine, and building materials was severely restricted.
- Gaza's economy collapsed, leaving its population heavily dependent on international aid.

Hamas, meanwhile, entrenched itself as both the de facto government of Gaza and the primary target of Israeli military campaigns, from Operation Cast Lead (2008–2009) to Protective Edge (2014) and beyond.

## Hamas and the Global Narrative

Hamas's dual identity, as both a political actor and an armed resistance movement, created a narrative paradox:

- To its supporters, Hamas was a legitimate resistance movement, standing up to occupation and offering services to communities long neglected by the Palestinian Authority.
- To Israel and its Western allies, Hamas was a terrorist organisation, indistinguishable from al-Qaeda or ISIS in its ideology and tactics.

This binary framing obscured the complexities of Hamas as both a product of, and a response to, decades of occupation, economic deprivation, and political marginalisation.

For much of the Global South, particularly in Arab and Muslim-majority countries, Hamas was seen less as an extremist group and more as a symptom of systemic injustice, an inevitable outgrowth of a situation in which political negotiation had repeatedly failed to deliver dignity, security, or sovereignty.

## The Paradox of Hamas

By the time of the Gaza war of 2023–2025, Hamas had become both indispensable and intractable. It was the dominant political force in Gaza, yet isolated diplomatically and economically. It provided essential services, yet ruled with authoritarian control. It claimed to defend Palestinian rights, yet its military strategies repeatedly provoked devastating reprisals that left ordinary Gazans to pay the heaviest price.

This paradox, resistance and governance, victimhood and violence, legitimacy and isolation, defined Hamas in the decades leading up to Gaza's destruction. It set the stage for the catastrophic spiral of violence that began on 7 October 2023.

## Section 6 – The Post-9/11 World: Terror as Policy

The attacks of 11 September 2001 reshaped global politics, foreign policy, and security doctrines. Nowhere was this transformation more consequential than in the Israeli-Palestinian conflict. What had been, for decades, a nationalist struggle for liberation and sovereignty was subsumed into the language and policy framework of the "War on Terror."

From that moment forward, Palestinian resistance, armed or otherwise, was increasingly viewed not through the lens of occupation and self-determination but as part of a global jihadist threat. The nuances of history, the legitimacy of Palestinian aspirations, and the asymmetry of power between occupier and occupied were flattened into a binary narrative: democracy versus terror, civilisation versus barbarism.

### The Immediate Aftermath of 9/11

The images of the Twin Towers collapsing burned into the collective consciousness of the United States and its allies. Overnight, the world entered a new political reality defined by fear, retaliation, and the expansion of state power.

For Israel, 9/11 was a geopolitical windfall. In Washington, where Israeli officials had long argued that Palestinian groups like Hamas and Hezbollah were indistinguishable from al-Qaeda, the tragedy provided an opportunity to align Israel's fight against Palestinian resistance with America's global war against terrorism.

Within days, Israeli officials began framing their decades-long conflict with Palestinians as part of the same struggle America now claimed as its own. Ariel Sharon, then Prime Minister, reportedly told U.S. leaders, "Now you understand us." It was a message that resonated deeply with an administration and a public reeling from unprecedented trauma.

### The Conflation of Resistance and Terrorism

The strategic conflation of Palestinian resistance with transnational jihadism was deliberate and effective.

- Hamas and Islamic Jihad, despite being locally rooted movements with no operational links to al-Qaeda, were branded as part of the same extremist network.

- The PLO, despite having renounced armed struggle and embraced diplomacy under Oslo, was tarnished by association whenever violence flared.

- Even non-violent movements, such as international solidarity campaigns or the Boycott, Divestment, and Sanctions (BDS) movement, were increasingly portrayed as fronts for extremism.

This framing erased the context of occupation from mainstream Western discourse. Acts of resistance were not analysed as responses to systemic dispossession or violence but as evidence of an irrational, implacable hatred of Israel and the West.

### The Second Intifada in a Post-9/11 World

The Second Intifada (2000–2005) erupted just before 9/11 but became inextricably linked to the new security paradigms that followed. Unlike the largely unarmed protests of the First Intifada, the second uprising was far more militarised, marked by suicide bombings, armed confrontations, and a devastating Israeli military response.

In the post-9/11 context, these attacks, horrific in their human toll, were no longer seen as acts of resistance within an occupied territory but as proof that Israel was, in the words of George W. Bush, "fighting the same war" as America.

This narrative alignment provided political cover for a series of escalatory Israeli policies:

- The construction of the Separation Barrier in the West Bank, justified as a counter-terrorism measure but widely criticised as a tool of annexation and demographic control.

- Targeted assassinations of Palestinian leaders, carried out with U.S.-supplied weapons and tacit approval.

- The tightening of the blockade on Gaza, particularly after Hamas's 2006 electoral victory and its subsequent takeover of the enclave in 2007.

**Policy Shifts in Washington and Beyond**

In Washington, the Bush administration's embrace of Israel's security narrative was comprehensive. Hamas and Hezbollah were formally designated as Foreign Terrorist Organisations. The Palestinian Authority, already weakened by corruption and internal division, was pressured to police resistance in the West Bank as a condition of continued financial support. This alignment was mirrored in European capitals, where counter-terrorism legislation blurred the lines between legitimate political advocacy and material support for terrorism. Charitable organisations operating in Palestinian territories were shut down, bank accounts frozen, and activists surveilled.

The effect was chilling: political space for Palestinian advocacy narrowed dramatically, while Israel consolidated its position as a strategic partner in the global fight against terror.

**The Media Ecosystem**

The Western media environment after 9/11 amplified these dynamics. With newsrooms adopting a security-first framing of global events, stories from Israel and Palestine were filtered through the prism of terrorism. Suicide bombings in Jerusalem or Tel Aviv dominated headlines, while Israeli incursions into Palestinian cities, the expansion of settlements, and the daily violence of occupation were relegated to secondary coverage or omitted altogether.

Language became a tool of control:

- Palestinians were almost always "militants" or "terrorists."
- Israeli actions were "operations," "responses," or "security measures."
- Civilian casualties in Gaza or the West Bank were framed as collateral damage, tragic but inevitable.

This asymmetry in coverage reinforced the perception, particularly in the United States, that Israel was a democratic bulwark under siege, while Palestinians were irredeemably violent.

**International Law and the Erosion of Norms**

The War on Terror also eroded the global commitment to international law. Precedents set by the United States, from indefinite detention at Guantanamo Bay to drone strikes and extraordinary renditions, created a permissive environment for Israel to pursue increasingly aggressive tactics without fear of meaningful international reprisal.

When Israel launched its first major assault on Gaza in 2008–2009, Operation Cast Lead, killing more than 1,400 Palestinians, including hundreds of children, the international response was muted. In Washington, the attacks were justified as a necessary response to "terrorism," despite widespread condemnation from human rights groups and UN investigators.

This permissiveness would repeat itself in 2012, 2014, 2021, and 2023, each time reinforcing the lesson that so long as Palestinian resistance was framed as terror, Israel's actions, no matter how disproportionate, would face little more than rhetorical criticism.

### The Role of Evangelical Zionism

Another key factor in the post-9/11 environment was the growing influence of evangelical Christian Zionism in the United States. For influential pastors, lobbyists, and Republican politicians, Israel was not just an ally but a theological necessity, a fulfilment of biblical prophecy.

This fusion of theology and politics created an unshakeable bipartisan consensus in Washington, where unconditional support for Israel became both a strategic imperative and a moral crusade. In this context, Palestinian resistance could only ever be framed as evil, a force to be eradicated, not a grievance to be addressed.

### The Global South Pushback

Yet even in the post-9/11 climate, the narrative was never uncontested. In much of the Global South, where the experience of colonialism and occupation remained raw, Palestinians continued to be seen as an oppressed people resisting a settler-colonial project.

In forums like the Non-Aligned Movement, Palestinian diplomats found sympathetic audiences, and in countries such as South Africa, Algeria, and Indonesia, the language of solidarity remained rooted in anti-apartheid and anti-imperialism.

But the power of Western media, finance, and diplomacy ensured that this counter-narrative rarely penetrated policymaking in Washington, London, or Brussels.

### The Long Shadow of 9/11

By the time of the Gaza war of 2023–2025, the legacy of 9/11 was unmistakable. The label of "terrorism" had been so thoroughly embedded in Western political discourse that it shaped initial responses to the 7 October attacks almost reflexively. The fact that the attack occurred after years of blockade, occupation, and periodic bombardments of Gaza barely registered in the first wave of coverage and official statements.

But as the war dragged on, and as images of mass civilian casualties saturated global media, the old certainties began to crack. Younger generations, particularly in the United States and Europe, rejected the binary framing of "terrorist" versus "democratic ally," demanding a more honest reckoning with the realities of occupation, apartheid, and asymmetrical violence.

### Language as a Tool of Power

The post-9/11 world taught Israel and its allies that language could be as powerful as weapons. By monopolising the term "terrorism," Israel neutralised criticism, delegitimised resistance, and secured decades of military, financial, and diplomatic support.

But that monopoly, like so much else, began to erode in Gaza between 2023 and 2025. The images of children starving in the rubble, of hospitals bombed, and of ministers speaking openly of erasure exposed the bankruptcy of a narrative that could no longer reconcile its language with the reality on the ground.

## Section 7 – Gaza 2023–2025: Resistance, Retaliation, and Reality

The events of 7 October 2023 and the catastrophic war that followed marked the most violent and consequential chapter in the history of the Israeli–Palestinian conflict since 1948. What began as a meticulously planned assault by Hamas rapidly spiralled into a devastating war of annihilation, exposing once again the asymmetry of power between one of the world's most advanced militaries and a besieged, impoverished civilian population.

This period forced the world to confront the reality that had been obscured for decades: that Palestinian resistance, in all its forms, armed, political, and civil, exists within the context of profound, sustained oppression, while Israel's response operates with almost no external restraint.

## October 7 – Shock and Symbolism

At dawn on 7 October 2023, Hamas launched Operation Al-Aqsa Flood, a coordinated and unprecedented assault that breached the heavily fortified perimeter between Gaza and Israel. Thousands of rockets overwhelmed the Iron Dome system, while Hamas fighters stormed border communities, military bases, and a music festival in the desert.

The toll was horrific:

- 1,200 Israelis killed, including civilians, police officers, and soldiers
- Over 200 hostages taken into Gaza, ranging from infants to elderly Holocaust survivors

For Israel, the attack was an existential shock, a brutal reminder of vulnerability that punctured the myth of invincibility carefully cultivated since the failures of 1973. For Hamas, the assault was intended as a symbolic rupture, a message to Israel, to Palestinians, and to the world that the status quo of blockade, occupation, and intermittent bombardment was no longer tolerable.

## Resistance or Terrorism?

The immediate framing of the attack revealed the enduring power of language. In Washington, London, and Brussels, leaders condemned the attacks as "unprovoked terrorism." Media outlets carried headlines invoking 9/11, Pearl Harbor, and the Holocaust.

Yet across the Global South, in Johannesburg, Jakarta, Brasília, and Ankara, the narrative was more complex. There, October 7 was understood, however reluctantly, as the inevitable outburst of a population subjected to 16 years of blockade, economic strangulation, and repeated cycles of collective punishment.

This tension, between terrorism and resistance, became the fault line of global discourse. It raised uncomfortable questions. Can an oppressed people under occupation ever be stripped of the right to resist? And if so, who decides the boundaries of legitimate struggle?

**The Overwhelming Retaliation**

Israel's response was immediate and overwhelming. Prime Minister Benjamin Netanyahu, facing a furious public and a collapsing political coalition, declared war and vowed to "eliminate Hamas completely."

Within hours, airstrikes blanketed Gaza, targeting not only Hamas positions but also apartment blocks, mosques, schools, and marketplaces. By the end of the first week:

- Over 4,000 Palestinians were dead, the majority women and children
- Entire neighbourhoods in Gaza City were reduced to rubble
- Electricity, water, and fuel were cut off, plunging the enclave into darkness

By the end of 2023, the death toll had climbed above 20,000, and by mid-2025, it exceeded 45,000, according to UN and independent monitoring bodies. The overwhelming majority were civilians.

**The Siege as Strategy**

The total siege imposed after October 7 transformed Gaza from an open-air prison into a death trap. Israel's defence minister, Yoav Gallant, declared:

"No electricity, no food, no water, no fuel. We are fighting human animals, and we will act accordingly."

This language was matched by policy. Food convoys were blocked or delayed, humanitarian workers were killed in airstrikes, and agricultural land was razed. By early 2024, UN agencies were reporting famine conditions in northern Gaza. By early 2025, children were dying of starvation daily, their emaciated bodies photographed and broadcast across the world in images that would become indelible symbols of the war.

**Hamas and the Calculus of Resistance**

Hamas, for its part, was playing a dangerous and deeply cynical game. The October 7 attack was partly strategic, an effort to force the issue of Gaza onto the international agenda, and partly suicidal, an acknowledgment that years of siege and blockade had created a situation where escalation felt inevitable.

In the months that followed, Hamas fighters continued to launch rockets and ambush Israeli troops in Gaza's labyrinth of tunnels, sustaining the narrative of resistance but at an enormous human cost to the civilian population.

Hamas's leaders, many of whom operated from bunkers deep underground, calculated that global outrage at the scale of Israeli retaliation would eventually shift the diplomatic terrain. In this, they were not entirely wrong. By late 2024, global opinion, and especially youth-led movements in the West, had turned sharply against Israel.

Yet for ordinary Gazans, the strategic calculations of both Hamas and Israel translated into an unrelenting nightmare.

**Digital Transparency and Global Witnessing**

If earlier wars in Gaza had been partially obscured by controlled access and media blackouts, the war of 2023–2025 unfolded in real time. Every smartphone in Gaza became a broadcast station, documenting the destruction with visceral immediacy.

- Videos of families pulling children from rubble went viral within minutes
- Live streams from bombed hospitals showed surgeries being performed without anaesthetic
- Aid workers documented starvation and disease in camps with global reach

This radical transparency changed the conversation. In the West, where official narratives had long dominated, younger audiences were confronted with unfiltered images that contradicted decades of framing. In the Global South, the images reinforced long-held beliefs about Israel as a colonial occupier acting with impunity.

**The Collapse of Narrative Control**

For decades, Israel had maintained a near-monopoly on the language of the conflict in the West: defensive wars, surgical strikes, collateral damage. But the scale of destruction in Gaza, combined with the unrelenting flow of evidence, made those narratives impossible to sustain.

Even sympathetic journalists, long accustomed to framing Israeli actions within a discourse of security and self-defence, found themselves unable to reconcile official statements with the reality on the ground. Reports from the New York Times, BBC, and Le Monde began to reflect the language of human rights organisations: collective punishment, war crimes, apartheid.

**The Global South and the Return of Moral Clarity**

Across the Global South, the events in Gaza were seen not through the lens of counterterrorism but through the history of colonial violence and liberation struggles. Leaders from South Africa, Brazil, and Indonesia drew explicit parallels between Gaza and their own histories of dispossession and resistance.

South Africa, invoking its apartheid legacy, filed its case against Israel at the International Court of Justice, accusing it of genocide. The move galvanised a wave of diplomatic realignment, with countries across Africa, Asia, and Latin America openly challenging Western narratives and calling for sanctions and accountability.

**Asymmetry Laid Bare**

By 2024, the asymmetry of the conflict had become impossible to ignore. On one side, a nuclear-armed state deploying advanced fighter jets, drones, and precision-guided bombs; on the other, a trapped population with no air defence, no safe zones, and no path to escape.

This was not a war between equals. It was the overwhelming application of force against a defenceless civilian population, and the world was watching.

**The Politics of Survival**

Inside Gaza, survival became the only politics that mattered. Families scavenged for food and clean water. Makeshift schools operated in bombed-out buildings. Communities organised ad hoc support networks, sharing what little they had.

For many Palestinians, the war reaffirmed the futility of appeals to international law or Western morality. Decades of negotiations, peace processes, and empty promises had delivered only siege, war, and death. Resistance, however costly, remained, for many, the only path to dignity.

**The Global Reckoning**

By mid-2025, the war in Gaza had fundamentally reshaped global discourse.

- In the Global South, solidarity with Palestine deepened, rooted in shared histories of oppression
- In the West, younger generations increasingly rejected the old narratives, demanding accountability and justice

- In international law, the words genocide, apartheid, and collective punishment were no longer confined to activists but echoed in courtrooms and parliaments

The reality of Gaza, the images, the testimony, and the sheer scale of destruction forced a reckoning, not only with Israel's policies but also with decades of silence and complicity from those who claimed to uphold a rules-based international order.

## Section 8 – The Politics of Labels: Who Gets to Define Terror

Language has always been the battleground of power in the Israeli–Palestinian conflict. For decades, the ability to define, to name, has shaped not just perceptions but also policy, law, and even morality. The word "terrorism" is the sharpest weapon in this arsenal, and its deployment has rarely been neutral.

To call an act or a group "terrorist" is to strip it of legitimacy. It is to foreclose debate, to deny historical context, and to silence nuance. But who decides what counts as terrorism? And why, in the Palestinian case, has that definition been wielded so selectively?

### The Power of Naming

The label of terrorism is rarely about what is done; it is about who does it and who controls the narrative.

When Hamas fighters crossed into southern Israel on 7 October 2023 and killed civilians, the global chorus of condemnation was swift and unequivocal. President Biden called it "pure, unadulterated evil." European leaders denounced the "barbaric terrorist assault." Headlines from *The New York Times* to *The Times of London* echoed the same word: terrorism.

Yet when Israel responded with overwhelming force, reducing entire neighbourhoods in Gaza to rubble, killing thousands of civilians, and openly weaponising starvation, that word was absent. Instead, the language was clinical, bureaucratic: "operations," "strikes," "security." Civilians became "collateral damage." The asymmetry in language mirrored and reinforced the asymmetry in power.

### Historical Double Standards

This double standard is not new. Throughout history, liberation movements have been branded as "terrorist" until they were no longer convenient to call so.

- The African National Congress (ANC) was designated a terrorist organisation by the United States and the United Kingdom well into the 1980s, even as Nelson Mandela languished in prison.

- The Irish Republican Army (IRA) was described as terrorist by London and Washington, even while clandestine back-channel negotiations laid the groundwork for the Good Friday Agreement.

- In Algeria, the FLN were terrorists to Paris until, suddenly, they were the negotiating partner in independence talks.

The Palestinian case follows the same pattern. The right to resist occupation, enshrined in international law under UN General Assembly Resolution 37/43 (1982), has been systematically delegitimised in Western discourse, while state violence by Israel is shielded by the language of defence and security.

### Occupation and the Right to Resist

International law is unambiguous: peoples under foreign occupation have the right to resist. The Fourth Geneva Convention and subsequent UN resolutions recognise the legitimacy of armed struggle against colonial domination and occupation.

This legal clarity, however, rarely finds expression in Western political or media discourse. The word "terrorist" has been weaponised to override legal nuance, reducing every act of

Palestinian resistance, whether a stone thrown at a checkpoint or a rocket fired over the Gaza fence, to an act of illegitimate violence.

By contrast, Israeli actions, even when they involve the indiscriminate killing of civilians, are framed as responses, as regrettable necessities in the pursuit of security.

### October 7 and the Global Divide

The October 7 attacks laid bare this global divide. In the West, the attack was almost universally condemned as terrorism, with little attention paid to the context of blockade, occupation, and decades of military aggression.

In the Global South, however, the narrative was markedly different. Leaders and commentators from South Africa to Brazil drew parallels with their own liberation struggles, framing October 7 not as an act of senseless barbarity but as the inevitable eruption of anger from a people denied dignity, sovereignty, and basic human rights for generations.

This divergence in interpretation exposed the power imbalance in global discourse: the West still largely dictates the language of legitimacy, but that dominance is eroding.

### The Role of Lobbying and Hasbara

Israel's dominance over the narrative has not been accidental. For decades, it has invested heavily in hasbara, the systematic promotion of its perspective in media, academia, and politics.

- Well-funded lobbying organisations such as AIPAC in the United States and similar groups in Europe have ensured that dissenting voices are marginalised or silenced.
- Language has been policed with remarkable discipline: terms like "disputed territories" replacing "occupied territories," or "security barrier" replacing "apartheid wall."
- Politicians, journalists, and academics critical of Israeli policy have been smeared as antisemitic, a tactic that

conflates legitimate critique of state policy with hatred of Jewish people.

This strategic policing of language has given Israel a powerful shield, one that has protected it even as the reality of occupation, apartheid, and systemic violence became increasingly visible.

**Digital Disruption and the Collapse of Monopoly**

The Gaza war of 2023–2025 shattered this monopoly. In the age of digital transparency, control of the narrative was no longer confined to press briefings and newspaper op-eds.

- Smartphones turned every witness into a journalist.
- Social media bypassed traditional gatekeepers, amplifying unfiltered images of destruction and suffering.
- Independent investigators and open-source intelligence groups dismantled official narratives in real time, geolocating airstrikes and verifying evidence of war crimes within hours.

Younger audiences, particularly in the United States and Europe, were no longer consuming news solely through mainstream outlets. They were seeing Gaza through TikTok, Instagram, and Telegram, platforms where the sanitized language of "counterterrorism operations" could not obscure the reality of dead children pulled from rubble.

**Terrorism as a Flexible Concept**

The elasticity of the term "terrorism" is what makes it so potent. It is applied expansively to those without power and sparingly, if at all, to those who wield it.

A homemade rocket fired from Gaza into southern Israel is terrorism; a 2,000-pound U.S.-made bomb dropped on a residential block in Rafah is a "strike."

A Palestinian protestor throwing a rock at an armoured vehicle is a terrorist; a soldier firing live rounds into a crowd of unarmed demonstrators is maintaining "security."

This double standard is not accidental. It reflects the reality that terrorism is defined by power: those who write the rules decide who wears the label and who escapes it.

**Historical Parallels: Ireland, Algeria, and South Africa**

History offers uncomfortable parallels.

- In Ireland, British authorities dismissed the grievances of Catholics in Northern Ireland for decades, branding the IRA and anyone sympathetic to its cause as terrorists, until political realities forced negotiations that recognised the legitimacy of nationalist aspirations.

- In Algeria, the French waged a brutal counterinsurgency against the FLN, insisting they were battling "terrorists," even as their own forces committed systematic atrocities.

- In South Africa, the ANC was vilified internationally until apartheid's collapse forced the world to confront the injustice of its position.

These examples underline a consistent truth: labels shift when power shifts. What is unthinkable to negotiate with today becomes legitimate tomorrow when the balance of power and public opinion changes.

**The Gaza Reckoning**

By 2025, the war in Gaza had eroded the reflexive power of the word "terrorism." While Western leaders clung to familiar talking points, younger generations increasingly rejected the binary framing of good versus evil, security versus terror.

Activists, academics, and independent journalists began reframing the debate, centring terms like occupation, apartheid, colonial violence, and collective punishment. In this reframing, the question was no longer whether Hamas was a terrorist organisation; it was why a people subjected to decades of systemic violence felt that violence was their only remaining voice.

**Language and Power in the Future**

The battle over language will continue to shape the conflict. The question of who gets to define "terrorism" will remain a function of power: political, military, and discursive.

But the monopoly is breaking. The Gaza war exposed the fragility of old narratives and empowered new ones, narratives that demand nuance, that refuse to erase context, and that insist on naming not just the violence of the oppressed but also the systemic, structural violence of the occupier.

# Section 9 – The Path Forward: Reframing the Conversation

The war in Gaza between 2023 and 2025 has done more than shatter buildings and lives; it has shattered the language that for decades defined the Israeli–Palestinian conflict in the global imagination. For years, the story was told in binaries: Israel as a beleaguered democracy defending itself; Palestinians as terrorists unwilling to make peace. That narrative, sustained by state power, media control, and diplomatic leverage, no longer holds.

The question now is how to reframe the conversation, how to build a discourse that acknowledges the complexities of the conflict, the shared traumas of both peoples, and the urgent need for language that does not obscure reality or dehumanise one side while sanctifying the other.

**Breaking the Binary**

The first step in reframing the conversation is to reject the false binary that has dominated for decades: security versus terror, victim versus aggressor, good versus evil.

The reality is infinitely more complex:

- Israel is both a state born of trauma, the Holocaust and centuries of antisemitism, and an occupying power enforcing systemic oppression over millions of stateless people.
- Palestinians are both a people with legitimate aspirations for sovereignty and dignity and, in some cases, represented by actors who have committed violence against civilians.

Acknowledging this complexity is not moral relativism; it is the foundation of any honest conversation about justice and peace.

## Restoring Context

Language without context is propaganda. The events of 7 October did not happen in a vacuum. They were the product of decades of occupation, settlement expansion, economic strangulation, and failed diplomacy.

To reframe the conversation, context must be restored. That means:

- Naming the occupation for what it is: a system of control, dispossession, and violence.
- Recognising the blockade of Gaza as collective punishment, not a neutral security measure.
- Situating acts of Palestinian violence within a historical continuum of oppression, without excusing or sanitising them.

Without context, discussions of "terrorism" or "security" will continue to obscure the structural realities that perpetuate the cycle of violence.

## The Role of Law and Accountability

Reframing the conversation also requires a return to law. International law, though imperfect, provides a framework for understanding the conflict in ways that are not hostage to political expediency.

- The right of occupied peoples to resist is enshrined in the UN Charter and the Fourth Geneva Convention.
- The illegality of settlements, annexations, and collective punishment is clear under international law.
- War crimes and potential genocide must be investigated and prosecuted, regardless of the perpetrators' power or alliances.

A discourse anchored in law, rather than ideology, creates a space where accountability is possible and where the humanity of both peoples can be recognised.

**The Generational Shift**

One of the most profound changes since 2023 is generational. In the United States and Europe, younger audiences are increasingly rejecting the old narratives. Polling across 2024 and 2025 shows:

- Majorities of Americans under 30 support conditioning or cutting military aid to Israel.
- In the UK, France, and Germany, young voters express deep scepticism of official narratives and strong support for Palestinian rights.

This shift is not driven by ideology but by visibility. Social media, open-source investigations, and digital activism have made it impossible to ignore the reality of occupation and asymmetrical violence. Younger generations are less willing to accept official talking points when unfiltered evidence is available at their fingertips.

**The Role of the Global South**

The Global South has long framed the Palestinian struggle as part of a broader history of anti-colonial resistance. What has changed since Gaza 2023–2025 is the confidence and clarity with which that perspective is being asserted in global forums.

- South Africa's genocide case at the International Court of Justice galvanised a new moral consensus in Africa, Asia, and Latin America.
- Leaders from Brazil, Indonesia, and Malaysia have called for sanctions, boycotts, and diplomatic isolation of Israel, challenging the Western monopoly over the discourse.
- The Non-Aligned Movement, once sidelined, has found renewed relevance in advocating for Palestinian rights.

Reframing the conversation means recognising that the West no longer owns the narrative and that global legitimacy increasingly depends on engaging with perspectives beyond Washington, London, and Brussels.

**Naming Structural Violence**

One of the failures of the old discourse was its refusal to name structural violence: the slow, grinding violence of checkpoints, home demolitions, arbitrary arrests, and economic strangulation.

The Gaza war made that violence impossible to ignore, but the reframing must go further. It must move beyond the spectacular violence of bombs and rockets to confront the daily realities of life under occupation:

- Children growing up in refugee camps with no hope of mobility or freedom.
- Farmers watching their land seized for settlements, their olive trees uprooted.
- Families navigating dozens of checkpoints just to reach work, school, or hospitals.

By naming these realities as violence and by recognising that they are not isolated incidents but systemic, the conversation can begin to move toward honesty.

**Challenging Weaponised Language**

Reframing the conversation also requires challenging the weaponisation of language. Criticism of Israeli policies is not antisemitism; calling for accountability is not delegitimisation; naming apartheid is not hate speech.

The conflation of criticism with bigotry has been one of the most effective tools in suppressing honest debate. Breaking that cycle means creating space for good-faith conversations that distinguish between the legitimate fight against antisemitism and the equally legitimate need to hold a state accountable for its actions.

**Building a Shared Language**

A reframed conversation will need a shared language, one that is precise, honest, and rooted in reality. That means:

- Calling the occupation an occupation.
- Naming apartheid where systems of law and segregation are separate and unequal.
- Describing violence accurately, whether it comes from a militant group firing rockets at civilians or a state deploying overwhelming force against a trapped population.

This shared language will not end the conflict, but it will strip away the distortions that have for too long obscured the path to any meaningful resolution.

**The Path Forward**

The path forward is not only about words; it is about power. But words shape power, and reframing the conversation is a necessary step toward any future that is less violent, less asymmetrical, and more just.

It means recognising the shared humanity of Israelis and Palestinians without erasing the reality of oppression and asymmetry. It means centring accountability, dignity, and law as the foundations of any peace. And it means rejecting the narratives that have, for decades, allowed violence to be justified, normalised, and forgotten.

The war in Gaza has created an opportunity, born of immense tragedy, to speak differently, to listen differently, and, perhaps, to imagine differently. Whether that opportunity is seized will depend not only on leaders and diplomats but on the millions of ordinary people who now see, in real time, what was once hidden.

## Section 10 – Conclusion: The Battle for Narrative

Every war is fought on two fronts: the battlefield and the narrative. In Gaza between 2023 and 2025, Israel deployed one of the most technologically advanced militaries in the world, while Palestinians, under siege, starved, and bombed, fought to survive and to be heard.

This chapter has traced how language, *"terrorist," "self-defence," "security," "resistance"*, has shaped the conflict for decades, distorting reality and legitimising violence. But Gaza changed everything. It fractured the monopoly Israel once held over the story, exposing the limits of propaganda in a world where digital transparency has eroded the old hierarchies of information.

### The End of Monopoly

For decades, Israel controlled the narrative in the West. It had the resources, the political leverage, and the media relationships to ensure that its framing of events dominated headlines and influenced policy. The story was always the same: a democratic state defending itself against irrational, hateful violence.

Gaza broke that. The sheer scale of destruction, the visibility of the suffering, and the open, dehumanising rhetoric of Israeli leaders created a chasm between official narratives and lived reality.

When images of starving children and bombed hospitals flooded timelines, when independent investigators geolocated and verified every strike within hours, the credibility of official statements crumbled. Younger generations, digital natives with access to unfiltered information, were no longer willing to accept state narratives at face value.

## A Shifting Moral Landscape

This collapse of narrative control has reshaped the moral landscape of the conflict:

- In the Global South, solidarity with Palestinians hardened into moral clarity, driven by historical memory and a shared understanding of colonial violence.

- In the West, younger generations began questioning the myths their parents and grandparents had accepted, seeing occupation, apartheid, and systemic violence for what they are.

- Within international law, the shift in discourse emboldened courts, investigators, and human rights bodies to speak with greater candour, using words like *apartheid*, *collective punishment*, and *genocide* without the hedging that once accompanied them.

## The Power of Words

Words do not end wars, but they shape the possibilities for what comes next. To call the October 7 attack *"terrorism"* without acknowledging the context of occupation and blockade is to freeze the conflict in a frame that absolves power and punishes the powerless. To describe the siege of Gaza as *"self-defence"* is to legitimise mass death and starvation as acceptable tools of policy.

Reframing the language is not about choosing sides; it is about telling the truth. And the truth is that this is not a war between equals. It is a conflict defined by asymmetry, in power, in weapons, in law, and in the ability to tell the story.

## The Lessons of History

History offers lessons for those willing to see them. In Ireland, the labels of *"terrorist"* and *"criminal"* were once used to delegitimise Irish resistance until negotiations reframed the conflict and produced the Good Friday Agreement. In South Africa, Nelson Mandela was a terrorist until the world recognised apartheid for what it was.

In each case, narrative shifts preceded political shifts. Language did not end the violence, but it created the space for solutions that had once seemed impossible.

The same could be true for Israel and Palestine, but only if the conversation moves beyond the binaries that have, for decades, trapped the conflict in cycles of violence and denial.

## Digital Transparency and Global Witnessing

The Gaza war underscored the power of digital transparency. Never before has a conflict been so visible, so immediate, and so relentlessly documented. Every smartphone became a witness. Every atrocity was geolocated, timestamped, and archived.

This radical visibility is irreversible. It has democratised information in ways that make future wars, and future narratives, fundamentally different. The tools of propaganda remain powerful, but their monopoly is gone. States can no longer rely on controlling the story when the story is being told in real time by those living it.

## The Moral Reckoning

By mid-2025, the world was facing a moral reckoning. The old narratives had collapsed, but new ones had yet to take firm hold. For some, this reckoning brought clarity: an understanding that justice and accountability must be the foundation of any path forward. For others, it brought denial and retrenchment, a desperate clinging to old myths in the face of overwhelming evidence.

The battle for narrative is not just about words. It is about power: who holds it, how it is exercised, and how it is justified. But language shapes the terrain on which power is contested, and in Gaza, that terrain has shifted irrevocably.

**What Comes Next**

The path forward will be defined by whether this moment of clarity becomes a catalyst for change or is buried under the weight of geopolitics and inertia.

- If the world continues to treat Palestinian lives as expendable, the cycle of violence will deepen, and the language of *"terrorism"* will once again become a convenient tool for erasing context and avoiding accountability.

- If, however, this moment is seized, if the conversation is reframed, if language is used to illuminate rather than obscure, then the possibility of justice, however distant, begins to take shape.

This is not naïve optimism. It is an acknowledgment that no conflict in modern history has been resolved without a shift in narrative: a reimagining of what is possible, who is legitimate, and what justice demands.

**A Battle Still Unfinished**

The battle for narrative is far from over. In the United States, political leaders remain largely tethered to the old language of unconditional support and counterterrorism. In Europe, fear of political backlash still mutes honest debate. In Israel, a traumatised public remains trapped in cycles of fear and vengeance, resistant to the idea that security cannot be built on the perpetual subjugation of another people.

But the ground has shifted. Gaza has ensured that future generations will not see the conflict as their parents did. The old frames have been cracked, if not entirely broken, and the demand for a more honest, more just discourse is growing louder.

## The Final Word

Language alone cannot end an occupation. It cannot rebuild Gaza, free the hostages, or heal the deep scars on both sides of this conflict. But language is where the work begins. It is where myths are dismantled, where silences are broken, and where new possibilities are imagined.

The battle for narrative is the battle for reality, and in Gaza, reality has forced its way into the open, undeniable and unignorable. The task now is to ensure that this clarity is not squandered, that the lessons of Gaza are not buried, and that the language of power is no longer allowed to obscure the humanity of those who have suffered the most.

# CHAPTER SEVEN:
# The Global Response to Gaza (2023–2025)

## Section 1 – Introduction: A World Watching in Real Time

The war on Gaza between October 2023 and mid-2025 was not just another bloody chapter in the decades-long story of occupation, resistance, and reprisal. It was a uniquely visible war, unfolding in real time before an audience of billions.

For the first time in modern history, every atrocity, every bomb dropped, every starving child was documented, shared, and archived — not by state media or journalists embedded with the military, but by ordinary people armed with smartphones and internet connections. The world was not reading about Gaza in history books or watching it on evening news bulletins days after the fact; it was watching Gaza live, unfiltered, and often unbearable.

### The Collapse of Narrative Control

For decades, Israel maintained a near-monopoly over the framing of the conflict in the West. Its hasbara machine — a finely tuned apparatus of state messaging, lobbying, and public relations — ensured that wars in Gaza or the West Bank were presented through a familiar script:

- Israel as the victim of "unprovoked attacks."
- Palestinians as "terrorists" who used civilians as human shields.
- Civilian deaths as "collateral damage," regrettable but unavoidable.

### But Gaza in 2023–2025 broke that monopoly.

The asymmetry of the violence — high-precision bombs, drones, and artillery pulverising one of the most densely populated and impoverished territories on earth — was impossible to reconcile with the old language of security and self-defence. Images of hospitals reduced to rubble, of children starving in the ruins of bombed-out neighbourhoods, were not mediated by official statements or carefully staged press briefings; they were streamed in real time, often by the people living — and dying — under the bombardment.

### Digital Witnessing

This was the first war of its kind: a digital war of witness.

- On TikTok, young Gazans uploaded videos showing the destruction of their homes, their families huddled in UN shelters, or the desperate queues for food and water.
- On Instagram, aid workers and doctors shared graphic footage of children undergoing surgery without anaesthetic as supplies ran out.
- On Telegram, citizen journalists geolocated strikes and documented evidence of war crimes with forensic precision.

The immediacy of this content changed everything. No longer could official statements about "surgical strikes" go unchallenged. No longer could casualty figures be dismissed as propaganda. The reality was there, inescapable, in every feed and on every screen.

### The End of the "Two-Sides" Narrative

In previous wars, the dominant frame in Western discourse was one of moral equivalence — "two sides" locked in an intractable conflict, with violence on both ends and blame to be shared.

Gaza 2023–2025 obliterated that narrative. The asymmetry was so stark, the suffering so visible, that framing the conflict as a war between equals became not just inaccurate but absurd.

A nuclear-armed state deploying state-of-the-art weaponry against a population with no air force, no navy, no escape routes, and almost no international protection: that was the reality, and the world could see it in real time.

Even in the United States — historically the most steadfast supporter of Israel — younger generations, armed with digital fluency and accustomed to fact-checking in real time, began to reject the language of equivalence and the justifications of state power.

### The "TikTok Effect"

The so-called "CNN effect" of the 1990s — when broadcast news drove political agendas by bringing distant wars into living rooms — has been replaced by what commentators now call the "TikTok effect."

This new paradigm is faster, decentralised, and harder to control:

- Speed: Graphic footage can reach millions within minutes of being recorded.
- Decentralisation: Narratives are no longer filtered through traditional media but emerge from countless voices on the ground.
- Authenticity: Raw, unpolished footage often carries more credibility than official statements or professional broadcasts.

This digital transparency gave the world a front-row seat to the war and, in doing so, stripped away the layers of abstraction that had allowed so many to look away in the past.

### Gaza and the Global Conscience

For the Global South, where memories of colonialism remain vivid and contemporary struggles against oppression continue, the Gaza war was recognised almost instinctively as a colonial war of domination and erasure.

From Cape Town to Jakarta, from Brasília to Nairobi, Gaza became a rallying point — a stark reminder of how power, when unchecked, strips humanity from those deemed expendable. In these contexts, there was no confusion, no hesitation in naming the violence for what it was: apartheid, ethnic cleansing, even genocide.

In the West, however, the shift was more gradual. At first, governments in Washington, London, Berlin, and Paris repeated familiar talking points of solidarity with Israel. But as the months wore on, and the images of mass graves, bombed hospitals, and starving children became impossible to ignore, cracks began to appear — first in civil society, then in the media, and finally, tentatively, in politics.

### A New Kind of Witness

What made Gaza 2023–2025 so different was the agency of ordinary people in shaping the narrative.

Gazans were not just subjects of other people's reporting; they were the reporters. They documented their own suffering, their own resilience, their own dead. The rawness of this self-documentation was impossible to co-opt or spin.

This agency shifted the moral terrain of the conversation. The West could no longer pretend not to know. Silence became complicity, and complicity became a political liability — particularly among younger voters and activists who refused to accept the old scripts.

### The Historic Parallel

The power of this moment is best understood in historical context. In the 1960s, images of fire hoses and police dogs attacking Black protesters in Birmingham helped galvanise the U.S. civil rights movement. In the 1980s, footage of township violence in South Africa helped build global momentum for sanctions against apartheid.

Gaza in the digital age was that dynamic multiplied a thousandfold: a flood of unfiltered, immediate testimony that made denial impossible and inaction morally indefensible.

**An Unfinished Reckoning**

By mid-2025, the shift was undeniable:

- In parliaments and campuses across the world, calls for accountability grew louder.
- International law, long muted in its language, began to speak with clarity about apartheid, war crimes, and genocide.
- Grassroots movements swelled, connecting the Palestinian struggle to broader fights for climate justice, anti-racism, and anti-colonial solidarity.

Yet the reckoning remains unfinished. Power does not relinquish its grip easily, and entrenched interests — in Washington, Tel Aviv, Brussels, and beyond — continue to fight to restore the old narrative.

But the digital witnessing of Gaza has irrevocably altered the terrain. The world was watching, and what it saw cannot be unseen.

## Section 2 – Western Governments: Unwavering Support, Growing Strain

In the hours after 7 October 2023, the reaction from Western capitals was swift, uniform, and unambiguous. Israel, they declared, had suffered an act of "pure terrorism." Leaders in Washington, London, Berlin, and Paris rushed to offer solidarity, pledging military, financial, and diplomatic support. Flags of Israel were projected onto national landmarks. The language was absolute: "Israel has the right to defend itself."

It was a script well rehearsed — one that had been played out during previous escalations in Gaza. But as the days turned into weeks, and as the scale of Israel's response grew, this script began to unravel. Western governments that had offered unconditional support found themselves increasingly out of step with their own populations, struggling to reconcile entrenched alliances with the moral clarity of images streaming from Gaza in real time.

## Washington: The Anchor of Unconditional Support

In the United States, President Joe Biden delivered one of the most forceful pro-Israel speeches in modern history just days after the October 7 attacks. Flanked by congressional leaders, Biden described Hamas as "pure evil" and pledged "ironclad" support for Israel. U.S. aircraft carriers were dispatched to the Mediterranean, precision-guided munitions were shipped to the IDF, and intelligence sharing intensified.

In Congress, bipartisan unity — rare in a polarised era — was on full display. Even lawmakers on the progressive left, traditionally more critical of Israel, hesitated in the immediate aftermath of October 7 to challenge the narrative of absolute solidarity.

But as Gaza descended into devastation — as footage of mass graves, bombed hospitals, and starving children circulated — that unity began to fracture. By December 2023, protests were erupting across U.S. cities, from New York to Los Angeles, with chants of "Ceasefire now!" and "Not in our name!"

By spring 2024, polling showed a dramatic generational divide. While older Americans still expressed strong support for Israel, younger voters — particularly under 35 — overwhelmingly opposed the war and called for restrictions on U.S. military aid. The Biden administration, facing a bruising re-election campaign, found itself squeezed between an entrenched pro-Israel establishment and a base increasingly unwilling to accept unconditional support for what they saw as collective punishment and ethnic cleansing.

The administration's response was telling. While publicly backing Israel, it began to apply quiet pressure behind the scenes, urging restraint and calling for "humanitarian pauses" — language that satisfied no one and underscored Washington's eroding moral authority.

## Britain: Solidarity and Tension

In the United Kingdom, Prime Minister Rishi Sunak was among the first world leaders to visit Israel after the October 7 attacks, standing shoulder to shoulder with Benjamin Netanyahu and declaring, "We stand with Israel."

But as the death toll in Gaza climbed and protests filled the streets of London, Manchester, and Glasgow, the government faced mounting pressure. Hundreds of thousands marched in weekly demonstrations, demanding a ceasefire and an end to arms sales to Israel. The sheer scale of the protests — the largest in Britain since the Iraq War — exposed a widening gap between public opinion and government policy.

The Labour Party, under Keir Starmer, initially mirrored the government's stance, with Starmer emphasising Israel's "right to self-defence" and refusing to call for a ceasefire. The backlash was immediate and fierce, particularly among younger voters and minority communities, many of whom accused Labour of moral cowardice and complicity in war crimes.

By early 2024, the political cost was evident. Local councillors resigned in protest, internal party dissent grew, and polls showed a sharp erosion of trust in Labour among key demographics. The UK's political establishment, long aligned with Washington on Middle East policy, found itself struggling to navigate a domestic landscape that had shifted decisively in favour of accountability and justice.

## Germany: History as Burden

In Germany, the response to October 7 was shaped by the country's unique historical burden. The memory of the Holocaust remains deeply embedded in German political consciousness, and support for Israel is often framed as an unquestionable moral obligation.

Chancellor Olaf Scholz declared within days of the attack that "Israel's security is Germany's reason of state", echoing a formulation used by successive German leaders since the 1990s. Berlin supplied weapons, intelligence, and diplomatic cover, while clamping down on pro-Palestinian protests in cities like Berlin and Frankfurt, often under the guise of preventing antisemitism.

But as the humanitarian catastrophe in Gaza worsened, cracks appeared. Prominent German academics, journalists, and even some politicians began questioning the government's stance. By mid-2024, Germany was facing an uncomfortable reality: its unwavering support for Israel was isolating it within the European Union, even as domestic protests swelled and younger Germans openly challenged the moral logic of silence in the face of atrocity.

The tension between historical responsibility and present-day ethics became the defining feature of Germany's Gaza debate — a debate that remains unresolved.

**France: Oscillation and Ambiguity**

In France, President Emmanuel Macron's response was initially aligned with the broader Western consensus. Condemnations of Hamas were unequivocal, and support for Israel was framed as both a moral and strategic imperative. But as the humanitarian crisis deepened, Macron shifted tone, calling publicly for a ceasefire and warning of the dangers of collective punishment.

France's internal dynamics complicated its response. With one of Europe's largest Muslim populations and a long history of tensions over identity, secularism, and integration, the Gaza war reignited polarised debates. Protests erupted in Paris, Marseille, and Lyon, sometimes met with heavy-handed policing. Macron, keenly aware of rising tensions, attempted to straddle the divide, but the result was often incoherence — a policy that satisfied neither pro-Israel advocates nor those demanding an end to French complicity in the war.

**Public Opinion vs. Political Power**

Across the West, a consistent pattern emerged: governments clung to old narratives, while public opinion shifted rapidly, particularly among younger generations. In the United States, Britain, Germany, and France, polling data from early 2024 onward revealed:

- Broad support for Israel among older voters, driven by decades of familiar narratives and mainstream media framing.
- Sharp opposition among younger demographics, who consumed information from alternative sources and were far less deferential to state or media authority.
- A growing consensus that unconditional support for Israel was incompatible with professed commitments to human rights and international law.

This generational divide translated into political volatility. Lawmakers in Washington faced unprecedented grassroots pressure. European governments were forced to respond to mass protests, university occupations, and calls for boycotts and divestment. The old calculus — that support for Israel carried little political risk — no longer held.

**The Strain of Real-Time Accountability**

What distinguished Gaza 2023–2025 from previous escalations was the immediacy of accountability. In the age of digital transparency, governments could no longer hide behind official statements or delayed reporting. Every missile strike, every starving child, every ministerial statement dehumanising Palestinians was documented, amplified, and archived.

This real-time witnessing created unprecedented pressure. Politicians were forced to respond to questions they had once been able to ignore. Journalists, confronted with evidence they could not dismiss, began to break from the script. The narrative control that had insulated Western governments for decades was eroding, and they knew it.

### Quiet Shifts, Public Stasis

By late 2024, subtle but significant shifts were underway behind closed doors. U.S. officials began warning Israeli counterparts about the strategic costs of a prolonged war. European diplomats explored alternative pathways to accountability, including sanctions and arms embargoes. But in public, leaders remained cautious, fearful of political backlash and the immense lobbying power of pro-Israel advocacy groups.

This dissonance — between private concern and public silence — became a defining feature of the Western response to Gaza. It exposed the limits of moral clarity in a geopolitical environment where alliances, arms contracts, and strategic calculations still trumped human rights.

## Section 3 – Europe: Between Solidarity and Silence

Europe's response to the Gaza war of 2023–2025 reflected the continent's complex history, political dynamics, and competing pressures. On the surface, there was broad alignment with Washington in the immediate aftermath of October 7, with statements of solidarity, diplomatic cover, and in some cases direct military support for Israel. But beneath that surface ran deep undercurrents of public dissent, generational shifts, and moral unease that exposed fault lines within the European Union and its member states.

### Germany: The Weight of History

No European country wrestled more visibly with its position than Germany. The Holocaust casts a long shadow over German politics, and since the 1990s, successive governments have framed unwavering support for Israel as a moral duty — encapsulated in the phrase, Israels Sicherheit ist deutsche Staatsräson ("Israel's security is Germany's reason of state").

After October 7, this stance hardened. Chancellor Olaf Scholz visited Tel Aviv within days, standing alongside Benjamin Netanyahu and pledging unconditional support. German arms exports to Israel spiked, and Berlin became a key diplomatic shield for Israel within the European Union.

At home, however, this posture collided with a shifting public consciousness. As images of destruction and starvation from Gaza flooded digital platforms, protests erupted across German cities. In Berlin, Frankfurt, and Hamburg, thousands marched weekly, demanding a ceasefire and an end to German complicity.

Authorities, citing concerns about antisemitism, banned several pro-Palestinian demonstrations and cracked down heavily on activists. The scenes — police hauling away students, flags torn down, placards confiscated — only deepened the perception that Germany's political class was out of step with the moral outrage building among younger generations.

By mid-2024, cracks began to show. Prominent German academics and journalists publicly criticised the government's silence in the face of what human rights groups increasingly called war crimes. A growing segment of the public began questioning whether historical guilt could justify present-day complicity in atrocities carried out in Gaza.

### France: Ambiguity and Tension

France's response was marked by oscillation and ambiguity, reflecting the country's fraught internal dynamics. President Emmanuel Macron initially aligned himself closely with Israel, condemning Hamas and pledging solidarity. Paris tightened security around synagogues and Jewish schools and authorised police crackdowns on early pro-Palestinian demonstrations, citing security concerns.

But as the death toll in Gaza mounted and protests swelled — from Paris to Marseille and Lyon — Macron's rhetoric shifted. By late 2023, he was calling for a humanitarian ceasefire, and by early 2024, for a sustained cessation of hostilities. France, historically more comfortable than Germany with positioning itself as a mediator, began to explore diplomatic initiatives aimed at de-escalation.

Yet this balancing act satisfied few. Supporters of Israel accused Macron of appeasing extremism, while pro-Palestinian activists condemned his failure to back stronger measures, such as sanctions or the suspension of arms exports.

France's large and diverse Muslim population added another layer of complexity. The Gaza war reignited long-simmering debates about identity, integration, and the place of Islam in French society, with far-right figures like Marine Le Pen seizing on the crisis to stoke fear and division.

## The United Kingdom: Political Paralysis

In the UK, Prime Minister Rishi Sunak adopted a posture of unwavering support in the early days of the war, projecting the Israeli flag on government buildings and travelling to Tel Aviv to signal solidarity. Like his counterparts in Washington and Berlin, Sunak framed the war as a fight against terror and made no public distinction between Hamas and the civilian population of Gaza.

But public sentiment told a different story. Massive demonstrations — the largest in Britain since the Iraq War — filled the streets of London, Manchester, and Glasgow every weekend. Chants of "Ceasefire Now" and "Free Palestine" reverberated through Westminster, amplified by younger voters and grassroots movements.

Labour leader Keir Starmer, initially echoing Sunak's line and refusing to call for a ceasefire, faced an internal revolt. Dozens of councillors resigned, members threatened to quit, and polls revealed a sharp decline in support among younger and minority voters. By mid-2024, Labour had softened its position, calling for an "immediate ceasefire" — a shift driven less by moral clarity than by political calculus.

The British debate exposed a stark reality: while the political class clung to the old language of alliance and security, the public was moving on, driven by unfiltered access to information and a growing intolerance for double standards in foreign policy.

### Ireland, Spain, and the Voices of Dissent

While major European powers vacillated, smaller nations carved out a more independent moral stance.

In Ireland, where the memory of colonialism and partition runs deep, the government and much of the public were openly critical of Israel's actions. Dublin condemned the collective punishment of Gaza, supported calls for international accountability, and amplified Palestinian voices in European forums.

Spain, under Pedro Sánchez, took a similarly assertive stance, calling for a permanent ceasefire and signalling its willingness to recognise a Palestinian state unilaterally. Norway and Belgium, though less prominent, echoed these positions, reflecting a growing frustration with the paralysis of larger European capitals.

These voices of dissent carried moral weight. They reminded the world that Europe was not monolithic and that some governments were willing to prioritise international law and human rights over strategic alignment with Washington and Tel Aviv.

### European Union: Paralysis and Division

At the level of the European Union, the Gaza war exposed deep divisions. Ursula von der Leyen, the European Commission President, faced intense criticism for her early, unqualified support for Israel, which many member states saw as exceeding her mandate.

While some countries — notably Hungary, the Czech Republic, and Austria — maintained hardline pro-Israel positions, others pushed for stronger calls for a ceasefire and accountability. The result was paralysis: the EU issued carefully worded statements calling for "restraint" and "humanitarian access" but failed to agree on concrete measures such as arms embargoes or sanctions.

This paralysis damaged the EU's credibility as a geopolitical actor. It revealed a bloc caught between competing identities — as a defender of human rights and as a strategic partner to Israel and the United States — and unable to reconcile the two.

Public Opinion and the Generational Divide

Across Europe, public opinion shifted dramatically over the course of the conflict. Polling throughout 2024 revealed consistent trends:

- Younger Europeans, especially those under 35, were far more critical of Israel and far more sympathetic to the Palestinian cause.
- Older generations, shaped by Cold War narratives and decades of pro-Israel framing, tended to support the status quo.
- Minority communities, particularly in countries with significant Muslim populations, were vocal and organised, driving sustained protests and grassroots campaigns.

These dynamics created political tension in capitals across the continent. Leaders who ignored the generational and demographic shifts risked alienating significant segments of their electorates, while those who attempted to engage with the new reality faced backlash from entrenched interests and powerful lobbying networks.

**The Collapse of Silence**

By mid-2025, it was clear that the old equilibrium was gone. The days when European leaders could issue platitudes about "restraint" while supplying arms and diplomatic cover were over. The visibility of the war, the immediacy of digital testimony, and the moral clarity of the images streaming out of Gaza made silence untenable.

Europe's challenge, moving forward, is whether it can reconcile its history — of complicity, of selective morality, of strategic alignment — with a future in which its publics demand consistency, justice, and accountability.

## Section 4 – The Global South: Moral Clarity and Leadership

If the response from Western capitals to the Gaza war of 2023–2025 was defined by hesitation, equivocation, and political calculation, the response from the Global South was striking in its clarity. Across Africa, Asia, and Latin America, leaders, intellectuals, and civil societies framed the assault on Gaza not as a complex, tragic "conflict" between equals, but as a colonial war of domination and erasure.

From the streets of Johannesburg to the parliaments of Brasília and Kuala Lumpur, the language was direct: apartheid, occupation, genocide. For much of the Global South, Gaza was not an isolated tragedy but a continuation of familiar histories — of empire, of dispossession, of resistance against overwhelming power.

### South Africa: From Apartheid to Advocacy

No country embodied this clarity more than South Africa. Its history of apartheid gave it not only a moral vocabulary but a lived experience of systemic dehumanisation and international complicity.

From the earliest days of the war, the African National Congress (ANC) government condemned Israel's actions in unflinching terms. President Cyril Ramaphosa described the blockade and bombardment of Gaza as "a crime against humanity," drawing direct parallels between the pass laws and racial hierarchies of apartheid-era South Africa and the checkpoints, permits, and segregation imposed on Palestinians.

But South Africa went beyond rhetoric. In December 2023, it filed a case against Israel at the International Court of Justice (ICJ), accusing it of genocide. The move electrified the Global South, positioning Pretoria as the moral vanguard in a fight for international accountability.

The symbolism was profound: the country that had once been branded a pariah state for its system of racial domination was now invoking the very architecture of international law — the same architecture that helped dismantle apartheid — to confront another state accused of systemic oppression.

The ICJ hearings in The Hague, where South African lawyers presented meticulously documented evidence of indiscriminate bombing, starvation, and dehumanising rhetoric from Israeli officials, were watched live across the world. For many, this was a watershed moment: a reminder that even in a system often paralysed by geopolitics, law could still be wielded as a tool of resistance.

**Latin America: Voices of Defiance**

Across Latin America, the response to Gaza was shaped by a deep history of anti-imperial struggle and a scepticism towards U.S. hegemony.

In Brazil, President Luiz Inácio Lula da Silva emerged as one of the most vocal critics of the war. From the earliest days of the assault, Lula condemned what he described as the "massacre of innocents", calling for an immediate ceasefire and accusing Israel of pursuing policies indistinguishable from apartheid. When pressed by Western leaders to moderate his language, Lula doubled down, arguing that silence in the face of atrocity was complicity.

Other regional leaders followed suit. Colombia's Gustavo Petro suspended arms deals with Israel, describing the Gaza offensive as "the same logic of extermination" that had characterised colonial violence in the Americas. Chile's Gabriel Boric, long a critic of Israeli policies, recalled his ambassador from Tel Aviv and pushed for coordinated Latin American pressure at the UN.

These responses resonated deeply across the region, where memories of dictatorship, repression, and externally supported violence remain vivid. Gaza was understood not as a distant tragedy but as a familiar story of power crushing the powerless — and of the necessity of solidarity in the face of that power.

### Asia and the Muslim World

In Asia, particularly in Muslim-majority nations, the response was immediate and visceral.

In Indonesia, the world's largest Muslim-majority country, millions took to the streets in Jakarta, Bandung, and Surabaya. The government of President Joko Widodo condemned the siege and called for international sanctions, framing the crisis as a test of the world's commitment to human rights and the rule of law.

Malaysia, under Prime Minister Anwar Ibrahim, was even more direct. Anwar accused Israel of "genocidal intent" and castigated Western governments for their double standards, noting that the same leaders who condemned Russia's invasion of Ukraine refused to apply the same moral clarity to Gaza.

In Pakistan, where solidarity with Palestine has been a political constant for decades, the government declared days of mourning, and protests brought major cities to a standstill. Even in countries with quieter official responses, like India, where geopolitical realignments have drawn New Delhi closer to Tel Aviv, civil society and opposition parties were vocal in their condemnation.

### The Power of Shared History

What united these diverse responses was a sense of historical recognition. For nations that had endured colonial rule, exploitation, and external domination, the images from Gaza were not abstract. They were reminders of their own histories — of plantations and concentration camps, of forced removals and imposed borders, of violence justified by the language of civilisation and progress.

This historical memory shaped not just rhetoric but policy. The Global South's clarity was not performative; it was grounded in a lived understanding of power, resistance, and the slow, grinding violence of structures designed to dehumanise.

### International Forums and New Alignments

At the United Nations, the Global South emerged as a bloc of moral clarity. While the United States wielded its veto repeatedly in the Security Council to shield Israel from censure, the General Assembly became a forum for growing defiance.

Resolution after resolution calling for a ceasefire passed with overwhelming support, with only a handful of countries — the U.S., Israel, and a shrinking group of allies — voting against.

The ICJ case brought by South Africa was a turning point, galvanising new forms of South–South cooperation. Countries across Africa, Asia, and Latin America submitted briefs in support of the case, signalling a new willingness to challenge Western dominance in international law and diplomacy.

This shift was not just symbolic. It marked the emergence of a new geopolitical alignment, one less deferential to Western power and more confident in asserting a moral and legal framework that holds even the powerful to account.

### Civil Society and Global Solidarity

Beyond governments, civil society across the Global South mobilised at an unprecedented scale.

- In Johannesburg, students occupied university campuses, demanding divestment from companies linked to the Israeli military-industrial complex.

- In São Paulo, labour unions organised strikes and boycotts targeting firms with ties to Israel.
- Across Asia, from Kuala Lumpur to Karachi, grassroots movements organised mass demonstrations, digital campaigns, and fundraising efforts for humanitarian relief.

This wave of activism created a feedback loop: grassroots pressure emboldened governments, and government action, in turn, legitimised grassroots mobilisation. It was a dynamic absent in much of the West, where activism often faced intense repression and accusations of antisemitism.

**Western Double Standards in the Spotlight**

One of the most consistent themes in the Global South's response was the highlighting of Western double standards. Leaders and commentators repeatedly pointed to the contrast between the West's robust response to Russia's invasion of Ukraine — with sanctions, military aid, and a moral discourse of sovereignty and human rights — and its silence, or worse, complicity, in the face of atrocities in Gaza.

This hypocrisy, long resented, became impossible to ignore. Editorials in major African, Asian, and Latin American newspapers drew the connection explicitly: the rules-based international order, they argued, is only as legitimate as its willingness to apply its principles universally.

**A Shift in Global Power**

By mid-2025, the war in Gaza had catalysed a geopolitical shift that had been building for years. The old unipolar order, in which the United States and its allies set the terms of global politics, was visibly eroding.

The Global South, emboldened by demographic weight, economic growth, and new alliances — from BRICS to regional blocs like ASEAN and the African Union — asserted a more independent and confrontational posture. Gaza became a rallying point, a moral and political touchstone for a world no longer willing to defer to the narratives of the Global North.

### The Moral Clarity of the Marginalised

The moral clarity of the Global South during the Gaza war was not accidental. It was born of history — of communities and nations that have lived under the boot of power and know, intimately, the cost of silence.

Where the West equivocated, the Global South spoke plainly. Where Western leaders clung to platitudes, leaders in Pretoria, Brasília, and Kuala Lumpur spoke of apartheid, genocide, and justice.

This clarity resonated globally, amplifying a truth that could no longer be ignored: that the narrative monopoly of the West was broken, and that in its place, a multipolar conversation — rooted in law, history, and lived experience — had begun to take shape.

## Section 5 – The UN, ICJ, and the Language of Law

The war in Gaza between 2023 and 2025 did more than expose the brutality of Israel's military campaign; it also laid bare the contradictions of the international system — a system ostensibly built to uphold the rule of law but too often paralysed by power politics. From the United Nations (UN) to the International Court of Justice (ICJ) and the International Criminal Court (ICC), Gaza became the ultimate test of whether the language of law could still carry meaning in an era of entrenched impunity.

### The United Nations: Paralysis and Outrage

At the UN Security Council, paralysis was immediate and predictable. Within hours of the October 7 attacks, the United States and its closest allies closed ranks around Israel, framing the event as a singular act of terrorism and blocking any language that hinted at proportionality, ceasefires, or accountability.

In the weeks that followed, as images of devastation in Gaza went viral and casualty figures mounted into the tens of thousands, multiple resolutions calling for an immediate ceasefire were vetoed by Washington, often with the backing of the United Kingdom.

This dynamic — decades in the making — was familiar but now starkly visible to a global audience more sceptical of Western intentions than ever before. Every veto cast by the United States was broadcast live and dissected in real time, sparking outrage in capitals from Pretoria to Brasília to Jakarta.

By contrast, in the UN General Assembly, where veto power does not exist, overwhelming majorities consistently voted for ceasefires and humanitarian access. In December 2023, 153 countries voted in favour of a ceasefire resolution, with only 10 opposed, including the U.S., Israel, and a handful of isolated allies. The image of near-total global consensus against the violence — and the isolation of the West — was one of the defining visuals of the war.

### The ICJ: South Africa's Case and the Return of Moral Clarity

The most significant legal challenge to Israel's actions came from South Africa, whose decision to bring a genocide case against Israel before the International Court of Justice (ICJ) was both historic and profoundly symbolic.

Filed in December 2023, the case alleged that Israel's actions in Gaza — the deliberate targeting of civilians, the destruction of critical infrastructure, the blocking of food, water, and medical aid, and the use of dehumanising language by senior officials — met the legal definition of genocide under the 1948 Genocide Convention.

When the ICJ convened its emergency hearings in January 2024, the world watched. South Africa's legal team, drawing on meticulous documentation from UN agencies, NGOs, and independent investigators, presented a chilling account:

- Entire neighbourhoods levelled without military justification.
- Starvation used systematically as a weapon of war.
- Ministers and Knesset members calling openly for Gaza to be "erased" and for Palestinians to be treated as "human animals."

Israel's defence, focused on its "right to self-defence" and the argument that civilian casualties were unintended, failed to convince many observers. The contrast between the two arguments — one rooted in evidence, the other in deflection — was striking.

In January 2024, the ICJ issued provisional measures ordering Israel to prevent genocidal acts, allow humanitarian aid into Gaza, and report on its compliance. Though the court stopped short of calling for an immediate ceasefire, the ruling was a watershed moment: for the first time, a major international court had formally acknowledged that there was a plausible case of genocide.

**The Impact of the Genocide Case**

The genocide case reverberated globally. In the Global South, it was celebrated as a triumph of law over impunity, a moment when the voices of the marginalised pierced the shield of Western power. Across Africa, Asia, and Latin America, the hearings were broadcast live, sparking mass viewing events and teach-ins in universities and community centres.

In the West, the reaction was more complex. Governments attempted to downplay the ruling, emphasising that the court had not yet found Israel guilty of genocide, but the language of "plausibility" and the stark imagery presented during the hearings began to seep into public discourse.

The ICJ case also placed enormous pressure on Western media, which had long avoided terms like "apartheid," "ethnic cleansing," or "genocide." By mid-2024, even mainstream outlets like the BBC,

The Guardian, and The New York Times began referencing the ICJ case directly, acknowledging its legal and moral significance.

**The ICC: Delayed Justice, Growing Pressure**

Parallel to the ICJ proceedings, the International Criminal Court (ICC) faced mounting pressure to act. For years, the ICC had been criticised for its reluctance to investigate alleged war crimes by Israel, a hesitation widely attributed to political pressure from Washington and Brussels.

The scale of the atrocities in Gaza — meticulously documented by human rights organisations and independent investigators — made continued inaction untenable. By late 2024, ICC Prosecutor Karim Khan had confirmed that his office was pursuing investigations into both Israeli actions in Gaza and Hamas's October 7 attack.

For Palestinians, who had long argued that the ICC was a court for the weak, not the powerful, this announcement was met with scepticism. But for legal scholars and activists, it represented a significant, if overdue, step toward accountability.

**Language as a Battlefield**

Throughout these legal battles, language itself became a point of contention. Israeli officials, backed by their Western allies, accused critics of "weaponising" international law, framing the genocide case as politically motivated.

But the evidence — satellite imagery of destroyed neighbourhoods, videos of starving children, public statements from senior Israeli figures — was impossible to ignore. The deliberate use of terms like "human animals," "flatten Gaza," and "no electricity, no food, no water" by officials gave legal weight to the argument that genocidal intent was not just plausible but demonstrable.

In this context, the language of law — precise, dispassionate, and rooted in decades of jurisprudence — provided a counterweight to the chaos of propaganda and misinformation. The courtrooms in The Hague became a rare space where the suffering of Palestinians was acknowledged with seriousness and dignity.

### Erosion of Western Legitimacy

The proceedings at the ICJ and ICC also accelerated the erosion of Western legitimacy in the eyes of much of the world. The sight of U.S. and European officials dismissing or undermining international courts — institutions they had once championed when prosecuting African leaders or Russian war crimes — fuelled accusations of hypocrisy.

For the Global South, Gaza became a case study in the double standards of the "rules-based international order." If law was only for the weak, if accountability stopped where power began, then the system itself was broken.

### The Symbolism of The Hague

The hearings in The Hague carried a symbolism that transcended the legal proceedings. Survivors testified, experts presented evidence, and international lawyers argued in meticulous detail about proportionality, intent, and the obligations of states under the Genocide Convention.

For Palestinians — long dehumanised, marginalised, and silenced — the simple act of having their suffering documented in a court of law was transformative. It was not justice, not yet, but it was a recognition that their voices and experiences could no longer be ignored or erased.

### The Future of Legal Accountability

By mid-2025, the ICJ case had entered a slower phase, with further hearings scheduled and final judgments years away. The ICC investigation, too, was moving at a glacial pace, hampered by political interference and the sheer complexity of gathering evidence in an active war zone.

But the symbolic and practical impact of these proceedings was undeniable:

- They shifted the global discourse, legitimising the language of apartheid, war crimes, and genocide in mainstream debate.
- They galvanised activism, giving movements for justice a legal framework to rally around.
- They signalled a shift in power, with the Global South increasingly willing to leverage international law against entrenched Western dominance.

## Section 6 – Global Protest Movements

If the courtrooms of The Hague gave the Gaza war of 2023–2025 its legal and moral vocabulary, the streets of the world gave it its heartbeat. From New York to Jakarta, São Paulo to Cape Town, millions of people mobilised in one of the largest and most sustained waves of global protest since the anti-apartheid movement of the 1980s or the anti-war protests of 2003.

These movements did more than express solidarity; they reshaped the narrative, forced reluctant governments to confront public outrage, and connected the Palestinian struggle to wider conversations about justice, race, and inequality.

The First Wave: Shock and Solidarity

In the days immediately following 7 October, protests erupted across the world. Initially, they were small and subdued — vigils for the dead in Israel and Gaza, calls for the release of hostages, and demands for restraint.

But as the scale of Israel's response became clear — as images of flattened neighbourhoods, dead children, and desperate families flooded social media — the protests grew exponentially.

215

- In London, hundreds of thousands filled the streets, waving Palestinian flags and chanting "Ceasefire Now" and "Free, Free Palestine."
- In New York, massive marches shut down bridges and key transport hubs.
- In Paris, despite attempts by police to suppress demonstrations, crowds gathered nightly, often clashing with authorities.
- In Jakarta, an estimated two million people rallied in front of the U.S. Embassy, in one of the largest single demonstrations in the world.

By the end of October 2023, the protests had become a global chorus of dissent, amplified by social media and coordinated across continents.

**A Generational Movement**

The protests were remarkable not just for their size but for their demographics. This was a movement led largely by young people, digital natives fluent in the language of online activism and unfiltered media.

For many, Gaza was their first direct political engagement — a cause that united students, activists, artists, and professionals across lines of race, class, and geography. University campuses in the United States, Canada, the UK, and Australia became flashpoints, with students occupying administrative buildings, demanding divestment from companies linked to the Israeli military, and holding teach-ins that connected Gaza to struggles against systemic racism and colonialism elsewhere.

This generational shift was particularly stark in the United States, where polling throughout 2024 showed a dramatic divide: older Americans clung to traditional pro-Israel narratives, while younger Americans overwhelmingly sympathised with Palestinians and questioned the moral and political logic of unconditional support for Israel.

## The Role of Social Media

At the heart of this mobilisation was social media, which transformed the protest movement into a global, decentralised network.

- TikTok became a platform for unfiltered testimony from Gaza, with videos of bombed-out hospitals and starving children going viral within hours.
- Instagram and X (formerly Twitter) amplified protest organisation, helping coordinate marches, sit-ins, and digital campaigns in real time.
- Telegram and other encrypted apps allowed activists to share strategies and bypass government surveillance in more repressive environments.

The immediacy of digital activism allowed protesters to challenge official narratives in real time. Governments could no longer rely on carefully crafted press briefings or mainstream media framing; the evidence of atrocity was everywhere, undeniable and immediate.

## State Responses: Repression and Resistance

The global scale and persistence of the protests triggered state pushback, particularly in Western democracies that had positioned themselves as guardians of free speech.

- In the United States, student protesters were smeared as antisemites, with some universities calling in police to break up encampments.
- In the UK, police invoked broad public order laws to arrest demonstrators, while ministers labelled chants such as "From the river to the sea" as hate speech.

- In France, pro-Palestinian demonstrations were initially banned outright, sparking clashes between protesters and police.
- Even in Germany, where public debate was already constrained by historical guilt, authorities cracked down heavily on activists, banning Palestinian flags at some rallies and shutting down cultural events deemed "politically sensitive."

These repressive measures often backfired, galvanising public anger and swelling the size of demonstrations. The sight of heavily armed police confronting peaceful marchers, particularly students and young people, became a potent symbol of the widening gap between governments and their citizens.

**Grassroots to Global**

By early 2024, the protest movement had evolved beyond spontaneous outrage into a coordinated, strategic campaign.

- Labour unions in countries like South Africa, Brazil, and Ireland threatened or enacted boycotts of companies complicit in the war.
- University campaigns for Boycott, Divestment, and Sanctions (BDS) gained momentum, winning high-profile endorsements from faculty and student organisations.
- City councils in progressive municipalities across the globe passed resolutions condemning the war and calling for an end to arms sales.

The movement's decentralised nature — without a single leader or organisational hub — made it difficult to suppress and resilient to attempts at co-optation or division.

**Echoes of Past Struggles**

Many observers drew parallels between the Gaza protests and earlier moments of mass moral mobilisation.

- Like the anti-apartheid movement of the 1980s, the Gaza protests combined grassroots activism, international solidarity, and legal strategies aimed at delegitimising an entrenched system of oppression.
- Like the anti-war marches of 2003, they mobilised millions across continents in opposition to what was widely seen as a war of choice, driven by ideology and impunity.
- But unlike those earlier movements, the Gaza protests unfolded in a digitally connected world, where images and information bypassed traditional gatekeepers, collapsing the distance between the suffering in Gaza and the streets of Western capitals.

## Corporate and Institutional Pressure

As the protests intensified, they began to exert real pressure on corporations, universities, and cultural institutions.

- Major brands faced boycotts and public backlash for perceived complicity or silence.
- Universities were pressed to disclose and divest from endowments tied to defence contractors supplying arms to Israel.
- Cultural figures — writers, musicians, and artists — used their platforms to speak out, often at great personal and professional risk.

By mid-2024, divestment campaigns were yielding tangible results, with several academic institutions and pension funds announcing partial or full withdrawals from companies linked to the Israeli military or settlement enterprise.

## The Diaspora Factor

The Palestinian diaspora played a pivotal role in sustaining and amplifying the protests.

- In London, second- and third-generation Palestinians became prominent organisers, connecting their family histories of displacement to the current catastrophe in Gaza.
- In the United States, Palestinian American activists leveraged their visibility and networks to keep Gaza at the forefront of political and media conversations.
- Across Latin America and Asia, diaspora communities bridged local struggles with global advocacy, framing Gaza as a universal story of oppression and resilience.

This interplay between local and global activism underscored the deeply interconnected nature of the movement, with solidarity rooted not just in ideology but in lived experience.

### Impact on Policy and Discourse

While the protests did not immediately shift government policies — particularly in Washington and key European capitals — they reshaped the political landscape in several key ways:

- They made silence costly for politicians, forcing even staunchly pro-Israel figures to acknowledge the humanitarian catastrophe.
- They accelerated the normalisation of critical language — apartheid, occupation, collective punishment — in mainstream political and media discourse.
- They laid the groundwork for long-term policy shifts, particularly as younger, more globally conscious generations enter positions of influence and power.

### A Movement That Won't Fade

By mid-2025, as Gaza lay in ruins and international investigations gathered momentum, the global protest movement showed no sign of fading. Instead, it began to evolve into a broader call for systemic change, linking Palestine to issues as varied as climate justice, indigenous sovereignty, and anti-racist struggles.

For many activists, Gaza had become the moral lens through which they viewed the world — a litmus test of whether principles like human rights and international law were truly universal or merely rhetorical tools of convenience.

## Section 7 – Media Transformation: From Control to Collapse

For decades, the story of Israel and Palestine in the Western media followed a familiar script: Israel as the embattled democracy fighting for its survival, Palestinians as either passive victims or irrational aggressors. This narrative was maintained by editorial discipline, political pressure, and structural biases that favoured official sources and excluded dissenting voices.

The Gaza war of 2023–2025 changed all of that. The old architecture of narrative control — carefully managed access, official briefings, and newsroom gatekeeping — collapsed under the weight of digital transparency. For the first time, the reality on the ground in Gaza could not be filtered, delayed, or sanitised.

### The Old Model of Narrative Control

Before Gaza, Western newsrooms operated within a framework that had been remarkably consistent since 1948:

- Heavy reliance on Israeli government and military sources for information and imagery.
- Limited access for journalists in Gaza, often mediated through official channels or "pool reporters."
- An editorial tendency to frame violence as cyclical and symmetrical, avoiding any acknowledgment of asymmetry in power or the structural violence of occupation.

In this old model, headlines often blurred reality. Bombing campaigns became "responses," civilians were "caught in crossfire," and the daily violence of checkpoints, raids, and land seizures was rarely covered outside specialist outlets.

### The Shock of October 7

The October 7 attacks initially reinforced these entrenched patterns. Western outlets rushed to cover Hamas's assault with wall-to-wall reporting, often echoing Israeli government talking points. The language was immediate and absolute: "terrorism," "massacre," "unprovoked violence."

But as Israel's retaliation escalated — and as images of devastation in Gaza spread online — this framing began to fray. The speed, volume, and visceral nature of the footage from Gaza forced mainstream outlets to confront a reality that their old scripts could no longer contain.

### Digital Witnessing and the Collapse of Control

At the heart of this transformation was the democratisation of media.

Every smartphone in Gaza became a camera, every resident a witness. Within minutes of an airstrike, images and videos were circulating globally, geolocated and verified by independent investigators. The gap between event and evidence collapsed.

Platforms like TikTok, Instagram, Telegram, and X bypassed traditional gatekeepers, making it impossible for official narratives to dominate unchallenged. Attempts by Israeli officials and their allies to frame the war as a defensive campaign against "terror" ran headlong into a torrent of unfiltered reality:

- Children pulled from rubble, their names and stories documented in real time.
- Hospitals bombed, their doctors live-streaming desperate pleas for supplies.
- Families broadcasting their final messages as bombs fell around them.

This immediacy shattered the illusion of narrative control. Viewers no longer needed journalists to interpret events; they could see them for themselves.

**Independent Journalism and Open-Source Investigations**

The rise of open-source intelligence (OSINT) and independent investigative journalism played a critical role in this shift.

Organisations like Bellingcat, Forensic Architecture, and Airwars, along with dozens of smaller digital collectives, used satellite imagery, geolocation, and metadata to verify strikes, trace the use of prohibited weapons, and debunk false claims.

Their work, often amplified by social media, forced mainstream outlets to confront uncomfortable truths and incorporate evidence that could no longer be ignored. By mid-2024, even traditionally cautious organisations like the BBC and The New York Times were referencing independent investigations in their coverage, marking a quiet but profound shift in editorial standards.

**The Generational Divide in Media Consumption**

This transformation was accelerated by a generational shift in how news is consumed.

For younger audiences, the primary sources of information were not evening broadcasts or legacy newspapers but digital platforms, where events unfolded in real time and narratives were contested openly. Trust in traditional media, already eroded by decades of bias and selective coverage, collapsed further as viewers saw stark discrepancies between what they witnessed online and what they read in mainstream headlines.

Polling across the United States, the UK, and Europe in 2024 showed a stark divide:

- Older generations largely continued to trust traditional outlets and government-aligned narratives.

- Younger generations, by contrast, were far more sceptical, more informed, and more likely to sympathise with Palestinians.

## Mainstream Media Under Pressure

Mainstream outlets found themselves in a crisis of credibility. Journalists and editors faced unprecedented scrutiny, both from audiences demanding accuracy and from governments exerting pressure to maintain old narratives.

In some cases, this tension produced remarkable moments of journalistic integrity: correspondents broke from official scripts to describe the reality of collective punishment, ethnic cleansing, and systemic dehumanisation. In others, it exposed the deep entanglement of media with power, as editors spiked or sanitised stories for fear of political backlash or accusations of bias.

By late 2024, some outlets began to shift their language, cautiously adopting terms long confined to human rights reports — "apartheid," "collective punishment," "genocide." These shifts did not happen in isolation; they were the product of relentless public pressure, digital transparency, and the collapse of old hierarchies of information.

### The Power of Imagery

Central to this transformation was the power of imagery.

- The photograph of a father cradling his dead child in the rubble of Gaza City.
- The live stream of a surgeon performing an operation by flashlight as generators failed.
- The viral video of a young girl, covered in dust and blood, asking, "Why do they hate us?"

These images transcended language, culture, and politics. They cut through decades of propaganda and forced viewers to confront the human cost of policies often described in abstract terms like "security" or "deterrence."

## Weaponised Narratives and Counter-Narratives

Israel and its allies fought back fiercely in the information war, deploying well-funded digital campaigns, lobbying technology companies to suppress pro-Palestinian content, and framing criticism of the war as antisemitism. Algorithms were tweaked, accounts shadow-banned, and content removed under the guise of safety or misinformation.

But these efforts largely failed to contain the shift. The volume of independent documentation and the speed of its dissemination overwhelmed attempts at suppression. The narrative monopoly had been broken, and no amount of digital gatekeeping could restore it.

## The Global South and Media Realignment

Outside the West, the transformation was even more pronounced. In the Global South, where state and independent media were less constrained by Western alliances, coverage of Gaza was blunt and unfiltered.

African, Asian, and Latin American networks broadcast the reality of the war without euphemism, often pairing live footage with historical context about colonialism, apartheid, and systemic oppression. This unflinching coverage reinforced the sense of a widening moral and narrative divide between the Global North and the rest of the world.

## A Permanent Shift

By mid-2025, the media landscape had undergone an irreversible transformation:

- Digital platforms had democratised information, making it impossible to control narratives in the way governments once did.

- Independent journalism had proven that accuracy and accountability were possible without the constraints of legacy media.
- Audiences, particularly younger generations, had grown more sceptical, more informed, and more willing to challenge official narratives.

The Gaza war of 2023–2025 will be remembered not only for its human cost but for the way it redefined information warfare, shifting power from the few to the many and exposing, in real time, the brutal realities of occupation and asymmetrical violence.

## Section 8 – Digital Transparency and the End of the Narrative Monopoly

The war in Gaza from 2023 to 2025 was not just a battle fought in the skies or the streets; it was also a battle for the truth, and this time, the truth could not be contained. What unfolded was a seismic collapse of the narrative monopoly that Israel and its Western allies had maintained for decades.

Digital platforms, in the hands of ordinary Gazans, journalists, and activists, flattened the information hierarchy. They exposed, in real time, the asymmetry of violence and the hollowness of official rhetoric. For the first time, the world saw Gaza not through government briefings or polished media soundbites but through the unfiltered lens of the people living — and dying — inside the enclave.

### The Power of the Smartphone

The smartphone became the defining weapon of narrative resistance.

Every strike, every rescue, every atrocity was captured in shaky, handheld footage — a mother screaming over the body of her child, a doctor weeping in an overcrowded ward, children clutching bread in queues that stretched for blocks. These images travelled faster than missiles, reaching audiences across the globe before traditional media could craft their headlines.

This immediacy stripped away the layers of abstraction that had insulated many viewers in the West from the realities of occupation. The destruction was not an event summarised in the evening news; it was unfolding live, in 4K clarity, on their phones.

## Breaking the Monopoly

For decades, Israel's public relations machinery, known as hasbara, had shaped global perceptions of the conflict. It framed Israel as a beleaguered democracy defending itself against irrational hatred, while Palestinian suffering was reduced to unfortunate collateral damage.

But the speed and reach of digital platforms made that framing untenable. In previous wars, official narratives could dominate for days, even weeks, before dissenting voices gained traction. By late 2023, those voices were instantaneous, decentralised, and amplified by millions.

Attempts to control the flow of information — through censorship, content takedowns, or algorithmic suppression — only highlighted the desperation of those trying to contain a narrative that had slipped irretrievably from their grasp.

## Citizen Journalism and Digital Forensics

This new reality was not just about volume but also about verification.

Independent investigators, journalists, and human rights organisations leveraged open-source tools to verify every image, every strike, every statement. Platforms like Bellingcat, Forensic Architecture, and Airwars turned social media into a vast archive of evidence, corroborating timelines, geolocating footage, and documenting war crimes with a level of precision that traditional media and governments could no longer dismiss.

This forensic transparency eroded trust in official statements and empowered activists and legal experts to hold powerful actors accountable in ways that had previously been unthinkable.

### The "TikTok Generation" and Generational Realignment

Much of this shift was driven by a generational transformation in media consumption.

Younger audiences — digital natives raised on platforms like TikTok, Instagram, and YouTube — bypassed traditional media entirely. They consumed raw, unfiltered footage directly from Gaza, often contextualised by activists, journalists, or ordinary citizens on the ground.

For these audiences, the cognitive dissonance between what they were witnessing online and what they were hearing from politicians and legacy outlets was impossible to ignore. Trust in mainstream institutions collapsed, and with it, decades of narrative conditioning.

Polling across 2024 and 2025 reflected this shift:

- In the United States, support for Israel among voters under 30 fell to historic lows, with a majority expressing sympathy for Palestinians.
- In Europe, similar generational divides emerged, particularly in the UK, France, and Germany, where younger voters were far more critical of Israeli policy and their governments' complicity.

### The Diaspora Amplifier

Palestinian diaspora communities around the world became crucial amplifiers of digital content from Gaza.

From London to Chicago, Kuala Lumpur to Santiago, diaspora activists used their platforms to contextualise the images, linking them to decades of displacement, dispossession, and resistance.

They translated, subtitled, and disseminated content, ensuring that language barriers did not impede the global flow of information.

This interplay between those in Gaza and those outside created a global digital ecosystem of solidarity and resistance, one that transcended borders and defied attempts at suppression.

**Attempts at Suppression**

Faced with this unprecedented transparency, states and corporations responded with familiar tools of control, but these efforts mostly failed.

- Platforms shadow-banned pro-Palestinian accounts, throttled hashtags, or removed content under vague "community guidelines."
- Governments pressured social media companies to take down posts deemed "incitement" or "misinformation."
- Lobby groups equated criticism of Israel with antisemitism, seeking to chill public discourse.

Yet the sheer volume and velocity of content made censorship impossible. Every deleted video spawned ten more uploads; every suspended account reappeared in seconds under a new handle. Suppression only amplified the sense of injustice and fuelled even greater engagement.

**Global South and the Media Divide**

In the Global South, where Western influence over information flows is weaker, coverage of Gaza was unflinching.

Television networks in South Africa, Brazil, Malaysia, and Turkey aired graphic footage nightly, often pairing it with sharp, unapologetic commentary about occupation, colonialism, and double standards in international law.

This media divide deepened the moral and political split between the Global North and South. In much of the South, the war was seen as a clear-cut case of oppression and resistance. In the

North, governments clung to outdated narratives even as their populations, armed with unfiltered access to the truth, grew increasingly sceptical.

### Mainstream Media in Crisis

For legacy media in the West, the war was an existential reckoning. Accused of bias, complicity, and selective reporting, major outlets faced unprecedented backlash. Protesters disrupted live broadcasts, journalists resigned in protest, and internal revolts erupted in newsrooms where reporters demanded more honest and accurate coverage.

Some outlets adapted, albeit cautiously. By early 2024, terms like "apartheid," "collective punishment," and even "genocide" began appearing in mainstream coverage — words that had been carefully avoided for decades. This shift was driven not by editorial bravery but by the collapse of control: audiences no longer tolerated euphemism when the truth was a swipe away.

### The Permanence of Transparency

By mid-2025, it was clear that the era of narrative monopoly was over. Digital transparency is irreversible. The tools of control — official briefings, embedded reporting, curated imagery — could no longer suppress the reality of asymmetrical violence broadcast live by those experiencing it.

This transformation carries profound implications for future conflicts. No state, however powerful, can now assume that its version of events will go unchallenged. Every bomb dropped, every atrocity committed, every lie told is subject to immediate, global scrutiny.

### The Psychological Shift

This transparency also produced a psychological shift. For decades, the suffering of Palestinians could be abstracted, sanitised, or ignored. But when the world saw Gaza in real time — when it watched families bury their children live on social platforms — that distance collapsed.

The war became intimate, personal, unavoidable. And with that intimacy came a moral clarity that eroded decades of manufactured consent.

**The End of Monopoly, the Start of Accountability**

Digital transparency did not stop the bombs. It did not prevent starvation. It did not dismantle the structures of occupation or apartheid.

But it did something profound: it shattered the shield of silence that had protected those in power for generations. It created the conditions for accountability — in courts, in parliaments, and in the court of global public opinion.

In that sense, the Gaza war marked a paradigm shift: the end of an era in which the powerful alone could write history, and the beginning of one in which the oppressed could tell their own stories, in their own voices, and be heard.

## Section 9 – The Backlash: Repression and Censorship

The collapse of Israel's narrative monopoly during the Gaza war of 2023–2025 triggered a ferocious backlash. Governments, corporations, and lobby groups across the West, shaken by the unprecedented visibility of Palestinian suffering and the rapid erosion of public support for the status quo, launched coordinated efforts to reassert control.

This backlash revealed both the fragility of democratic norms and the lengths to which entrenched power structures would go to preserve an eroding paradigm. What followed was a campaign of repression, censorship, and intimidation, aimed at silencing dissent and re-establishing a monopoly over the narrative.

## Criminalising Protest

From the United States to the United Kingdom, and from France to Germany, the first front of the backlash was the criminalisation of protest.

- In the United States, universities, once bastions of free expression, became battlegrounds. Students leading pro-Palestinian demonstrations were suspended, expelled, or even arrested. Police raids on campus encampments, often in the dead of night, drew chilling parallels to civil rights and anti-war crackdowns of previous eras.
- In the UK, ministers branded protesters "hate marchers" and pushed for new public order laws to curb demonstrations. Marches in London, Manchester, and Birmingham were surveilled extensively, with participants later receiving police warnings or visits.
- In France, Interior Minister Gérald Darmanin invoked "public order" to ban demonstrations outright in the early weeks of the war. Those who defied the bans faced violent dispersal by riot police.
- In Germany, protests were routinely banned or broken up, with Palestinian flags confiscated and activists detained. Berlin, in particular, became a flashpoint, with heavy-handed policing drawing international criticism.

These repressive measures often backfired, galvanising movements rather than deterring them. Images of heavily armed police dragging away peaceful demonstrators, often students or young activists, spread widely online, reinforcing perceptions that Western democracies were abandoning their own professed values.

## The Weaponisation of Antisemitism

Perhaps the most pervasive tool of suppression was the weaponisation of antisemitism.

Criticism of Israeli policy, even when grounded in human rights law, independent investigations, or first-hand evidence, was increasingly conflated with antisemitism. Activists, academics, and journalists who spoke out were smeared, blacklisted, or subjected to professional reprisals.

- At major universities in the United States, prominent scholars faced campaigns for dismissal after criticising the war.
- In the UK, politicians and activists who condemned the bombing of Gaza were publicly accused of supporting extremism or promoting hate.
- In Germany, cultural events were cancelled, and artists with any history of pro-Palestinian statements were disinvited from exhibitions and festivals.

This conflation was deliberate. By collapsing the distinction between criticism of a state and hatred of a people, governments and lobby groups sought to delegitimise dissent, painting any challenge to the status quo as inherently dangerous.

**Corporate and Institutional Pressure**

The backlash extended beyond governments into the corporate and institutional spheres.

- In the private sector, employees who expressed solidarity with Gaza on social media were fired or disciplined.
- In media organisations, editors instructed reporters to avoid using terms like "apartheid," "occupation," or "collective punishment," fearing backlash from advertisers or political figures.
- At cultural institutions, artists and writers were disinvited from events or had contracts terminated for speaking out.

One particularly high-profile case involved a Pulitzer Prize-winning journalist who was dropped by a major US newspaper after publicly criticising American military aid to Israel. Such cases sent a chilling message: that even in ostensibly liberal democracies, certain truths were unspeakable.

**Algorithmic Suppression**

Digital platforms, now the primary battleground for narrative, became sites of algorithmic censorship.

- Videos from Gaza documenting bombings, mass graves, and starvation were flagged as "graphic content," throttled, or removed outright.
- Pro-Palestinian hashtags were shadow-banned or quietly suppressed, while accounts of prominent activists were suspended without explanation.
- Users reported that posts critical of Israeli policy disappeared mysteriously or received dramatically reduced reach.

These measures were often justified under the guise of "safety" or "misinformation," but internal leaks from several platforms revealed intense political pressure from Western governments and lobbying groups to "moderate" pro-Palestinian content.

Despite these efforts, the decentralised nature of digital activism made total suppression impossible. Every deleted video spawned countless reposts; every suspended account was replaced within minutes. Suppression became a story of its own, fuelling anger and amplifying distrust of mainstream platforms.

**Fear and Self-Censorship**

The cumulative effect of legal crackdowns, professional reprisals, and digital suppression was a climate of fear and self-censorship.

- In newsrooms, journalists admitted privately that they avoided certain language or stories for fear of losing their jobs.

- In universities, students spoke of lowering their profiles online, deleting posts, or using pseudonyms to protect themselves from retaliation.
- In cultural spaces, artists described the "invisible line" they dared not cross, lest they be blacklisted.

This atmosphere of intimidation mirrored other moments in history when power, threatened by truth, sought to silence dissent. Yet, as in those moments, repression often had the opposite effect, radicalising a generation that refused to accept enforced silence.

**Resistance and Resilience**

Against this backdrop of repression, movements for justice adapted and innovated.

- Activists turned to encrypted platforms to coordinate and share information safely.
- Legal defence funds and solidarity networks emerged to support those facing retaliation.
- Independent media and grassroots journalism flourished, providing unfiltered coverage when mainstream outlets hesitated.

This resilience underscored a central lesson of Gaza: that while power can suppress speech temporarily, it cannot erase a truth that has already been witnessed and archived.

**The Global South: Immunity to Suppression**

In the Global South, the backlash was less pronounced. Free from the same political and corporate pressures that constrained discourse in the West, media and public debate remained unflinchingly honest.

South African, Brazilian, and Indonesian outlets aired graphic coverage nightly, unafraid to use the language of apartheid, ethnic cleansing, and genocide. Governments in these regions openly criticised Western censorship, framing it as yet another example of hypocrisy and double standards.

This divergence deepened the moral and political divide between the Global North and South, reinforcing the sense that the West's grip on global narratives was slipping.

### The Paradox of Suppression

By mid-2025, the backlash had produced a paradox: while repression intensified, it also validated the very critiques it sought to suppress.

Every arrest, every censorship attempt, every smear campaign became further evidence of a system desperate to defend the indefensible. Far from silencing dissent, these efforts often amplified it, fuelling a deeper, more sustained engagement with the Palestinian cause, particularly among younger generations.

### The Limits of Control

The lesson of the Gaza war was clear: in the digital age, narrative control is no longer absolute. States and corporations can still exert enormous pressure, but they can no longer monopolise information. The truth, once documented and shared, is impossible to erase.

This does not mean victory is inevitable. Power adapts, and so do the tools of suppression. But the era in which atrocities could be hidden, denied, or spun into submission is over.

### Toward a New Public Sphere

The backlash to the collapse of the narrative monopoly also revealed something deeper: the emergence of a new, global public sphere, one less deferential to traditional power structures and more attuned to evidence, context, and justice.

In this new sphere, ordinary people are no longer passive consumers of information. They are producers, curators, and amplifiers of truth, capable of challenging — and often dismantling — the narratives of the powerful in real time.

## Section 10 – Conclusion: A Changed World

By the summer of 2025, the war in Gaza had resolved none of the core disputes — the occupation persisted, settlements continued to expand, and millions of Palestinians remained trapped under a system of apartheid and dispossession. Yet, despite the absence of structural change, something profound and irreversible had shifted.

The world's perception of Israel, of Zionism, and of the Palestinian struggle had been fundamentally altered, and the old narratives that had framed the conflict for decades no longer held the same power.

### The Collapse of the Old Story

For decades, Israel's story in the West was simple and effective: a democracy in a hostile region, defending itself against implacable enemies motivated by hatred rather than history. That story, maintained through powerful lobbying, disciplined media messaging, and geopolitical alignment, allowed Israel to wage war after war with minimal scrutiny and virtually no accountability.

Gaza 2023–2025 shattered that illusion. The asymmetry of the violence — a nuclear-armed state unleashing its military might on a besieged, impoverished civilian population — was captured in such stark, unfiltered detail that denial became impossible. The narrative of self-defence rang hollow in the face of starvation, collective punishment, and open calls from Israeli officials for the erasure of Gaza and its people.

### The Digital Reckoning

The most significant shift came from the digital transparency that defined the war.

Every strike, every atrocity, every act of resistance was documented and disseminated in real time. Gaza was no longer a distant abstraction but an immediate, intimate reality in millions of feeds worldwide. This proximity to suffering transformed the conflict from a geopolitical issue into a moral crisis.

Younger generations, unbound by the historical narratives that shaped their parents and grandparents, saw through the euphemisms and demanded honesty. For them, terms like apartheid, colonialism, and genocide were not inflammatory rhetoric but accurate descriptions of what they were witnessing with their own eyes.

### A Global Shift

The Global South, long sceptical of Western narratives, responded with a clarity and unity that exposed the deep hypocrisies of the so-called rules-based order. From South Africa's genocide case at the ICJ to mass mobilisations in Indonesia, Brazil, and Kenya, Gaza became a symbol of resistance to a system of global power that shields the strong while punishing the weak.

This global realignment was not just rhetorical. It signalled the emergence of a multipolar moral order, where the West no longer held a monopoly on defining reality. For much of the world, the Palestinian struggle was no longer a niche issue; it had become emblematic of broader struggles against colonialism, exploitation, and systemic injustice.

### The West in Crisis

In the West, the shift was slower but no less profound.

Governments clung to the old language of solidarity and security, but their publics — especially the young — moved in another direction entirely. Polling in the United States by early 2025 showed unprecedented levels of scepticism towards Israel, with majorities under 30 supporting restrictions on military aid and calling for accountability.

In the UK, France, and Germany, the same generational divide played out, with students and activists driving sustained movements for divestment, sanctions, and political accountability. The old calculus — that support for Israel was cost-free politically — no longer applied. Every statement, every vote, every shipment of arms became a point of contention, challenged openly in the streets, in parliaments, and online.

### The Power of Language

Perhaps the most significant transformation was linguistic.

The words used to describe the conflict shifted, sometimes subtly, sometimes dramatically. "Self-defence" gave way to "collective punishment." "Operations" were recognised as sieges and massacres. "Conflict" was reframed as occupation.

This linguistic shift matters because language shapes reality. For decades, the erasure of context — the stripping away of history and power dynamics — allowed the conflict to be misrepresented as a dispute between equals. By 2025, that erasure was no longer possible. The discourse had caught up with the evidence.

### The Limits of Power

Israel remains a regional powerhouse, backed by the economic, military, and diplomatic might of the United States and Europe. But power is no longer uncontested. The war in Gaza demonstrated that while bombs can flatten buildings, they cannot erase memory, and they cannot restore a monopoly over the story.

Every atrocity is archived. Every statement is saved. Every act of violence is documented and distributed globally. In this environment, impunity becomes harder to sustain, and the costs of repression — diplomatic, economic, and reputational — grow heavier with each passing year.

### A New Moral Clarity

The world that emerged from Gaza in 2025 is one in which moral clarity is sharper, if still contested.

- In the Global South, the Palestinian cause is entrenched as a central moral and political issue, a litmus test for global justice.
- In the West, the battle over narrative continues, but the balance has shifted. Generational change, digital transparency, and grassroots mobilisation have eroded the automatic alignment between Western publics and the policies of their governments.
- In the international legal arena, the language of accountability — genocide, apartheid, war crimes — is no longer confined to activists and scholars; it is now the language of courts and institutions.

**The Unfinished Reckoning**

And yet, despite these shifts, the reckoning remains unfinished. Gaza lies in ruins, its people traumatised and dispossessed. The occupation continues. The machinery of dispossession in the West Bank grinds on. In Israel, hardline politics still dominate, buoyed by fear, anger, and a sense of siege.

But change, once unthinkable, is now inevitable. The collapse of the narrative monopoly has created a new space for accountability, for solidarity, and for truth-telling. Whether that space can be translated into structural change — into justice, dignity, and freedom — remains an open question.

**Looking Ahead**

The Gaza war of 2023–2025 will be remembered not only for its human cost but for the profound shift it catalysed. It marked the moment when the old order cracked, when power could no longer fully control perception, when the oppressed seized the means to tell their own story and to be heard.

The next chapters of this history — of resistance, resilience, and reckoning — are still being written. What is certain is that the world after Gaza is a world in which silence is no longer possible, and denial is no longer credible.

# CHAPTER EIGHT:
# Resistance and the Politics of Terror

## Section 1 – Introduction: Defining Resistance

Few words are as politically charged as "resistance" and "terrorism." They do not merely describe actions; they carry with them entire worldviews. To call someone a "resistance fighter" is to dignify their struggle, to root it in justice and the right to self-defence. To call them a "terrorist" is to criminalise their existence, to strip them of legitimacy, and to render their cause beyond the pale of moral or political sympathy.

Nowhere has this distinction mattered more than in the story of Palestine. For over seven decades, Palestinians have been caught between their claim to a legal and moral right to resist occupation and a global system that often collapses their struggle into the single, loaded word: terrorism.

### The Legal Right to Resist

International law does not exist in a vacuum; it reflects the struggles of the twentieth century. Following the Second World War, as empires crumbled and colonies fought for independence, the international system had to grapple with the legitimacy of anti-colonial struggle. The UN General Assembly passed multiple resolutions affirming "the legitimacy of the struggle of peoples under colonial and alien domination" — explicitly recognising armed struggle as lawful in certain contexts.

The Fourth Geneva Convention (1949) and the Additional Protocols (1977) also reinforced the idea that peoples under foreign occupation have the right to resist, including by force, provided that such actions distinguish between combatants and civilians. This framework became a cornerstone of anti-colonial legitimacy in the 1960s and 70s, when movements from the FLN in Algeria to the

241

ANC in South Africa sought recognition not as "terrorists" but as freedom fighters.

In principle, then, Palestinians possess the same legal entitlement: the right to resist an occupation that is widely recognised as illegal and oppressive. In practice, however, their actions have been judged not by law but by politics.

### The Politics of Labeling

Zionism, from its earliest days, has relied heavily on the politics of language. To secure international support, it framed the creation of Israel as a story of return and survival. To defend its wars, it relied on the vocabulary of "security" and "self-defence." And to delegitimise Palestinian resistance, it instinctively reached for the word "terrorism."

This was not unique to Israel. The British described the Irish Republican Army (IRA) as terrorists; the French branded the Front de Libération Nationale (FLN) in Algeria as terrorists; the apartheid regime in South Africa did the same to the African National Congress (ANC). Only decades later, after independence had been won and history rewritten, were these movements re-cast as liberation struggles. Nelson Mandela, once denounced as a terrorist, became a global icon of peace.

The irony is stark: many of the same Western governments that now celebrate Mandela and the ANC continue to brand Palestinians in almost identical terms to those once used against South Africans.

Part of the difficulty lies in the asymmetry of power. Israel is a nuclear-armed state with one of the most advanced militaries in the world. Palestinians, by contrast, are a stateless and fragmented people, denied sovereignty, heavily policed, and subjected to military occupation in the West Bank and blockade in Gaza.

In such conditions, resistance rarely resembles conventional warfare. Instead, it has taken the form of guerrilla attacks, uprisings, stone-throwing, and in more recent decades, rockets and suicide bombings. Each of these has been seized upon to reinforce the narrative that Palestinians are "terrorists," conveniently ignoring the context that makes such tactics — however morally fraught — the weapon of the weak.

Here lies the crux: Israel's wars are almost always framed as wars between two sides, while in reality they are wars of a state against a stateless population. When Palestinians fight back, their actions are labelled terrorism; when Israel deploys fighter jets, drones, and tanks, its actions are framed as legitimate defence.

It would be dishonest to romanticise all forms of Palestinian resistance. Some tactics — particularly the targeting of civilians, whether in suicide bombings or indiscriminate rocket fire — are violations of international humanitarian law. To acknowledge Palestinians' right to resist does not mean endorsing every act committed in the name of that struggle.

But to collapse the entire spectrum of resistance into the single word "terrorism" is to erase the political reality of occupation itself. It is to deny Palestinians the very legitimacy that was extended to virtually every other anti-colonial movement of the twentieth century.

This double standard is not accidental; it is central to how Zionism defends itself. For if Palestinian resistance were recognised as legitimate, then Israel's project — the settlements, the occupation, the sieges — would stand exposed not as self-defence but as colonial domination.

The Gaza war of 2023–2025 brought this debate into sharp relief. Israel insisted it was waging war against Hamas, a terrorist organisation bent on its destruction. Yet the images that reached the world showed something different: a state deploying overwhelming firepower against a trapped civilian population.

For many outside the corridors of Western power, the dissonance became impossible to ignore. If the ANC were right to resist apartheid, why not Palestinians under occupation? If Algerians had the right to fight French colonial rule, why not Gazans under siege?

The debate was no longer abstract; it was playing out live on global screens. And with each bomb, each starvation, each statement calling Palestinians "human animals," the credibility of branding all resistance as terrorism eroded further.

### Conclusion: Setting the Stage

Defining resistance, then, is not just a semantic exercise. It is the foundation of how the world understands the Palestinian struggle. To accept Israel's framing is to erase Palestinian agency and to normalise endless occupation. To reclaim the language of resistance is to situate Palestinians where they belong: in the long continuum of peoples who have fought against colonialism, domination, and erasure.

The chapters that follow will trace this contested history — from the rise of the PLO to the emergence of Hamas, from the first intifada to the Gaza wars of the twenty-first century. Through it all runs a single thread: the fight not only for land and freedom but for the right to be seen not as terrorists, but as a people resisting the denial of their very existence.

## Section 2 – The Rise of the PLO

The story of the Palestine Liberation Organization (PLO) is the story of Palestinians attempting to reclaim political agency in a world determined to deny them one. Established in 1964, at the height of Arab nationalism, the PLO emerged as a coalition of factions united by a single, powerful aim: the liberation of Palestine from Zionist control. For Palestinians scattered across refugee camps in Lebanon, Jordan, and Gaza, the PLO became more than an institution — it was the embodiment of their statelessness, their dispossession, and their determination to resist.

## Arafat and the Birth of Palestinian Nationalism

Though formally created under the auspices of the Arab League, the PLO quickly evolved into an independent actor under the leadership of Yasser Arafat and his faction, Fatah. Arafat's genius lay not in military strategy but in symbolism: he turned the PLO into the sole legitimate representative of the Palestinian people, giving a scattered and silenced nation a political voice.

His trademark keffiyeh and speeches before world forums symbolised not only resistance but survival. In 1974, Arafat addressed the United Nations General Assembly, famously declaring: "I have come bearing an olive branch and a freedom fighter's gun. Do not let the olive branch fall from my hand." It was a statement of profound duality — a willingness to seek peace, but only on terms that preserved dignity and sovereignty.

## From Refugee Camps to Guerrilla Bases

The PLO's early years were defined by guerrilla warfare and spectacular acts of defiance. Operating from bases in Jordan, and later Lebanon, PLO factions carried out cross-border raids, hijackings, and attacks on Israeli targets. These tactics were designed to draw international attention to the Palestinian cause, which had been all but erased from diplomatic discourse after 1948.

For Palestinians in exile, these actions were seen as acts of resistance — the only means left to a people denied land, statehood, and representation. For Israel and its Western allies, they were proof that Palestinians were irredeemably violent, reinforcing the framing of the PLO as a terrorist organisation.

This tension between perception and intent would haunt the PLO throughout its existence. Each attack brought visibility but also condemnation. Each guerrilla victory came at the cost of reinforcing Israel's narrative of existential threat.

## Black September and the Limits of Host States

The PLO's presence in Jordan culminated in the crisis known as Black September (1970). King Hussein, threatened by the PLO's growing autonomy and its challenge to Jordanian sovereignty, launched a bloody crackdown, killing thousands of Palestinians and forcing the PLO leadership into exile in Lebanon.

This moment was formative. It revealed the vulnerability of a movement without a state — dependent on the goodwill of host governments, yet often undermining their authority. It also underscored the PLO's precarious position: at once a liberation movement and a destabilising force in fragile regional politics.

## Lebanon, Civil War, and Internationalisation

In Lebanon, the PLO established a state-within-a-state, controlling camps and neighbourhoods, levying taxes, and operating as a government in exile. But Lebanon's fragile sectarian balance could not withstand the strain. The Lebanese Civil War (1975–1990) drew the PLO deep into conflict, further blurring the lines between liberation struggle and regional entanglement.

Israel seized the opportunity. In 1982, it launched a full-scale invasion of Lebanon, besieging Beirut and forcing the PLO leadership into exile once more, this time in Tunis. The invasion culminated in the Sabra and Shatila massacre, where Israeli-allied militias slaughtered thousands of Palestinian refugees as Israeli forces looked on. The horror shocked the world, and for the first time, Israel faced widespread condemnation even in Western capitals.

The PLO, though battered, gained a new kind of legitimacy: it was no longer possible to erase Palestinians from the global conversation. Their suffering had been made visible, and their representatives could no longer be ignored.

## Intifada and Transformation

The First Intifada (1987–1993) was a turning point. Unlike the PLO's exiled leadership, this uprising was grassroots — led by ordinary Palestinians in the West Bank and Gaza. Children throwing stones at tanks, women organising community resistance, and neighbourhood committees mobilising strikes captured the world's imagination.

The Intifada exposed both the brutality of Israeli occupation and the limits of the PLO's old guerrilla tactics. Arafat and the PLO, watching from Tunis, quickly aligned themselves with the uprising, claiming leadership but also recognising that the struggle was evolving.

It was in this context that the PLO took its boldest step: recognising Israel in exchange for international recognition of the Palestinian right to self-determination. The Oslo Accords (1993) marked both a breakthrough and a betrayal in the eyes of many Palestinians. For some, it was the first step toward statehood. For others, it was a capitulation that entrenched occupation rather than ending it.

## From Liberation Movement to Political Authority

The post-Oslo years transformed the PLO into the Palestinian Authority (PA), tasked with limited self-rule in parts of the West Bank and Gaza. Arafat returned to Palestinian soil, cheered as a hero, yet burdened with the impossible task of governing without sovereignty.

The shift from resistance movement to quasi-government created profound contradictions. The PLO, once the symbol of defiance, now found itself policing its own people under Israeli and Western pressure. Its legitimacy eroded, and space opened for new actors, particularly Hamas, who would present themselves as the true heirs of resistance.

**Resistance or Terror? The PLO's Legacy**

The PLO's journey illustrates the core dilemma of Palestinian resistance: how to fight for liberation without being defined by violence. To its supporters, the PLO was the vanguard of a dispossessed nation, keeping alive the hope of return and statehood. To its enemies, it was a terrorist organisation that rejected peace and sought Israel's destruction.

Over time, the PLO gained international recognition — observer status at the UN, diplomatic offices worldwide, and a seat at the negotiating table. But this recognition came at a price: concessions, compromises, and the erosion of its revolutionary legitimacy.

Today, the PLO is often seen as a shadow of its former self — bureaucratic, corrupt, and sidelined by the rise of Hamas. Yet its historical role remains undeniable. It was the PLO that first gave Palestinians a political voice, that forced the world to acknowledge their existence, and that kept alive the principle of resistance at a time when it might otherwise have been extinguished.

**Conclusion: The Stage for Hamas**

The PLO's story sets the stage for the next chapter: the rise of Hamas. Where the PLO once embodied Palestinian resistance, Hamas would claim the mantle of authenticity, rejecting the compromises of Oslo and presenting itself as both an Islamist alternative and a continuation of the struggle.

The transition from PLO dominance to Hamas ascendancy is not simply a change of leadership; it represents a profound shift in the nature of Palestinian resistance — from secular nationalism to Islamist militancy, from international diplomacy to local governance, from exile to siege.

To understand that shift, we must examine the origins, ideology, and trajectory of Hamas — a movement that would redefine not only

Palestinian resistance but also how the world understood Zionism's opponents.

## Section 3 – Lebanon, Intifadas, and the Limits of Armed Struggle

The trajectory of the Palestinian resistance movement cannot be understood without grappling with its displacement across the Middle East. Forced into exile, the PLO and its factions became entangled in the politics of their host countries. Each exile produced both opportunity and catastrophe: visibility on the world stage, but also repeated confrontation with powerful states unwilling to cede their sovereignty to a stateless movement. Lebanon, and later the West Bank and Gaza during the intifadas, revealed both the resilience of Palestinian resistance and its limits when confronted with overwhelming force.

### Lebanon: The State Within a State

After being expelled from Jordan in 1970 during the brutal events of Black September, the PLO leadership established itself in Lebanon. Here, among the sprawling refugee camps of Beirut, Tyre, and Sidon, the Palestinians constructed a de facto state within a state. They ran schools, clinics, and social services, levied taxes, and fielded militias. For many Palestinians, Lebanon represented a rare moment of semi-autonomy, even if it was fragile and dependent on Lebanese tolerance.

But the PLO's armed presence destabilised Lebanon's delicate sectarian balance. Christian militias viewed the PLO as an existential threat; Syria sought to manipulate the conflict to secure its own influence; and Israel, watching from the south, saw the PLO's Lebanese bases as launching pads for cross-border raids. The stage was set for tragedy.

## The Israeli Invasions and Sabra and Shatila

Israel invaded Lebanon in 1978 and again, far more comprehensively, in 1982. The second invasion saw Israeli forces lay siege to Beirut itself, pounding the city with artillery and airstrikes in an attempt to crush the PLO once and for all. Under US mediation, Arafat and the PLO leadership were evacuated to Tunis, leaving behind a void in Palestinian leadership inside the camps.

The most searing memory of this period remains the Sabra and Shatila massacre. In September 1982, Christian Phalangist militias allied with Israel entered the refugee camps of Sabra and Shatila in West Beirut, killing thousands of civilians. Israeli forces surrounded the camps, sealing the perimeter and providing flares to light the night sky as the killing went on. An Israeli commission later found Defence Minister Ariel Sharon indirectly responsible, forcing his resignation, though he would return decades later as Prime Minister.

For Palestinians, the massacre symbolised their vulnerability — stateless, exiled, and dependent on the goodwill of others. For the world, it was a moment of reckoning: even Israel's allies could not deny the horror. Images of the dead filled television screens, prompting the first real wave of mass condemnation against Israeli policy in Western capitals.

## The First Intifada: Stones Against Tanks

If Lebanon was a story of exile and massacre, the First Intifada (1987–1993) was the opposite: a spontaneous, grassroots uprising inside the occupied territories themselves. It began in Gaza after a fatal traffic incident involving an Israeli military vehicle, but quickly spread to the West Bank.

The Intifada was remarkable not for its firepower — Palestinians had almost none — but for its mass participation. Children throwing stones at heavily armed soldiers became the defining image. Women organised neighbourhood committees, schools continued in secret after closures, and strikes paralysed the occupation's administrative machinery.

The Israeli response was brutal. Then-Defence Minister Yitzhak Rabin infamously ordered soldiers to "break the bones" of protesters. Thousands were killed or injured, tens of thousands imprisoned. Yet the uprising succeeded in transforming global perceptions: Palestinians were no longer seen merely as refugees or hijackers but as a people living under daily military occupation, resisting with whatever tools they had.

### The PLO in Exile vs the People on the Ground

The Intifada also exposed a rift between the PLO leadership in Tunis and the Palestinians on the ground. Arafat sought to harness the uprising for political leverage but was physically distant and politically constrained. The uprising was largely leaderless, coordinated through local committees rather than centralised command.

This dynamic foreshadowed future tensions: Palestinian resistance rooted in grassroots activism versus leadership operating in exile, subject to external pressures and dependent on negotiations. The Intifada, for all its limitations, revealed the power of popular resistance to capture global attention in ways guerrilla warfare never had.

### The Oslo Accords and the Trap of Diplomacy

The First Intifada set the stage for the Oslo Accords (1993), negotiated secretly in Norway. In exchange for recognising Israel, the PLO was granted recognition as the representative of the Palestinian people and limited autonomy in parts of the West Bank and Gaza under the newly created Palestinian Authority (PA).

At the time, Oslo was heralded as a breakthrough. Yet the accords left Israel in control of borders, resources, and security. Settlements continued to expand; checkpoints multiplied. For many

Palestinians, Oslo felt less like liberation and more like a trap —
transforming their resistance movement into a subcontracted
authority managing the occupation rather than dismantling it.

The limits of armed struggle had become clear, but the limits of
diplomacy were now equally visible. Palestinians were stuck
between the futility of guerrilla warfare and the illusion of statehood
offered by negotiations.

### The Second Intifada: From Stones to Suicide Bombs

Disillusionment exploded in the Second Intifada (2000–2005),
triggered by Ariel Sharon's provocative visit to the Temple
Mount/Haram al-Sharif in Jerusalem. Unlike the first uprising, this
one was far more militarised. Suicide bombings, armed clashes, and
rocket fire defined the period. Israel responded with overwhelming
force, reoccupying West Bank cities, demolishing homes, and
constructing the Separation Wall that carved deep into Palestinian
land.

The Second Intifada marked a shift in global perception.
Whereas the First Intifada had generated sympathy by highlighting
the imbalance of power, the Second Intifada's violence against
civilians allowed Israel to reassert its narrative of fighting
"terrorism." The devastation in Palestinian society was immense:
thousands killed, infrastructure destroyed, the economy shattered.

The dream of Oslo collapsed entirely, but so too did the moral
clarity of the Palestinian struggle in the eyes of much of the
international community.

### The Limits of Armed Struggle

By the mid-2000s, Palestinians faced a bitter reality. Armed
struggle had secured visibility but not liberation. Diplomacy had
delivered recognition but not sovereignty. Each uprising, each exile,
each massacre revealed the structural asymmetry at the heart of the
conflict: Palestinians were stateless, fragmented, and constrained,

while Israel wielded overwhelming military, diplomatic, and economic power.

Yet resistance persisted, because occupation persisted. Out of the failures of both the PLO's diplomacy and the intifadas' exhaustion, a new actor would rise: Hamas. Born during the First Intifada, Hamas promised both an Islamist vision of resistance and a rejection of Oslo's compromises. It would come to dominate Palestinian politics in Gaza and redefine the global debate about resistance and terrorism.

### Conclusion: From Lebanon to Gaza

The story of the PLO in Lebanon, the intifadas, and the Oslo process reveals a cycle of resilience and limitation. Palestinians resisted with guns, with stones, with strikes, and with negotiations. Each method achieved something — visibility, recognition, international sympathy — but none dismantled the structures of occupation.

This cycle left a vacuum into which Hamas would step, presenting itself as the uncompromising alternative. If the PLO had grown too close to diplomacy, Hamas promised unrelenting resistance. If stones and strikes had limits, Hamas offered rockets and suicide bombings. Whether one saw it as liberation or fanaticism, Hamas would become the defining force of Palestinian resistance in the twenty-first century.

## Section 4 – The Rise of Hamas

If the PLO embodied the first great phase of Palestinian resistance — secular, nationalist, and internationally focused — then Hamas represented the second. Born in the crucible of the First Intifada (1987), Hamas combined grassroots activism, Islamist ideology, and uncompromising militancy into a force that would permanently reshape Palestinian politics and the global discourse on resistance. For supporters, it was the authentic voice of a people betrayed by endless negotiations. For critics, it was the epitome of terrorism, proof that Palestinians were incapable of compromise. For Israel, it was both a mortal threat and, paradoxically, a useful enemy.

### Origins: From the Mosque to the Movement

Hamas — an acronym for Harakat al-Muqawama al-Islamiya ("Islamic Resistance Movement") — was formally established in December 1987, just days after the First Intifada erupted. But its roots stretch further back to the Muslim Brotherhood in Gaza, where Sheikh Ahmed Yassin and his followers had been building networks of mosques, schools, and charities since the 1970s.

Initially tolerated, even quietly encouraged by Israel, these Islamist networks were seen as a counterweight to the secular, leftist factions of the PLO. The Israeli military administration granted licences for Islamic associations while cracking down hard on PLO-linked activists. The strategy was short-sighted. What Israel thought was a religious distraction from nationalism became a potent fusion of both: Islamist identity married to national liberation.

### Charity, Social Services, and Popular Legitimacy

Unlike the PLO leadership exiled in Tunis, Hamas was rooted in the daily life of Palestinians in Gaza. It built clinics, distributed food, supported widows and orphans, and ran schools. These networks gave it a legitimacy the Palestinian Authority (PA) would later struggle to match.

For ordinary Palestinians, Hamas was not just a militia but a social lifeline. This dual character — both a political-military organisation and a welfare provider — mirrored the strategies of movements like Hezbollah in Lebanon. It allowed Hamas to claim moral authority not only on the battlefield but in the neighbourhoods of Gaza's impoverished camps.

From its inception, Hamas framed armed struggle (*muqawama*) as a religious duty. Its founding charter of 1988 declared that "Palestine is an Islamic land" and that the conflict was not merely political but existential. This uncompromising rhetoric set Hamas apart from the PLO, which by the 1990s was negotiating with Israel under the Oslo framework.

The early 1990s saw Hamas pioneer the use of suicide bombings inside Israel, targeting buses, markets, and cafés. These attacks shocked Israeli society and shifted global perceptions: Palestinians were no longer seen only as stone-throwing youths or exiled guerrillas but as suicide bombers — a label that the media and Western governments eagerly equated with terrorism.

For Hamas, these tactics were framed as asymmetric warfare: a response to tanks, helicopters, and occupation. For Israel and its allies, they were proof of barbarity, cementing Hamas's place on international terror lists.

**The Oslo Years: Opposition and Division**

The signing of the Oslo Accords (1993) marked a turning point. Where Arafat and the PLO saw recognition and the first steps toward a Palestinian state, Hamas saw betrayal. It rejected Oslo outright, arguing that negotiations legitimised occupation and permanently abandoned the right of return for millions of refugees.

This division split Palestinian politics. The PLO, transformed into the PA, now carried the burden of governance, security coordination, and diplomacy. Hamas, free from the compromises of state-building, positioned itself as the uncompromising voice of resistance. Every Israeli settlement expansion, every checkpoint humiliation, every broken promise of Oslo vindicated Hamas's rejectionist stance.

### The Second Intifada and the Rise of Rockets

During the Second Intifada (2000–2005), Hamas moved to the forefront of the armed struggle. Its suicide bombings inside Israel became infamous, killing hundreds and spreading fear across Israeli cities. At the same time, Hamas began developing rockets — crude at first, but symbolically powerful.

By launching rockets over the border into Israel, Hamas redefined the battlefield. The message was clear: Palestinians could strike back, even if their weapons were vastly inferior. For Israelis, the rockets represented an intolerable threat to civilian life. For Palestinians, they were symbols of defiance in the face of overwhelming military superiority.

### Elections and the Gaza Takeover

In a twist few expected, Hamas also demonstrated political muscle. In 2006, it contested the Palestinian legislative elections — and won a majority, defeating Fatah in a stunning upset. International observers judged the elections largely free and fair, but the result was immediately rejected by Israel, the US, and the EU. Aid was cut off, sanctions imposed, and Hamas was politically isolated.

The division soon turned violent. In 2007, after months of street battles, Hamas forcibly expelled Fatah from Gaza, seizing full control of the Strip. From that moment, Palestinian politics split into two rival governments: Fatah in the West Bank, Hamas in Gaza. The dream of a unified national movement lay in ruins.

For Israel, Hamas's takeover provided both a justification and a strategy: Gaza could be isolated, blockaded, and treated as a hostile enclave. For Palestinians in Gaza, Hamas's rule meant both resilience and repression — resistance to Israel, but also authoritarian control at home.

## The Siege of Gaza

Since 2007, Gaza has been under a near-total blockade imposed by Israel and Egypt, restricting the movement of people and goods. The siege devastated the economy, crippled infrastructure, and left over two million people trapped in what has often been called "the world's largest open-air prison."

Hamas's survival under siege became central to its identity. It presented itself as the guardian of Palestinian dignity, standing firm where the PA had capitulated. Each war with Israel — in 2008–09, 2012, 2014, and beyond — deepened this dynamic. While the cost in civilian lives was catastrophic, Hamas claimed victory simply by surviving.

For Israel, the siege was both containment and provocation: a way to weaken Hamas while also ensuring it remained the dominant force in Gaza, conveniently dividing Palestinians and undermining the possibility of a unified state.

## The Global Perception of Hamas

The world remains divided on Hamas. To Israel and the West, it is a terrorist organisation beyond redemption. To much of the Global South, it is a resistance movement operating under conditions of siege and occupation. To many Palestinians, it is both: a flawed, authoritarian actor and yet the only group willing to stand up to Israel militarily.

What is undeniable is Hamas's role in reshaping the discourse on resistance. Where the PLO moved toward negotiation and compromise, Hamas embodied rejection and defiance. Where international law recognised a right to resist, Hamas pushed that principle to its violent limits, testing how far the world was willing to apply it.

### Conclusion: Hamas and the Future of Resistance

Hamas's rise signalled a profound shift in Palestinian resistance. It replaced the secular nationalism of the PLO with Islamist militancy, shifted the locus of struggle from exile to Gaza, and forced the world to confront the messy reality of asymmetric warfare in the 21st century.

Hamas's story is not simply one of terrorism or resistance; it is a story of a people trapped between occupation and authoritarianism, between despair and defiance. Its legacy is contested, its tactics divisive, but its central role in the Palestinian struggle cannot be denied.

As we move forward, the next section will explore the heart of the debate: Terrorism or Resistance? — and why the label matters so profoundly in shaping the legitimacy of Palestinian struggle and the global future of Zionism.

## Section 5 – Terrorism or Resistance?

The struggle over Palestine has never been fought only on the ground; it has also been waged in the realm of language. Few terms carry as much weight as "terrorism." To apply it is to strip a movement of legitimacy, to place it outside the boundaries of lawful or moral struggle. To withhold it is to acknowledge a claim to resistance, to dignity, to the universal right to oppose oppression. For decades, Palestinians have lived under the shadow of this word, their every act of defiance measured against it.

### The Power of a Word

"Terrorism" is not merely a description of violence against civilians. It is a political category, one that governments wield selectively. In the 20th century, countless liberation movements — from the Irish Republican Army (IRA) to the African National Congress (ANC) and the Front de Libération Nationale (FLN) in Algeria — were branded terrorist organisations by the very powers they opposed. Yet today, their leaders are celebrated as statesmen and heroes. Nelson Mandela, once condemned as a terrorist, won the Nobel Peace Prize.

The Palestinian case follows this familiar pattern, with one key difference: the label of terrorism has proven far stickier. Where the ANC or FLN eventually broke through the narrative barrier, Palestinians continue to find their resistance reduced, almost reflexively, to "terror."

### International Law and the Right to Resist

The legal framework is clear in principle. Under international law, peoples under foreign occupation have the right to resist, including by armed struggle, provided they distinguish between combatants and civilians. The UN General Assembly reaffirmed this repeatedly during the decolonisation era, granting legitimacy to anti-colonial movements across Africa and Asia.

By this standard, Palestinians resisting occupation ought to be recognised as exercising a lawful right. Yet in practice, this recognition has been systematically denied. The reason lies not in the law but in politics: Israel, backed by the United States and its allies, has framed nearly every act of Palestinian resistance as terrorism, and Western governments have echoed the claim.

### The Civilian Question

The sharpest point of contention lies in the targeting of civilians. Suicide bombings during the Second Intifada, indiscriminate rocket fire from Gaza, and hostage-taking have all been cited as violations of humanitarian law. And indeed, they are. International law requires combatants to distinguish between civilian and military targets. By attacking civilians, Hamas and other groups have undermined their legal and moral claims.

But the debate rarely ends there. Israel's own conduct — systematic bombing of civilian areas, collective punishment through siege and blockade, and open calls by ministers for the eradication of Gaza — also violates the same principles. Yet Israel's actions are consistently framed as "self-defence," even when disproportionate.

Here lies the double standard: Palestinians are judged solely by their worst tactics, while Israel is judged by its intentions, however lethal its results.

### Framing the Intifadas

The contrast between the First and Second Intifadas illustrates how tactics shape perception. The First Intifada, with its images of stone-throwing youth confronting soldiers, generated enormous sympathy for Palestinians. It highlighted the asymmetry of power and made it difficult to deny the reality of occupation.

The Second Intifada, by contrast, was marked by suicide bombings and armed attacks on civilians. However rooted in despair, these tactics allowed Israel to reassert its narrative: that it was fighting terror, not suppressing a liberation struggle. International sympathy waned, and the label of terrorism became entrenched.

This dynamic underscores the cruel bind facing Palestinians: peaceful protest is ignored or crushed, armed resistance is condemned as terrorism, and the occupation continues regardless.

### Selective Use of Terrorism

The political selectivity of the term is evident when comparing Palestine with other struggles. The ANC, the FLN, and even Zionist militias such as the Irgun and Lehi, which attacked British forces and civilians in the 1940s, were once labelled terrorists. Yet Israel itself was born partly out of groups that used tactics identical to those for which Palestinians are condemned.

The King David Hotel bombing (1946) by the Irgun killed 91 people, mostly civilians. The Deir Yassin massacre (1948) by Zionist militias killed over 100 Palestinian villagers. These acts are rarely framed as terrorism today; instead, they are folded into Israel's founding narrative. Palestinians, however, are offered no such historical forgiveness.

### Dehumanisation and Terrorism as Identity

For Israel, branding Palestinians as terrorists is not just about delegitimising tactics — it is about delegitimising identity. Officials frequently describe Palestinians in sweeping, dehumanising terms: as "human animals," as "terrorists from birth," as a people beyond redemption. By collapsing Palestinian identity into terrorism, Israel justifies policies that would otherwise be indefensible: sieges, mass bombings, starvation as a weapon of war.

The Western adoption of this framing compounds the effect. To question Israel's use of force becomes, in some contexts, tantamount to excusing terrorism. This rhetorical trap silences debate, narrows political space, and entrenches impunity.

### The View from the Global South

Outside the Western orbit, the framing looks very different. In the Global South, where anti-colonial struggles remain living memory, Palestinians are widely seen as part of the same lineage. South Africa's ruling ANC, once condemned as terrorists, openly supports the Palestinian cause and draws direct parallels between apartheid and occupation. In Latin America, Asia, and Africa, the label of terrorism is understood for what it often is: a political weapon wielded by the powerful to criminalise resistance.

This divergence deepens the moral divide. In much of the Global South, Hamas may be criticised for its tactics, but Palestinians as a whole are not stripped of legitimacy. In the West, by contrast, the word terrorism continues to function as a near-total erasure.

### Gaza 2023–2025: A Turning Point?

The Gaza war may prove to be the breaking point for this discourse. As images of mass starvation, bombed hospitals, and children buried under rubble circulated globally, the old narrative began to falter. When Israel insists it is fighting terrorists while levelling entire neighbourhoods, the credibility gap grows impossible to ignore.

For a new generation — particularly in the West — the question is no longer whether Palestinians have the right to resist, but why their resistance has been denied legitimacy for so long. Polling in 2024–25 showed unprecedented shifts in opinion: young Americans and Europeans increasingly reject the blanket label of terrorism and see Palestinians as engaged in a liberation struggle.

The language is changing. What was once taboo — calling Israel an apartheid state, questioning its self-defence narrative — is now mainstream. This shift suggests that the word terrorism may finally be losing its power to erase Palestinian claims.

## Conclusion: Resistance Beyond Labels

The question of whether Palestinian actions constitute resistance or terrorism will not be resolved easily. The reality is that both truths exist: Palestinians have a legal and moral right to resist occupation, and some of the methods employed by groups like Hamas have violated the laws of war. But to collapse the entire struggle into the label of terrorism is to erase its context, its history, and its legitimacy.

If history teaches anything, it is that today's terrorists are often tomorrow's statesmen. What matters is not the label imposed by the powerful but the underlying justice of the cause. For Palestinians, that cause remains the same: liberation from a system of domination that denies them their land, their rights, and their future.

The next section will turn to the dehumanisation within the Zionist narrative — how Palestinians have been systematically portrayed not as a people with legitimate rights but as enemies to be eradicated, and how this rhetoric has shaped both policy and perception.

## Section 6 – Dehumanisation and the Zionist Narrative

If the word "terrorism" has functioned as a weapon of political erasure, then dehumanisation has been its moral foundation. To sustain the idea that an entire people can be treated as a security threat, Israel and its defenders have relied on a rhetoric that strips Palestinians of individuality, dignity, and humanity. This process is not incidental. It is central to how the Zionist project has justified the ongoing dispossession of Palestinians and normalised violence that, in almost any other context, would be deemed intolerable.

### The Language of Erasure

Words matter. They frame the boundaries of the possible. Israeli leaders, from the founding generation to the present, have often deployed language that presents Palestinians not as neighbours or even adversaries, but as obstacles to be removed.

- In 1969, Prime Minister Golda Meir declared: "There was no such thing as Palestinians… They did not exist."
- In 1983, Menachem Begin referred to Palestinians in Lebanon as "two-legged beasts."
- In 2014, Israeli politicians used phrases like "mowing the lawn" to describe recurring bombardments of Gaza, reducing human lives to routine maintenance.
- During the Gaza war of 2023–25, several Knesset members and ministers openly called for Gaza to be "erased" and for Palestinians to be treated as "human animals."

Such language is not fringe rhetoric; it has been uttered from the highest offices of the state. It serves a clear purpose: to desensitise, to legitimise violence, and to frame Palestinians as a population undeserving of protection.

### Origins of Dehumanisation in Israeli Society

To understand why cruelty towards Palestinians has become not only permissible but, at times, celebrated within Israeli society, we must look at a convergence of history, ideology, and social conditioning.

### The Legacy of Trauma and Siege Mentality

The Holocaust left an indelible mark on Jewish consciousness, embedding a deep sense of existential insecurity. Zionism channelled this trauma into a narrative of perpetual survival, in which Palestinians became the latest incarnation of an eternal enemy. When survival is the central national myth, empathy for the "other" is easily sacrificed. Palestinians are not seen as neighbours but as threats to Jewish existence itself.

### Education and Socialisation

From school curricula to military training, Israeli society normalises separation and suspicion. Palestinian history is often erased from textbooks; Arabs are depicted as hostile or primitive. Mandatory military service immerses Israeli youth in the daily control of Palestinian lives — at checkpoints, in raids, in occupations. Cruelty becomes routinised, not as sadism but as duty.

### Normalisation of Violence in Public Culture

The sight of settlers celebrating new outposts or crowds gathering to cheer bombardments is shocking to outsiders but not anomalous within a culture where Palestinians are systematically dehumanised. During the Gaza war of 2023–25, footage circulated of Israelis sitting on hillsides near Sderot with picnic blankets, watching the bombardment of Gaza as though it were a spectacle. Some clapped as plumes of smoke rose from residential towers; others livestreamed the destruction on social media, presenting the annihilation of Palestinian neighbourhoods as entertainment. Children were filmed laughing and chanting slogans as airstrikes shook the horizon.

### Religious and Nationalist Rhetoric

For some Israelis, especially within religious-nationalist circles, Palestinians are cast as biblical enemies — Amalek, Philistines, perpetual foes to be conquered or destroyed. This fuses nationalism with divine sanction, making cruelty not only permissible but sacred.

### Impunity and International Shielding

Decades of unpunished violence — from massacres to settlement expansion — have fostered a culture of impunity. When the international community defends or excuses Israeli actions, cruelty carries no cost. It becomes possible to enact it openly, even proudly.

### Collective Denial and Projection

Finally, there is a psychological mechanism at play: by projecting violence onto Palestinians ("they are terrorists, they want to kill us"), Israelis displace their own aggression. This allows society to commit acts of cruelty while still seeing itself as perpetually innocent.

This is not about "DNA" but about a system of ideology, trauma, and impunity that has shaped Israeli society over decades. When children grow up in a world where Palestinians are portrayed as animals, when soldiers are rewarded for violence, and when leaders openly call for annihilation, cruelty becomes a form of belonging. The tragedy is not that Israelis are uniquely monstrous, but that a system of occupation and ideology has normalised monstrosity — and that it unfolds so openly, so unashamedly, because the world has allowed it to.

### From Security to Dehumanisation

Israel's security doctrine has always emphasised overwhelming force, deterrence, and the prevention of threats before they emerge. But over time, the rhetoric of security has fused with rhetoric of dehumanisation. Instead of distinguishing between militants and civilians, Israeli discourse often collapses the two, portraying Palestinians as a collective danger.

This was starkly visible during the 2023–25 Gaza war. Ministers spoke of cutting off food, water, and electricity to the entire population, framing it not as collective punishment but as legitimate warfare. When children were killed, officials claimed responsibility lay with Hamas, who had "used them as human shields." The implication was that Palestinian lives were already forfeit, their humanity already discounted.

### The Role of Dehumanisation in Policy

Language is not just talk; it shapes policy. When Palestinians are described as "human animals," the bombing of residential towers becomes easier to justify. When an entire population is framed as complicit in terrorism, the starvation of two million people under blockade can be reframed as strategy.

Dehumanisation underpins practices such as:

- Home demolitions, punishing entire families for the alleged actions of one member.
- Administrative detention, holding Palestinians indefinitely without trial.
- Checkpoint humiliation, reducing daily life to a gauntlet of subordination.
- The blockade of Gaza, treating civilians as leverage in a war of attrition.

Each of these practices violates international law, yet each is normalised within Israeli society and often defended in international forums by invoking the dehumanising frame of collective guilt.

### Western Adoption of Dehumanising Frames

The power of Zionist discourse lies not only in its domestic use but in its export to Western capitals. Politicians in the U.S. and

Europe frequently repeat Israeli talking points that cast Palestinians as indistinguishable from Hamas, as inherently violent, or as uniquely dangerous.

During debates in Western parliaments, phrases like "Israel has the right to defend itself" are invoked almost automatically, even when the defence in question involves mass civilian casualties. Rarely is the right of Palestinians to defend themselves even mentioned. This rhetorical asymmetry rests on the assumption that Palestinians are not full subjects of international law, but objects to be managed.

The result is a policy environment where dehumanisation travels freely: from Knesset speeches to Congressional hearings, from Israeli media to British tabloids. Palestinians are cast not as people with rights but as a problem to be solved.

**Media and the Devaluation of Palestinian Lives**

The dehumanising narrative is reinforced in media coverage. Studies of Western reporting show stark differences in how Palestinian and Israeli deaths are described. Israeli casualties are individualised — names, ages, backstories. Palestinian casualties are aggregated — numbers, statistics, anonymous masses.

This imbalance creates a moral hierarchy of grief: Israeli lives are mourned, Palestinian lives are counted. The implicit message is that one life is worth more than another, that Palestinian suffering is inevitable, regrettable, but ultimately disposable.

During the Gaza war, this disparity became glaring. Even as death tolls reached tens of thousands, major outlets often foregrounded Israeli suffering, with Palestinian losses relegated to secondary paragraphs. Social media disrupted this pattern by humanising Palestinians directly — children speaking into cameras, families broadcasting their last moments — but legacy media often lagged behind.

## Dehumanisation and International Law

International law rests on the principle of distinction: civilians must be distinguished from combatants. Dehumanisation erases that distinction. When Israeli officials describe Gaza as a nest of terrorists, they invite policies that disregard civilian protection altogether.

The rhetoric of dehumanisation also undermines accountability. War crimes become harder to prosecute when entire populations are framed as guilty. Starvation, collective punishment, and indiscriminate bombing can be defended as legitimate military tactics if civilians are presumed to be indistinguishable from militants.

This erosion of legal norms is not only a Palestinian tragedy. It threatens the very foundations of humanitarian law. If an entire people can be stripped of their humanity in one context, the precedent weakens protections for all.

## The Psychological Toll

Dehumanisation is not only external; it shapes internal identity. Generations of Palestinians have grown up hearing themselves described as animals, terrorists, or demographic threats. This constant barrage of denial and degradation produces trauma, anger, and resistance. It fosters a sense of exclusion from the human community, a perception that international law and moral concern stop at their borders.

At the same time, it entrenches Israeli psychology. If Palestinians are animals, then Israelis are perpetual victims, forever under threat, forever justified in pre-emptive violence. This cycle of mutual entrapment sustains conflict by making empathy politically impossible.

**Breaking the Spell**

And yet, dehumanisation is fragile. During the Gaza war of 2023–25, social media provided a counter-narrative that rehumanised Palestinians in real time. Names, faces, voices, and stories circulated globally, undermining the official rhetoric. The image of a doctor operating on children by torchlight, the voice of a young girl pleading for food, the funeral of entire families killed in a single strike — these broke through the abstractions of "terror" and "security."

For many around the world, this was the first time Palestinians appeared not as faceless masses but as fully human, living under impossible conditions. The spell of dehumanisation cracked, even if it has not yet been fully broken.

**Conclusion: Humanity Denied, Humanity Asserted**

Dehumanisation has been one of Zionism's most effective tools. By reducing Palestinians to less than human, it has justified decades of dispossession and violence. But this tool is increasingly contested. The global circulation of Palestinian voices, the exposure of official rhetoric, and the growing scepticism of younger generations have begun to reverse the narrative.

Resistance, then, is not only physical or political. It is also linguistic and moral: the struggle to reclaim humanity in a discourse that denies it. As long as Palestinians are seen as "terrorists" first and people second, the cycle of violence will continue. But as more of the world begins to see them as mothers, fathers, children, and neighbours, the power of dehumanisation weakens.

**Reflection: Watching Gaza Burn**

During the Gaza war of 2023–25, a disturbing phenomenon unfolded on Israel's southern hills. Families brought folding chairs and picnic baskets to ridgelines overlooking the Strip. Children clapped as bombs fell; adults pointed their phones at the plumes of smoke, streaming destruction live to social media. Some cheered when apartment blocks collapsed into rubble.

To outsiders, this looked like barbarity made public. To those participating, it was framed as a kind of national theatre — proof of strength, vengeance, or even entertainment. It captured, in one grotesque image, what decades of dehumanisation had produced: a society where cruelty could be performed openly, without shame, because Palestinians were no longer seen as people at all.

## Section 7 – Global Shifts in Perception

The question of Palestinian resistance has always been shaped not only by what happens in Gaza, the West Bank, or Israel itself, but also by how the world perceives it. For decades, Zionism relied on a favourable global narrative: Israel as a democracy under siege, Palestinians as faceless aggressors. That framing is now crumbling. The wars of the 21st century — especially Gaza 2023–2025 — have accelerated a profound shift in global perception. From the streets of Johannesburg to the campuses of New York, from the parliaments of Latin America to the online spaces of Gen Z, the Palestinian struggle is increasingly seen not through the prism of "terrorism" but as part of the universal story of anti-colonial resistance.

### The Global South's Moral Clarity

The Global South has long viewed the Palestinian struggle through the lens of its own anti-colonial history. In South Africa, the ruling African National Congress (ANC) explicitly links Israel's occupation to its own experience of apartheid. Leaders like Nelson Mandela made this connection clear decades ago: "We know too well that our freedom is incomplete without the freedom of the Palestinians."

In Latin America, countries such as Bolivia, Brazil, and Chile have taken strong stances in solidarity with Palestine, often recalling their own histories of dictatorship and resistance. In Asia, Indonesia and Malaysia, as Muslim-majority nations with colonial legacies, frame the Palestinian cause as a moral duty.

The Global South's clarity stems from recognition: Palestinians are not an anomaly but the latest chapter in the long book of peoples resisting domination. Where the West hesitates, the South speaks plainly, calling occupation what it is and recognising resistance as a legitimate response.

### The Crisis of Western Narratives

In the West, the narrative has been slower to shift, but cracks are widening. For decades, Israel enjoyed bipartisan support in the U.S. and near-consensus in Europe. The default script — "Israel has the right to defend itself" — remained almost unchallenged in parliaments and newsrooms.

But the Gaza war of 2023–2025 created a credibility crisis. As bombs levelled hospitals, as famine spread under blockade, as children filled morgues, the old script rang hollow. Governments continued to defend Israel, but their citizens increasingly did not. Mass protests in London, Paris, Berlin, New York, and Toronto revealed a widening gulf between rulers and ruled.

Polling in the U.S. showed generational divides sharper than ever: while older Americans remained broadly supportive of Israel, younger Americans overwhelmingly sympathised with Palestinians. In the UK, support for Israel fell to historic lows, particularly among youth and minority communities. The same trends appeared in France, Germany, and Canada.

Western leaders found themselves out of step with their own populations — defending policies their citizens increasingly viewed as indefensible.

### Universities and the Battle for Legitimacy

University campuses became epicentres of this shift. Students mobilised encampments, divestment campaigns, and boycotts reminiscent of the anti-apartheid movement. Professors and academic unions issued statements condemning the occupation and calling for sanctions.

The backlash was intense: accusations of antisemitism, donor pressure, police crackdowns. Yet the protests persisted, spreading across continents. For many students, Palestine became a defining moral issue of their generation — as Vietnam was in the 1960s or South Africa in the 1980s.

This mattered not just symbolically but strategically: today's students are tomorrow's policymakers, journalists, and business leaders. Their rejection of the old narratives signals a long-term transformation in Western political culture.

### Social Media and the End of Monopoly

The engine of this shift was social media. For the first time, Palestinians could speak for themselves directly to the world. Videos from Gaza, livestreams from West Bank villages, testimonies from refugee camps circulated globally within minutes.

This unfiltered visibility undermined decades of narrative monopoly. Where once Palestinians were portrayed only through the lens of official briefings or mainstream media, they now appeared as mothers, children, doctors, teachers — as people. The contrast between polished government press conferences and raw footage of bombed neighbourhoods was too stark to ignore.

Social media also connected struggles. Activists drew parallels between Gaza and Ferguson, between West Bank checkpoints and racial profiling in Western cities. Hashtags like #PalestineSolidarity and #FromTheRiverToTheSea became rallying cries, uniting movements across borders.

### Celebrities, Culture, and Visibility

Cultural figures — musicians, actors, writers — played an unexpected role in shifting perception. Artists used their platforms to speak out, often at great personal and professional risk. Concert boycotts, film festival statements, and viral speeches helped normalise open criticism of Israel in circles once dominated by silence.

The backlash was fierce: contracts cancelled, shows pulled, reputations smeared. But the chilling effect was weaker than in previous decades. Each silencing attempt sparked new waves of solidarity. The cultural sphere, like the academic one, became a key front in the battle for legitimacy.

### The Generation Gap

Underlying these shifts is a generational divide. For older generations, support for Israel was rooted in memories of the Holocaust, Cold War alliances, and decades of political conditioning. For younger generations, shaped by social media and global activism, the Holocaust feels distant, while Gaza is immediate.

This generational shift matters profoundly. As younger voters, journalists, and politicians rise, their scepticism toward Israel and sympathy for Palestinians will shape future policy debates. What is unthinkable in today's parliaments — arms embargoes, sanctions, recognition of Palestine — may be commonplace tomorrow.

### The Role of Law and Human Rights Language

Another driver of shifting perception is the growing authority of human rights discourse. Reports by Amnesty International, Human Rights Watch, and even Israeli NGOs like B'Tselem have labelled Israel's system an apartheid regime. The International Court of Justice and International Criminal Court have taken up cases of potential war crimes and genocide.

These developments legitimise the language long used by activists but dismissed as extreme. When mainstream institutions adopt the language of apartheid and genocide, the moral ground shifts. Governments may still defend Israel, but the legal and discursive terrain is no longer entirely in their control.

### The Palestinian Narrative Reclaimed

For decades, Palestinians were spoken about but rarely heard. Today, that is changing. Palestinian journalists, writers, and ordinary citizens are telling their own stories, reclaiming narrative authority. The power of testimony — a mother describing her child's death, a doctor live-streaming from a besieged hospital — pierces through propaganda and demands recognition.

This reclamation of narrative is itself a form of resistance. It asserts Palestinians not as terrorists or statistics but as human beings with names, voices, and rights. It dismantles dehumanisation at its root.

### Conclusion: The Tide Turns

Global perception is not uniform, nor is it irreversible. Western governments still arm and defend Israel. The word "terrorism" continues to shape discourse. But the tide is turning. In the Global South, solidarity is entrenched. In the West, younger generations are shifting the debate. Social media has shattered old monopolies. Human rights language has entered the mainstream.

For Zionism, this is an existential challenge. Its legitimacy has always depended not only on military might but on international acceptance. If the world no longer believes the narrative, the foundation weakens. Resistance, once silenced as terror, is being reinterpreted as part of the universal struggle for freedom.

The next section will explore the consequences of this transformation: how world opinion, once an asset to Israel, is becoming a liability — and how the collapse of narrative control may signal the fall of Zionism itself.

## Section 8 – Conclusion: The Unfinished Debate

The story of Palestinian resistance is not one of easy answers. It is a narrative shaped by tragedy, resilience, compromise, and contradiction. At its heart lies a profound tension: the right of a people to resist occupation versus the global system's refusal to recognise that right when exercised by Palestinians.

This chapter has traced that tension across decades — from the rise of the PLO to the ascendancy of Hamas, from the grassroots defiance of the Intifadas to the contested framing of "terrorism." Along the way, one truth emerges: the debate is far from settled. It remains unfinished, not only in the realm of politics but in the moral consciousness of the world.

### Resistance as Universal, Palestine as Exception

History offers countless examples of peoples resisting colonial domination: Algerians against France, Indians against Britain, Vietnamese against the U.S. and France, South Africans against apartheid. Each was once labelled violent, illegitimate, even terrorist. Each is now celebrated as part of the global march toward freedom.

Palestinians belong within this same lineage. Yet uniquely, their struggle continues to be denied that recognition. Zionism has succeeded, for decades, in presenting their resistance as an aberration — not freedom fighting but fanaticism. This exceptionalism reveals less about Palestinians themselves than about the power structures that uphold Israel. The refusal to extend to Palestinians what was extended to Algerians or South Africans is a testament to the persistence of Western double standards.

### The Limits of Violence, the Limits of Diplomacy

If the history of resistance teaches anything, it is that no single tactic guarantees success. Guerrilla warfare brought visibility but also alienation. Suicide bombings shook Israeli society but eroded global sympathy. Rockets symbolised defiance but provoked crushing reprisals. Diplomacy, meanwhile, brought recognition but little sovereignty, exposing the PLO to charges of capitulation.

This cycle underscores the cruel bind: Palestinians are condemned when they fight and ignored when they negotiate. Peaceful protest is often met with bullets; armed resistance is branded terrorism. In this paradox lies the unfinished nature of the struggle. It is not only a fight for land but for the basic right to resist at all.

**Dehumanisation as a Barrier to Resolution**

The persistence of dehumanisation ensures that the debate over resistance remains poisoned. When an entire people are cast as "terrorists" or "human animals," their claims are never heard on their own terms. They are judged not by the justice of their cause but by the rhetoric of their oppressors.

Breaking this cycle requires more than political change; it requires a transformation of imagination. Palestinians must be seen not as a security problem but as human beings with rights, dignity, and history. Until that shift occurs fully, resistance will always be framed in terms that deny its legitimacy.

**Global Shifts and Their Potential**

Yet change is underway. The cracks in Zionism's narrative monopoly are widening. The Global South speaks with increasing clarity, recalling its own anti-colonial past. Younger generations in the West reject the double standards of their governments. Human rights language, once dismissed as fringe, now shapes mainstream discourse.

These shifts do not resolve the debate, but they tilt its trajectory. What was once unthinkable — calling Israel an apartheid state, recognising the right of Palestinians to resist — is now part of global conversation. The unfinished debate may not be resolved overnight, but its contours are changing in ways that Zionism cannot easily control.

### The Future of Palestinian Resistance

Where, then, does Palestinian resistance go from here? The answer remains uncertain. Hamas remains entrenched in Gaza, its legitimacy bolstered by defiance but undermined by authoritarianism and its targeting of civilians. The PLO and PA remain weak, bureaucratic, and compromised. Grassroots movements persist, from the Great March of Return to digital activism, but their impact is often contained by overwhelming force.

Perhaps the future lies in plurality: resistance that is military, diplomatic, digital, cultural, and legal all at once. Perhaps it lies in shifting the battlefield from violence to visibility, from rockets to rights language. Or perhaps, as in other liberation struggles, the combination of global solidarity and internal resilience will eventually break the deadlock. What is certain is that the demand for freedom cannot be extinguished, however it is expressed.

### The Debate as a Measure of Zionism's Fragility

The persistence of the resistance-terrorism debate is itself revealing. If Zionism were secure, it would not need to silence, censor, and criminalise every expression of Palestinian defiance. If Israel's legitimacy were unassailable, it would not collapse so heavily on the rhetorical crutch of "terrorism."

The unfinished debate is not a sign of Palestinian weakness but of Zionism's fragility. It reveals that Israel's moral authority is contested, its narrative power diminished, its justifications increasingly hollow. In the court of global opinion, the case is shifting. What remains unfinished is not only the Palestinian struggle but the project of Zionism itself.

## Conclusion: The Struggle Continues

The debate over Palestinian resistance — whether it is terrorism or liberation — remains unresolved. But perhaps resolution is not the point. Perhaps what matters is that the debate itself continues, refusing erasure, refusing silence. Each act of resistance, however flawed or contested, keeps alive the truth that Palestinians are not passive victims but active agents of history.

The struggle continues, unfinished but unextinguished. And in that persistence lies the greatest challenge to Zionism: the refusal of a people to disappear, the insistence on their humanity, and the unyielding demand that the world recognise both.

# CHAPTER NINE:
# The Politics of Zionism in Crisis

## Section 1 – Introduction: From Strength to Fragility

For much of its history, Israel thrived on a narrative of strength. To its allies, it was the small nation that survived against impossible odds; to its own people, it was the fulfilment of an ancient promise, a homeland reborn from ashes. The world was encouraged to see Israel as a miracle: democratic in a sea of authoritarianism, innovative in a region stereotyped as stagnant, resilient in the face of existential threat.

This narrative was not just propaganda. It became the foundation of Zionism's claim to legitimacy. Israel was not merely another state; it was an exceptional one, born in tragedy yet destined for survival. Every military victory, every economic achievement, every diplomatic breakthrough reinforced the image of a people who had not only returned to history but mastered it.

And yet, this image concealed as much as it revealed. Strength was often projected to mask fragility. The constant invocation of existential threat — whether from Arab neighbours, Palestinian resistance, or Iranian ambitions — reflected not only real dangers but a deeper insecurity. From its inception, Israel was a state that depended on exceptional support — first British, then American — to survive. Its military supremacy was real, but it was underwritten by billions in foreign aid, diplomatic shielding, and the impunity granted by powerful allies.

By the 2020s, this contradiction between image and reality could no longer be ignored. Israel remained militarily formidable, but politically it was unstable, socially divided, and morally compromised. The Gaza wars of 2023–25 stripped away the last vestiges of its moral narrative. What had once been described as "self-defence" now appeared to much of the world as something far darker: deliberate, systematic, and genocidal violence against a trapped civilian population. The UN's Commission of Inquiry would eventually use the word "genocide" — a word Israelis had long claimed as uniquely their own.

Internally, the cracks were just as visible. Israeli politics had descended into paralysis, with repeated elections failing to produce stable governments. Corruption scandals, most notably surrounding Benjamin Netanyahu, consumed the political system. The judiciary, long one of the few independent checks on executive power, came under sustained assault from a government determined to shield itself from accountability. The so-called "startup nation" — hailed abroad for its innovation and dynamism — found itself unable to maintain even the basic integrity of democratic institutions.

At the centre of this unravelling stood Benjamin Netanyahu, the man who came to personify both the promise and the decay of Zionism. For three decades, Netanyahu dominated Israeli politics, outlasting rivals, manipulating coalitions, and presenting himself as indispensable. His longevity was not an accident. He understood the mechanisms of fear, division, and narrative better than anyone. To the world, he was Israel's polished spokesman, fluent in English, adept at media, able to cast Israel's wars as part of the West's eternal struggle against terror. To Israelis, he was the master tactician, the man who could always deliver — or at least survive.

But Netanyahu's dominance came at a cost. His repeated entanglements with corruption revealed a leader less interested in vision than in survival. His willingness to empower extremists exposed how Zionism had drifted from its early claim of democracy to an authoritarian populism rooted in racism and dehumanisation. His reliance on perpetual conflict — especially in Gaza — showed how war itself had become the mechanism of political survival.

What makes this crisis unique is that it is not merely personal, but structural. Netanyahu did not invent corruption, extremism, or war as politics. He inherited them, refined them, and embodied them. His story reveals the deeper logic of Zionism in the 21st century: a movement that once justified itself as the rebirth of a people, now reduced to the preservation of power at any cost.

These contradictions are stark:

- Israel claims to be a democracy, yet it denies millions of Palestinians under its control any political rights.
- It claims to be a moral state, yet its leaders now stand accused of genocide at the UN.
- It claims to be strong, yet its politics are consumed by corruption, and its survival depends on endless conflict.

In this chapter I will take you through that transformation. It traces how Zionism moved from strength to fragility, from democracy to decay, from legitimacy to international indictment. And at the centre of this story is Netanyahu — not because he is uniquely corrupt or uniquely powerful, but because he is the mirror in which Zionism now sees itself. His corruption scandals, his attacks on the courts, his reliance on far-right allies, his wars in Gaza — all these are not aberrations, but symptoms of a deeper crisis.

Zionism in the age of Netanyahu is no longer about building the future. It is about buying time. It is about survival — not for the people as a whole, but for the political elite who hold them hostage. As Israel stands accused of genocide abroad and slides toward authoritarianism at home, the myth of strength has given way to the reality of fragility.

This is the paradox at the heart of Zionism's politics today: a state that projects invincibility but is trapped in dependence, a democracy that erodes itself to save its leaders, a nation that once claimed to rise from genocide now accused of committing one. The story of Benjamin Netanyahu is the story of that paradox — the man and the myth, the survivor and the saboteur, the guardian and the gravedigger of Zionism itself.

## Section 2 – Netanyahu: The Man and the Myth

Benjamin Netanyahu is not simply another Israeli prime minister. He is the central figure of modern Zionism, the man who more than any other has defined Israel's politics, image, and trajectory in the 21st century. To his admirers, he is Israel's indispensable statesman, a modern-day Churchill who held firm against terror and international pressure. To his critics, he is a corrupt opportunist, a salesman of fear who clings to power through division and war. Both views contain truth. But above all, Netanyahu is the product — and embodiment — of a Zionism that has shifted from state-building vision to survivalist cynicism.

### The Family Inheritance

Netanyahu's political inheritance began at home. His father, Benzion Netanyahu, was a historian of the Spanish Inquisition and a devoted follower of Ze'ev Jabotinsky, the founder of Revisionist Zionism. Unlike mainstream Labour Zionism, which often cloaked itself in socialist ideals and the dream of coexistence, Revisionist Zionism was uncompromising. It taught that Jews could secure their homeland only through force, through an "iron wall" that would crush Arab resistance until surrender was the only option.

This was the worldview Benjamin inherited: Zionism not as negotiation but as domination. His father's fierce belief in Jewish exceptionalism and suspicion of Arabs shaped a young man who would later frame every political challenge in existential terms. To Netanyahu, politics was not about compromise; it was about survival and supremacy.

**Formed in America, Branded for Export**

Unlike Israel's founding generation, Netanyahu spent much of his formative years abroad. He attended high school in Philadelphia, studied architecture and management at MIT, and briefly pursued political science at Harvard. These years in America were decisive. They gave him not only fluent English but a deep understanding of U.S. political culture.

Where his Israeli contemporaries learned the idiom of kibbutz and military command, Netanyahu absorbed the language of American television, marketing, and political spin. He became the first Americanised Israeli leader, equally at home on CNN as in the Knesset. His ability to speak to U.S. audiences directly, in their idioms and soundbites, would later make him an unrivalled advocate for Israel in Washington.

This dual identity — Israeli militarism fused with American polish — became the core of Netanyahu's political brand. He was not just a politician; he was a salesman, capable of packaging Zionism for export as the West's frontline defence against terror.

**The Entebbe Legacy**

The defining myth of Netanyahu's career was not his own, but his brother's. In 1976, Yonatan Netanyahu led the famous commando raid to rescue hostages at Entebbe Airport in Uganda. He was killed in the operation and instantly became a national hero.

Benjamin inherited this aura of sacrifice. Though he himself had served in Israel's elite Sayeret Matkal unit, his military career was unremarkable compared to his brother's. Yet he positioned himself as the custodian of Yonatan's legacy, turning his brother's death into a personal and political inheritance. The myth of Entebbe became a cornerstone of his career, allowing him to drape himself in heroism without having lived it.

This dynamic — trading on tragedy for political capital — would repeat itself throughout his career. Just as he used his brother's death to elevate his image, he would later use national crises and wars to fortify his own position.

## The Master Salesman

Netanyahu first rose to prominence not in Israel but on the world stage. As Israel's ambassador to the United Nations in the 1980s, he mastered the art of public diplomacy. His telegenic style, polished American English, and knack for soundbite politics made him a favourite on U.S. talk shows. At a time when Israel was increasingly isolated after its invasion of Lebanon and the Sabra and Shatila massacre, Netanyahu reframed the debate.

He presented Israel as the frontline state in the global war on terror, years before that phrase would dominate Western politics. He argued that terrorism, not occupation, was the defining issue of the conflict. This rhetorical shift — away from colonialism and toward terrorism — resonated with Western audiences and cemented Israel's narrative as a victim rather than an occupier.

In the 1990s and beyond, Netanyahu carried this same formula into Israeli politics. He was not a builder like Ben-Gurion, not a general like Rabin, not a diplomat like Peres. He was, above all, a communicator — a man who understood that in an age of television and later social media, politics was less about policy than about performance.

## The Myth and the Reality

The myth of Netanyahu was powerful because it fused personal tragedy, ideological inheritance, and media mastery. He was the son of a historian who preached iron resolve, the brother of a fallen hero who embodied sacrifice, and the Americanised spokesman who could sell Israel to the world. To many, he seemed irreplaceable — the man who could hold the line against Iran, against Hamas, against international criticism.

But the reality was more cynical. Netanyahu was not a visionary but a tactician. His career was marked less by bold strategy than by relentless manoeuvring. He thrived not by resolving crises but by perpetuating them, because crises kept him indispensable. He spoke of democracy abroad while undermining it at home. He invoked morality while entangling himself in corruption scandals. He presented himself as Israel's guardian while leaving the nation more divided, isolated, and morally compromised than ever.

Netanyahu was, in short, the perfect embodiment of Zionism in its late stage: a movement sustained not by ideals but by fear, division, and perpetual survivalism. His myth masked the decay, but it also revealed it. In him, Zionism's contradictions — between democracy and occupation, between morality and brutality, between strength and fragility — became impossible to ignore.

## Section 3 – Corruption and the Courts (Expanded, with Genocide Box)

If Netanyahu's early career was built on myth, his later years were defined by scandal. By the end of the 2010s, the prime minister who sold himself as Israel's indispensable guardian faced multiple criminal indictments. The charges — bribery, fraud, and breach of trust — painted a picture not of a leader above politics, but of one deeply entangled in its murk. Lavish gifts from billionaires, backroom deals with media barons, and sweetheart arrangements designed to secure favourable coverage all pointed to a man whose appetite for power was matched only by his willingness to bend the rules.

For many Israelis, the spectacle was disillusioning. Netanyahu had been in power for so long, dominating every election cycle, that his corruption trials seemed almost like the natural by-product of his rule. Yet the implications were profound. At stake was not merely one man's political survival, but the integrity of Israel's democracy itself. If the prime minister could bend the judiciary to his will, then the idea of Israel as a state governed by law — the claim that distinguished it from its neighbours — would collapse.

## The War on the Judiciary

Netanyahu's response was not contrition but confrontation. He denied all charges, dismissed the investigations as political witch-hunts, and accused the judiciary of conspiring with "leftist elites" to remove him from office. It was a strategy drawn directly from the populist playbook of Donald Trump: cast yourself as the victim, delegitimise the courts, and turn corruption into a badge of persecution.

In 2023, this battle reached its climax. Netanyahu's government introduced sweeping reforms designed to strip the Supreme Court of its independence. These measures would have allowed parliament to override judicial rulings and given the executive near-total control over judicial appointments. The effect was clear: the judiciary, long one of the few checks on Israeli executive power, would be neutered.

The public response was explosive. Hundreds of thousands of Israelis poured into the streets week after week in the largest protests in the country's history. The demonstrations brought together secular liberals, former generals, business leaders, and even reservists — a cross-section of society united in the belief that democracy itself was at stake. For a moment, it seemed that Netanyahu had overplayed his hand. The myth of indispensability was crumbling; the man who once sold himself as the saviour of democracy was now its gravedigger.

## The Gaza War Intervenes

But fortuitously, history intervened. In October 2023, Hamas launched a devastating attack on Israel, killing civilians and exposing the vulnerabilities of its vaunted security establishment. The country was thrown into shock, fear, and rage. Netanyahu, who only weeks earlier had faced unprecedented opposition, was suddenly repositioned as a wartime leader.

The protests dissipated. The focus shifted from democracy to survival, from the courts to Gaza. Netanyahu's trial slowed, overshadowed by the daily spectacle of war. For him, it was a political reprieve. For Israel, it was a disaster. A society that had been on the brink of holding its leader accountable found itself once again trapped in his narrative of crisis.

### The UN Names Genocide

In June 2025, the UN Independent International Commission of Inquiry delivered its most damning verdict yet:

*"The Commission finds that Israel is responsible for the commission of genocide in Gaza... It is clear that there is an intent to destroy the Palestinians in Gaza through acts that meet the criteria set forth in the Genocide Convention."*

— *Navi Pillay, Chair of the Commission*

The report detailed how Israeli authorities and security forces committed four of the five genocidal acts defined under the 1948 Genocide Convention:

- Killing
- Causing serious bodily or mental harm
- Inflicting conditions of life designed to bring about destruction
- Imposing measures to prevent births

It described a pattern of starvation, indiscriminate bombardment, destruction of healthcare and education, and even systematic sexual and gender-based violence. Responsibility, it concluded, lay with Israel's leadership "at the highest echelons," where ministers openly denigrated Palestinians as "human animals."

Israel's ambassador dismissed the 70-page report as "cherry-picked," but the language was unambiguous: genocidal intent was the only reasonable inference.

UN Secretary-General António Guterres later condemned Israel's strike on Hamas leaders in Doha, Qatar — a U.S. ally and host of a major American base — as a "flagrant violation of sovereignty and a threat to regional peace." That single attack brought the war into the heart of a friendly state, triggering outrage at the Security Council and exposing how far Israel was willing to go, shielded by Western silence.

*"When clear signs and evidence of genocide emerge, the absence of action to stop it amounts to complicity."*

— *Navi Pillay*

### Corruption as Structure, Not Scandal

What is striking about Netanyahu's corruption saga is not merely the personal details, but what it reveals about Zionism itself. Corruption here is not an aberration; it is the logical outcome of a system built on impunity. Just as Israel has evaded accountability for decades of occupation, so too could its prime minister evade accountability for personal misconduct. The erosion of law abroad mirrored its erosion at home.

This is why Netanyahu's trials matter beyond his personal fate. They show how Zionism in its late stage became hollowed out, its institutions weakened, its morality compromised. The leader who claimed to embody the state had, in truth, bent it around his own survival.

### Section 4 – War as Political Survival

For Benjamin Netanyahu, war has never been merely a matter of security. It has been the stage upon which his political survival depends. Time and again, his leadership has coincided with military escalation, and time and again those escalations have served to protect him — not only from external threats but from domestic accountability. Gaza, in particular, has become both the testing ground of Israeli military doctrine and the shield behind which Netanyahu defends his place in power.

### A Pattern of Escalation

Netanyahu's political career reveals a striking pattern: moments of personal or political weakness often coincide with sudden military action. When his popularity waned, operations in Gaza — *Pillar of Defence* (2012), *Protective Edge* (2014), and later wars — provided a rallying point. Each time, the government insisted that it had no choice but to act. Each time, Netanyahu rebranded himself as the indispensable wartime leader.

The 2023–25 Gaza war followed the same script but on a scale unlike anything before. Hamas's October 2023 attack had indeed been catastrophic for Israel, exposing intelligence failures and shattering the image of invulnerability. For any other leader, such a failure might have ended a career. For Netanyahu, it became the pretext for entrenchment. By recasting the disaster as proof of Israel's existential vulnerability, he transformed a political liability into a mandate for indefinite war.

### From Security to Survival

Officially, the war was about defeating Hamas. In practice, it became a vehicle for Netanyahu's own survival. The daily bombardments, the calls for "total victory", and the refusal to engage seriously with ceasefire proposals all served to extend the war's timeline. The longer the conflict raged, the less attention the public and media paid to Netanyahu's corruption trial or his failed judicial reforms. The prime minister who had been on the verge of political collapse was suddenly indispensable once more.

The costs were staggering. Tens of thousands of Palestinians were killed, famine spread across Gaza, and Israel itself became more isolated than ever on the international stage. Yet domestically,

Netanyahu held on. In the atmosphere of siege, criticism was muted, protests against his corruption evaporated, and the narrative of survival trumped all else.

## The Genocide Connection

The UN Commission of Inquiry's determination that Israel was committing genocide did not shake Netanyahu's government — it emboldened it. To admit guilt would have been to admit vulnerability; instead, the accusations were spun as proof that the world was biased, that Israel was under attack not just from Hamas but from the international community itself.

This rhetorical judo turned legal condemnation into political capital. Just as he had dismissed the courts at home as corrupt, Netanyahu dismissed the UN and the ICC as illegitimate. For his supporters, he was the leader standing against a hostile world, the last line of defence against both terrorists and hypocritical global institutions. War and defiance fused into one survival strategy.

## The Qatar Strike

Perhaps the clearest example of this logic was the Israeli strike in Doha, Qatar, in 2025. The target was Hamas's political leadership, but the message was broader: Israel would pursue its enemies anywhere, even on the soil of a U.S. ally hosting an American base. For Netanyahu, the risk of alienating allies was secondary to the political gains of appearing uncompromising.

The attack was condemned as a flagrant violation of sovereignty and a threat to regional stability. Yet Netanyahu framed it as proof of his resolve, daring others to stop him. In the process, he not only escalated the war but deepened his own indispensability: in a moment of international outrage, only he could stand firm, only he could carry the burden of leadership.

**War Without End**

The tragedy of Netanyahu's wartime strategy is that it creates a politics without exit. Defeat Hamas completely? Unlikely. Negotiate peace? Politically suicidal. End the war without "total victory"? Impossible under the narrative he himself had created. And so, the war became endless, because endless war was the condition of his political survival.

This logic was corrosive not only to Palestinians, who bore the brunt of the violence, but to Israel itself. The longer the war continued, the more the country's institutions were hollowed out, the more its international standing deteriorated, and the more its society was defined by fear and division. Yet for Netanyahu, these costs were acceptable. Better a nation in crisis than a prime minister in prison.

**Survival at Any Cost**

Netanyahu's reliance on war to sustain his leadership exposes a grim truth about late-stage Zionism. Once a project of state-building, it has become a project of self-preservation — not of the people, but of the political elite. War is not the by-product of this crisis; it is its engine.

For Netanyahu, the lesson of his career is simple: peace threatens him, war sustains him. His genius has been to convince much of Israel — and many of its allies abroad — that what sustains him also sustains them. The result is a state caught in perpetual conflict, where war itself has become the foundation of political order.

## Section 5 – The Far-Right Coalition and the Erosion of Democracy

If corruption hollowed Israel's institutions and war prolonged Netanyahu's career, it was his alliances with the far right that permanently reshaped the political landscape. Once confined to the margins, ultranationalist and religious-extremist parties were brought into the heart of government under Netanyahu. Their presence not only kept him in office but fundamentally altered the nature of Zionism itself: from a movement that once paid lip service to democracy and pluralism into a project increasingly defined by racism, authoritarianism, and the language of annihilation.

### From Fringe to Power

Figures such as **Itamar Ben-Gvir** and **Bezalel Smotrich** were long considered political pariahs, too extreme even for Israel's right-wing mainstream. Ben-Gvir, once convicted of incitement to racism and support for a terrorist organisation, had built his career on calls for the expulsion of Arabs. Smotrich, a settler leader, openly advocated annexation of the West Bank and the dismantling of any prospects for Palestinian statehood.

In previous decades, leaders like Yitzhak Rabin or Ariel Sharon, though hawkish, had sought to keep such voices at arm's length. Netanyahu, by contrast, embraced them. Facing declining support and desperate for parliamentary majorities, he brought them into his coalition. The result was a government more extreme than any in Israel's history, one that treated positions once considered radical as mainstream policy.

### Legislating Extremism

With the far right in power, policies that had once been rhetorical provocation became concrete proposals. Plans for **annexing large swathes of the West Bank** were openly discussed. Settler violence, once condemned by the state, was increasingly excused or even enabled. Ministers spoke not only of defeating Hamas but of the wholesale "erasure" of Gaza.

The rhetoric of dehumanisation that had long circulated at the margins — Palestinians as "two-legged beasts," as "human animals," as "Amalek" — was now echoed from cabinet tables.

What had once been whispers became policy debates. The state no longer merely tolerated racism; it institutionalised it.

## The Assault on Democracy

This far-right ascendancy dovetailed with Netanyahu's own attacks on Israel's judiciary. Judicial reforms were not only about shielding the prime minister from prosecution; they were also about creating space for the far right's agenda. A weakened Supreme Court would be less able to block settlement expansion, less able to rule against discriminatory laws, less able to protect minority rights.

In this sense, Netanyahu's personal survival and the far right's ideological goals aligned. Both required dismantling the last institutional checks on executive power. Both required silencing dissent and framing opposition as treachery. Together, they pushed Israel further down the road of illiberalism, transforming it from a flawed democracy into a state where authoritarian impulses reigned unchecked.

## Religion, Nationalism, and the New Zionism

What emerged under Netanyahu's far-right coalition was a new fusion of religious zealotry and ultranationalism. For Ben-Gvir and Smotrich, the conflict with Palestinians was not about borders or security but about divine destiny. Palestinians were not neighbours to be compromised with but biblical enemies to be vanquished.

This rhetoric resonated with settler movements emboldened by government backing. Violence against Palestinians in the West Bank surged, with homes torched, villages attacked, and military authorities turning a blind eye. Ministers defended such actions as expressions of "legitimate frustration." In this climate, the language of annihilation ceased to be taboo. It was, increasingly, the grammar of governance.

## Western Complicity

What made this shift even more striking was the response abroad — or rather, the lack of it. Western governments that once expressed concern over settlement expansion or the erosion of democracy now offered near-total support. Leaders in Washington and London repeated Netanyahu's talking points about "self-defence," even as his far-right allies called for the destruction of Gaza and the expulsion of its people.

The silence was telling. It revealed not only the reach of Zionist influence but also the bankruptcy of Western democratic rhetoric. How could the UK or U.S. condemn authoritarian drift elsewhere while embracing it in Israel? How could they claim to uphold international law while ignoring its most flagrant violations? Netanyahu's coalition exposed not only the fragility of Israel's democracy but the hypocrisy of its allies.

## A System Transformed

By allying with the far right, Netanyahu did more than save his premiership. He changed the character of the state. Zionism, once able to present itself as democratic even while occupying millions, could no longer maintain the pretence. With extremists in government, the mask slipped. The world saw a state that had institutionalised dehumanisation, embraced authoritarianism, and normalised calls for ethnic cleansing.

For Netanyahu, this was a bargain worth making. For Israel, it was a bargain that deepened its crisis. What had once been a state striving to balance democracy and occupation was now openly abandoning democracy altogether. The erosion was no longer subtle; it was structural.

## Section 6 – Netanyahu and the Diaspora

If Netanyahu's alliances with the far right transformed Israel at home, his role abroad was no less consequential. For decades he served as the polished salesman of Zionism to the world. To Washington and London, he was the articulate statesman, fluent in English and adept at speaking in the idioms of Western politics. He cast Israel as not just another state but as the frontline outpost of Western civilisation, a partner in the global struggle against terrorism.

Yet as his domestic politics grew more extreme, this carefully curated image began to fracture — not only in international diplomacy but within the Jewish diaspora itself. The very communities once relied upon as Israel's strongest advocates grew increasingly divided, disillusioned, and in many cases alienated from the project Netanyahu represented.

### The American Stage

No Israeli leader understood the United States better than Netanyahu. Having grown up in America and mastered its political culture, he became a natural fit for Congress, think tanks, and Sunday talk shows. His speeches often echoed the rhythms of American patriotism: moral clarity, good versus evil, freedom against tyranny.

In the U.S., this framing resonated powerfully, especially with conservative Christians. Evangelical churches saw Israel not only as a geopolitical ally but as the fulfilment of biblical prophecy. Netanyahu harnessed this support with remarkable skill, forging ties that bound Israel to the American right as firmly as to the Jewish diaspora.

But this alliance came at a cost. By aligning so closely with American evangelicals and right-wing politics, Netanyahu alienated large swathes of liberal American Jews, who increasingly saw Israel not as a beacon of justice but as an embarrassment.

## The Growing Rift with American Jews

Generational change accelerated this rift. Older American Jews, shaped by memories of the Holocaust and Israel's early vulnerability, tended to view Israel through a lens of sympathy and solidarity. Younger Jews, however, raised in a world of social justice movements and instant access to global media, saw images of checkpoints, bombed-out Gaza neighbourhoods, and settlers torching Palestinian homes.

For them, the Israel of Netanyahu did not embody Jewish values of justice and compassion. It looked instead like a state built on occupation, racism, and militarism. The slogan "Not in our name" became a rallying cry for young Jewish activists across U.S. campuses and synagogues. Organisations like Jewish Voice for Peace and IfNotNow emerged as vocal critics, challenging the once-unquestioned assumption that diaspora Jews and Israel spoke with one voice.

## Europe and the UK

In Europe and the UK, the same tensions played out. Netanyahu cultivated close ties with conservative governments, particularly those willing to overlook Israeli settlement expansion in exchange for trade or security partnerships. Yet among Jewish communities, especially in Britain, divisions deepened.

The spectacle of British leaders like Keir Starmer declaring themselves "supporters of Zionism" while downplaying Palestinian suffering sharpened the sense of moral unease. For many diaspora Jews, the issue was no longer about Israel's survival but about the ethical cost of uncritical support. The charge of genocide during the Gaza war of 2023–25 pushed this unease into open conflict, as synagogues, community groups, and families split over whether supporting Israel now meant complicity in atrocity.

## Netanyahu's Dual Image

This duality — admired abroad, resented at home — became Netanyahu's defining paradox. To Congress, he could bring the chamber to its feet with thunderous applause. To diaspora communities, he could sell the image of Israel as a democracy under siege. But to growing numbers of Jews worldwide, he represented a betrayal: a leader who had traded the ethical core of Judaism for the cynical power politics of perpetual war.

Netanyahu leaned heavily on fear to bridge this gap. He argued that criticism of Israel was a new form of antisemitism, that to oppose Zionism was to oppose Jewish survival itself. This conflation of Jewish identity with Israeli state policy was his most powerful weapon — and also his most corrosive. It left little room for Jews to dissent without being branded as traitors, and it further eroded the distinction between genuine antisemitism and legitimate criticism of state policy.

## Diaspora Support in Decline

The long-term consequences of this estrangement are profound. Israel's claim to speak for world Jewry has always been central to Zionism's legitimacy. If diaspora Jews increasingly reject that claim, the moral foundation of Zionism weakens. Netanyahu's tenure accelerated this process. By tethering Israel to the far right, by presiding over wars branded as genocidal, he made support for Israel more divisive than ever within the very communities it claimed to represent.

The irony is striking. Netanyahu, who once positioned himself as the great protector of the Jewish people, may ultimately be remembered as the leader who drove the deepest wedge between Israel and the diaspora. His global statesmanship, so polished on the surface, concealed a growing crisis of legitimacy underneath.

## Section 7 – Netanyahu as a Symbol of Zionism's Decay

In every era of Israel's history, one leader has come to embody the spirit of the moment. David Ben-Gurion symbolised state-building. Golda Meir represented resilience in crisis. Menachem Begin gave voice to the Revisionist right. Yitzhak Rabin, before his assassination, carried the fragile hope of peace. In Benjamin Netanyahu, we find the embodiment of something different: the decay of Zionism itself.

### The Survivor, Not the Builder

Netanyahu is not remembered for creating or reforming institutions, nor for advancing peace, nor even for visionary strategy. His gift has been survival — political, personal, and rhetorical. He has outlasted rivals, scandals, and even wars that might have destroyed another leader. But this survival has come at a cost. In his pursuit of power, Netanyahu hollowed out Israel's institutions, empowered extremists, and turned perpetual war into a governing principle.

This is why he is more than a corrupt politician; he is a symbol of what Zionism has become. Once imagined as a movement of renewal, of moral rebirth after catastrophe, Zionism in Netanyahu's hands became a movement of fear, division, and self-preservation.

### From Vision to Cynicism

The Zionism of Ben-Gurion, for all its contradictions, had a vision: to create a state for Jews, to secure their survival, to establish sovereignty after centuries of statelessness. The Zionism of Netanyahu has no such horizon. It is not about building a future; it is about managing a present. It sustains itself through endless cycles of fear, pointing always to existential threats that justify authoritarian measures, war crimes, or outright genocide.

This shift from vision to cynicism is perhaps the starkest marker of decay. A project that once sought legitimacy through moral argument now survives through raw power and manipulation. It is a Zionism emptied of ideals, left only with survival instincts and slogans.

### The Dehumanisation at the Core

Central to this decay is the normalisation of dehumanisation. Under Netanyahu and his far-right allies, language once confined to the fringes — Palestinians as "animals," Gaza as "a nest of terrorists," whole populations marked for erasure — became the language of the state. Ministers openly called for killing not just fighters but "their mothers and babies." Crowds gathered to cheer bombings as entertainment. Children were raised to see cruelty not as shameful but as natural.

This is not an aberration; it is the endpoint of a movement that has long defined itself against an "other." For decades, Zionism justified itself by portraying Palestinians as obstacles to be removed rather than people to be lived with. Netanyahu did not invent this logic, but under his rule it became fully exposed, impossible to deny.

### Western Shield, Global Isolation

Another element of the decay lies in the growing gap between protection and legitimacy. With the unwavering backing of the United States and key allies like the UK, Netanyahu could act with impunity. Bombings, annexations, judicial takeovers — all were excused as matters of "self-defence." Yet globally, Israel grew increasingly isolated. UN reports spoke of genocide. European publics turned against it. The gap between elite support and popular outrage widened until Israel stood as a pariah state, protected diplomatically but delegitimised morally.

Netanyahu symbolises this paradox. He is the man who could still bring a standing ovation in Washington while presiding over international condemnation in The Hague. He embodies both the shield and the isolation — the impunity at the top and the shame at the base.

## The Man as the Movement

In the end, Netanyahu's career tells us as much about Zionism as about himself. His corruption, his reliance on war, his alliances with extremists, his estrangement from the diaspora — all are not merely personal flaws but structural realities of the Zionist project in its late stage. He is the mirror in which the movement sees its reflection: tarnished, brittle, and dependent on coercion rather than consent. He represents the transition from a Zionism of builders to a Zionism of survivors, from a movement that promised rebirth to one that delivers only decay. In this sense, Netanyahu is not just a leader of Israel. He is its symbol, the face of a Zionism that has lost its moral compass and, perhaps, its future.

## Conclusion – The Politics of Zionism in Crisis

By the mid-2020s, Benjamin Netanyahu stood as both the survivor and the symbol of a movement in decline. His story was not only that of a man who evaded accountability, but of a state that evaded it too. His corruption trials revealed how fragile Israeli democracy had become. His assault on the judiciary showed how easily institutions could be bent to personal will. His embrace of the far right normalised racism and authoritarianism in the very heart of government. And his wars in Gaza revealed how violence itself had become the engine of political survival.

The UN's determination that Israel was committing genocide did not mark a turning point inside the country; it marked a moment of entrenchment. Where others saw atrocity, Netanyahu saw an opportunity to rally his supporters, to turn condemnation into proof of indispensability. It was a grim inversion: the same man who claimed to speak for the Jewish people against the shadow of past genocide was now leading a state accused of committing one.

This is what makes Netanyahu more than just another Israeli leader. He personifies the crisis of Zionism in the 21st century. No longer about building a future, Zionism under his stewardship became about clinging to the present. No longer about ideals, it became about fear. No longer about legitimacy, it became about survival.

And yet, survival at any cost comes with its own price. By tying Israel's fate to his own, Netanyahu ensured that the state itself would bear the consequences of his corruption, his wars, and his compromises. In the process, he revealed the hollowness of the myth that had sustained Zionism for so long: that it was strong, moral, and democratic. Instead, the world saw fragility, impunity, and decay.

As this chapter has shown, the politics of Zionism today are not merely in crisis; they are symptomatic of a deeper collapse. The question that remains is not whether Netanyahu will fall — eventually he will — but whether Zionism can survive the rot he has come to symbolise. For the first time, the movement that once claimed to rise above history now faces the possibility of being consumed by it.

In the next chapter I will turn from Netanyahu the man to the broader movement he represents. If Chapter 9 revealed the decay of Zionism through the prism of one leader, Chapter 10 will examine how that decay has been amplified by social division, dehumanisation, and a culture of impunity — and why, for many around the world, the project of Zionism now stands accused not of fulfilment, but of betrayal.

# CHAPTER TEN –
# Society in Fracture:
# Zionism's Crisis of Legitimacy

## Section 1 – Introduction: From Democracy to Division

For decades, Israel presented itself as the only democracy in the Middle East. It was a refrain repeated in speeches, textbooks, and diplomatic exchanges. It was a claim that resonated powerfully in the West: here was a nation that shared the same institutions, the same values, the same democratic ideals as 'us'. To support Israel, Western leaders insisted, was not simply a matter of geopolitics but of solidarity with democracy itself.

By the 2020s, however, this claim had begun to collapse under the weight of reality. The façade of democracy had always been selective, granting rights and representation to Jewish citizens while denying them to millions of Palestinians under occupation. What had once been concealed by rhetoric was now laid bare by practice. Zionism, in its late stage, revealed not the promise of democracy but its fragmentation, its erosion, and, for many, its outright betrayal.

### The Erosion of the Democratic Mask

The image of Israel as a democracy rested on two fragile foundations. First, that within its internationally recognised borders, citizens could vote, organise, and participate in political life. Second, that the occupation of millions of Palestinians could be treated as temporary, an unfortunate but necessary security measure that would one day be resolved.

Both claims collapsed in the 21st century. Inside Israel proper, the rise of the far right and the assault on the judiciary gutted the independence of institutions. What had once been presented as a robust parliamentary system became little more than a platform for the dominance of one man and his extremist allies. Meanwhile, the

302

occupation ceased even to be disguised as temporary. Settlement expansion, annexationist rhetoric, and the normalisation of military control made it clear that Palestinians were not awaiting statehood but condemned to permanent subjugation.

The result was a state that spoke the language of democracy while practising the politics of apartheid. It was not only critics abroad who recognised this contradiction. Israeli society itself began to fracture along deep and dangerous lines.

## Fault Lines in Israeli Society

The crisis of legitimacy was not only external. It was internal. The myth of unity, the idea that "we are all in this together", no longer held. Instead, Israeli society was riven by divisions.

• Secular vs religious: Secular Israelis, once dominant in politics and culture, found themselves increasingly outnumbered and outmanoeuvred by religious nationalists and ultra-Orthodox communities who sought to redefine the state in theological terms.

• Left vs right: The political left, once the engine of Zionism, had collapsed into near irrelevance, leaving the right and far right to define the national agenda.

• Jewish vs Palestinian citizens of Israel: Palestinian citizens, roughly 20% of the population, lived under formal citizenship yet faced systemic discrimination, exclusion from power, and constant suspicion of disloyalty.

These fractures were not incidental. They were the product of a movement that had long defined itself against an "other". In the early decades, Zionism used the "other" as justification for unity. By the 21st century, however, the constant invocation of existential threat no longer united Israelis. It divided them, turning every social and political question into a battlefield.

## Gaza as a Mirror

The Gaza conflict of 2023 to 2025 crystallised these divisions. For Netanyahu and his allies, Gaza was proof that only perpetual war could sustain the state. For the far right, it was a divine mandate to annihilate an enemy people. For secular liberals, it was evidence of moral collapse and international isolation. For Palestinian citizens of Israel, it was a reminder that their identity placed them perpetually under suspicion, caught between loyalty to the state and solidarity with their people.

Gaza was not simply a war zone. It was a mirror in which Israeli society saw itself, fractured, angry, fearful, and incapable of consensus. What was revealed was not unity under threat but disunity under exposure.

## The Collapse of Consensus

What made this moment so striking was the collapse of that consensus. In the past, Israel had relied on a shared narrative that, whatever its flaws, it was a democracy defending itself against implacable enemies. That narrative no longer held. Too many contradictions had become visible.

• How could a state claim democracy while ruling millions without rights

• How could it claim morality while being accused of genocide by the UN

• How could it claim unity when its own citizens were more divided than ever before

These questions were not confined to activists or outsiders. They were asked within Israel itself, often in the streets during protests or in conversations across fractured families. The sense of a shared project, Zionism as collective destiny, was dissolving.

**From Democracy to Division**

I have tried in this chapter to explore that dissolution. I hope it shows how the language of democracy has given way to the politics of division, how dehumanisation has corroded not only the treatment of Palestinians but the cohesion of Israeli society itself. It looks at how violence in the West Bank and Gaza has normalised impunity, how the diaspora has broken away, and how the charge of genocide has eventually shattered global legitimacy.

If Netanyahu represents the politics of survival, Israeli society represents the cost of that survival: fractured, embittered, and increasingly hollow. Zionism once promised not only a homeland but a democracy. Today it offers neither. What remains is division, internal, external, and moral.

## Section 2 – The Language of Dehumanisation (Expanded)

If societies are measured by the language they use, Israel in the 21st century revealed its moral condition in the words of its leaders. The dehumanisation of Palestinians, once a subtext whispered in private or confined to the fringes, became the vocabulary of mainstream politics. Ministers, generals, and settlers no longer spoke of compromise or coexistence. Instead, they spoke of erasure, annihilation, and cleansing. What had long been denied as slander was now broadcast as policy.

**From Euphemism to Annihilation**

In the early years of the state, Israel's leaders often cloaked their language in euphemism. Ben-Gurion and his successors spoke of "security", "self-defence", and "redeeming the land". Yet even then, the logic of dehumanisation was present. As Ben-Gurion himself acknowledged in 1938:

"Let us not ignore the truth among ourselves: politically, we are the aggressors and they, the Palestinians, defend themselves. The country is theirs because they inhabit it, while we seek to settle here."

This candid admission was quickly buried beneath decades of mythmaking. By the 21st century, however, such euphemisms gave way to something far starker. Ministers declared Palestinians "human animals", invoked biblical commandments to "wipe out Amalek", and spoke of mothers and babies as legitimate targets.

The dehumanisation was no longer a hidden current. It was the flood tide of political rhetoric.

**Children of Cruelty**

Perhaps most disturbing was the way this language filtered into everyday culture. Reports emerged of Israeli families gathering on hilltops near Gaza to watch bombardments, treating the explosions as entertainment. Videos circulated of children chanting "Death to Arabs" in schoolyards or at football matches. Settler youths posed for photographs with burning Palestinian homes in the background.

This was not simply propaganda from outside critics. It was documented in Israeli media, recorded in testimonies, and acknowledged by educators and human rights groups. A culture of cruelty had taken root, in which violence was not only justified but celebrated.

How does such a culture emerge? Psychologists point to the siege mentality deeply embedded in Zionism, the constant invocation of existential threat, and the projection of fear onto an "other" cast as subhuman. When leaders frame an entire people as animals, parasites, or biblical enemies, cruelty becomes not only permissible but righteous.

**The Gaza War as Spectacle**

The Gaza war of 2023 to 2025 intensified this trend. Bombing campaigns were cheered on social media with hashtags celebrating destruction. Right-wing politicians boasted of the scale of devastation. One minister declared: "There are no innocents in Gaza."

Civilian suffering was dismissed not as collateral damage but as a legitimate goal. Starvation was framed as strategy. Even humanitarian aid was described as a weapon to be withheld until Palestinians surrendered. In this context, cruelty was not a by-product of war; it was its essence.

The spectacle of destruction replaced the discourse of defence. Israel no longer claimed reluctantly to protect itself. It claimed proudly to annihilate.

**From Dehumanisation to Genocide**

The UN Commission of Inquiry later concluded that such rhetoric and actions demonstrated genocidal intent. The language of leaders, the policies of starvation and mass bombardment, and the systematic targeting of civilians all pointed to a deliberate effort to destroy a people.

This was not accidental. Genocide always begins with words, with the denial of humanity and the reduction of people to pests, beasts, or enemies of God. In Israel's case, the language had long been present but constrained. Under Netanyahu's far-right coalition, the constraints fell away. The mask slipped, and the language of annihilation became the official discourse of the state.

**The Cost of Cruelty**

The cost of this dehumanisation is not borne only by Palestinians. It corrodes Israeli society itself. A people taught to see cruelty as natural cannot sustain democracy. A culture that celebrates bombardment cannot also nurture compassion. Children raised to chant for death will not grow up to build peace.

This is the deeper tragedy of Zionism in its late stage. By defining Palestinians as less than human, it has deformed Israelis themselves. What began as a project of national rebirth has become a project of moral decay, in which survival is purchased at the price of humanity.

## Section 3 – Violence in the West Bank and Gaza

Language shapes reality, but in Israel and the occupied territories, the dehumanising words of leaders and settlers were not left as rhetoric. They translated directly into acts of violence. By the mid-2020s, the West Bank and Gaza were theatres of unrelenting brutality, where settlers attacked villages with impunity and the Israeli military imposed sieges that starved millions. What had once been dismissed as sporadic or exceptional became systemic, a culture of violence legitimised by the state.

### Settler Pogroms in the West Bank

In the West Bank, settler violence escalated to levels unseen in decades. Palestinian homes were torched, olive groves uprooted, and families beaten in the night. Entire villages were attacked by mobs who marched under the protection, or indifference, of Israeli soldiers. Human rights organisations documented a sharp rise in so-called "price tag" attacks, acts of collective punishment carried out against Palestinians in response to any resistance, real or imagined.

The brazenness was striking. Settlers posted videos of their assaults online. Politicians excused the violence as "understandable frustration". Ministers in Netanyahu's government openly encouraged settlement expansion, and some suggested that Palestinian villages should be "emptied". What once might have been condemned as fringe vigilantism became state-sanctioned terror against an occupied population.

### The Gaza War as Total War

In Gaza, violence was elevated to the level of policy. After the Hamas attacks of October 2023, Israel launched a campaign that quickly surpassed any previous conflict in scale and ferocity. Entire neighbourhoods were flattened, hospitals destroyed, and aid convoys blocked. Civilian infrastructure, including water plants, schools, and refugee shelters, was deliberately targeted.

The siege was total. Fuel and electricity were cut. Food and medicine were withheld. International organisations reported famine conditions across Gaza, with children dying of hunger in full view of the world. Israeli officials spoke openly of using starvation as a weapon, claiming that "no aid should enter until the hostages are released".

This was not the accidental consequence of war. It was its deliberate design. The goal was not only to weaken Hamas but to render Gaza unliveable. In the words of one Israeli minister: "We will erase Gaza from the face of the earth."

## Impunity as Policy

The common thread between West Bank pogroms and the Gaza war was impunity. Settlers knew they would not be punished. Soldiers knew their actions would not be questioned. Ministers knew their words would not be challenged by allies abroad.

This impunity was reinforced by Israel's closest partners. Washington repeated the mantra of "Israel's right to self-defence" even as evidence of war crimes mounted. London echoed the same language, framing atrocities as regrettable but necessary. The international shield allowed violence to expand unchecked, creating a situation in which cruelty was not hidden but flaunted.

## The Collapse of the Moral Army Myth

For decades, Israel had promoted the image of the "most moral army in the world". That myth collapsed in Gaza. Drone footage of bombings, testimonies of aid workers, and satellite images of devastation all circulated globally in real time. The world could see what was happening: the deliberate targeting of civilians, the destruction of livelihoods, and the attempt to break a people's will through suffering.

In the West Bank, the same collapse played out on a smaller scale. Settlers who once acted in the shadows now carried out attacks in broad daylight, confident that cameras or courts would not hold them accountable. The distinction between state violence and private terror dissolved. Both served the same purpose, and both drew from the same culture of impunity.

### Violence as the Logic of Zionism

What these events revealed was not an aberration but the logic of late-stage Zionism. A movement that defined itself through exclusion, expansion, and fear inevitably produced violence as its organising principle. Where compromise was impossible and equality unthinkable, domination became the only option.

In Gaza, this meant the attempt to destroy an entire population. In the West Bank, it meant gradual ethnic cleansing by attrition: burning fields, demolishing homes, denying permits, and driving people away through constant terror. Both reflected the same mindset, that Palestinians were not partners to live with but obstacles to be removed.

### The Consequences of Normalised Violence

The consequences extended far beyond the occupied territories. The culture of impunity that allowed soldiers to bomb hospitals and settlers to torch homes also corroded Israeli democracy itself. A state that normalises violence abroad inevitably imports it at home, turning politics into warfare and opponents into enemies.

The fractures I described in Section 1, between secular and religious, left and right, and Jewish and Palestinian citizens, were sharpened by this normalisation. Violence was not only external; it became the default mode of politics within Israel itself.

## Section 4 – The Diaspora Breaks Away

For decades, Zionism's claim to legitimacy rested not only on state power but on its connection to the wider Jewish world. Israel presented itself as the homeland of all Jews, the centre of Jewish identity, the protector of a people scarred by centuries of persecution. To criticise Israel was often framed as a betrayal of Jewish solidarity itself.

But by the 2020s, this narrative began to fracture. Among Jewish communities abroad, especially in the United States and Europe, support for Israel was no longer automatic. Generational change, shifting moral priorities, and the undeniable evidence of occupation and war crimes produced a rupture between Israel and its diaspora. The movement that once claimed to unite Jews across the globe was now dividing them.

**The American Shift**

The most striking shift came in the United States, home to the world's largest Jewish population outside Israel. For older generations, Israel remained a sacred cause, a guarantee against a repeat of the Holocaust, and a homeland to be defended regardless of flaws. Synagogues rallied for Israel, community leaders aligned with AIPAC, and criticism of Zionism was often silenced as antisemitism.

But younger Jews, raised in an era of social justice movements, saw Israel differently. They saw images of checkpoints, bombed-out schools in Gaza, and settlers torching Palestinian villages. They compared these with the struggles of Black Lives Matter, of Indigenous peoples, and of other oppressed groups. To them, Israel did not embody safety or justice; it embodied oppression.

Organisations such as If Not Now and Jewish Voice for Peace emerged as powerful dissenting voices, declaring "Not in our name" and challenging the conflation of Judaism with Zionism. On U.S. campuses, Jewish students joined pro-Palestinian protests, sometimes facing backlash from older community leaders who accused them of betrayal and called them 'self-hating Jews'. The rift was generational, ideological, and irreconcilable.

## Europe and the UK

In Europe, the picture was similar. In the UK, the Labour Party's internal battles over antisemitism had once made criticism of Israel politically toxic. Yet by the Gaza war of 2023 to 2025, the scale of devastation made silence impossible. Jewish groups such as Na'amod openly declared opposition to occupation and settlement expansion. British Jews, particularly younger ones, increasingly rejected unconditional support for Israel, insisting that Jewish values demanded solidarity with the oppressed rather than the oppressor.

Elsewhere in Europe, the pattern repeated. Once-unquestioned support for Zionism gave way to moral unease, then to open dissent. Demonstrations in cities such as Paris, Berlin and Dublin saw Jewish activists marching alongside Palestinians, carrying banners declaring "Jews Against Genocide".

## The Gaza Catalyst

The Gaza war was the catalyst for this rupture. The images of starvation, mass bombardment and children pulled from rubble were impossible to reconcile with the rhetoric of "the most moral army in the world". Diaspora Jews who had long defended Israel found themselves unable to explain, let alone justify, what they were seeing.

The UN's genocide determination deepened the crisis. For many diaspora Jews, the charge cut to the core of identity. How could a state founded in the shadow of the Holocaust now stand accused of genocide? How could they defend Israel without becoming complicit in atrocity? For many, the answer was simple: they could not.

## The Weaponisation of Antisemitism

Netanyahu and his allies responded by doubling down on a familiar strategy: equating anti-Zionism with antisemitism. Criticism of Israel, they insisted, was nothing more than Jew-hatred in disguise. Internationally, this tactic had some effect, silencing politicians and institutions fearful of being branded antisemitic.

But within the diaspora itself, the strategy backfired. Younger Jews resented being told that to oppose war crimes was to betray their heritage. They saw in this conflation not the protection of Jews but the exploitation of Jewish suffering to justify state violence. The more Netanyahu weaponised antisemitism, the more alienated many diaspora Jews became.

## A Broken Bond

The result was a profound rupture. For the first time since 1948, Zionism could no longer claim the unqualified loyalty of global Jewry. The idea that Israel spoke for all Jews collapsed under the weight of dissent. Instead of a source of unity, Israel became a source of division. Families split, synagogues fractured, and community organisations fought bitterly over whether to criticise or defend the state.

This rupture carries profound consequences. Zionism's moral claim has always been tied to its status as the collective project of the Jewish people. If that claim is rejected by growing numbers of Jews themselves, the project stands exposed as parochial rather than universal, and coercive rather than consensual.

## Ireland's Contrast

Ireland offers a striking counterpoint. Having endured its own colonial subjugation, Ireland became one of the most vocal critics of Israeli settlements and the Gaza war. Where diaspora Jews fractured over Israel's actions, Ireland's position was forged by its history, a sense of empathy for Palestinians rooted in the lived memory of occupation, partition, and the denial of national rights.

This contrast underscores the uniqueness of the diaspora rupture. Support for Israel is no longer guaranteed even among those for whom it was meant to be most natural. The moral centre of Zionism is shifting, and for many, collapsing.

## Section 5 – The Charge of Genocide

Few words carry as much weight as genocide. It is the crime of crimes, the ultimate condemnation under international law, and the spectre that has haunted Jewish history since the Holocaust. For Israel, a state founded in the wake of that catastrophe, to be accused of genocide against another people was not merely a legal challenge. It was a profound moral rupture. By the mid-2020s, that accusation was no longer confined to activists or critics. It was being levelled by the United Nations itself.

### The UN Commission of Inquiry

In June 2025, the UN Independent International Commission of Inquiry published its most damning report yet. Chaired by Navi Pillay, the former UN High Commissioner for Human Rights, the Commission concluded bluntly:

"The Commission finds that Israel is responsible for the commission of genocide in Gaza… It is clear that there is an intent to destroy the Palestinians in Gaza through acts that meet the criteria set forth in the Genocide Convention."

The report identified four of the five genocidal acts defined in the 1948 Genocide Convention:

• Killing members of the group.

• Causing serious bodily or mental harm.

• Inflicting conditions of life calculated to bring about physical destruction.

• Imposing measures intended to prevent births.

These were not abstract accusations. The Commission documented starvation as policy, systematic bombardment of civilian infrastructure, deliberate obstruction of humanitarian aid, and rhetoric from senior ministers calling for the annihilation of Gaza's population.

**Truth Under Fire: Silencing the Witnesses**

One of the starkest indicators of intent in Gaza has been the unprecedented killing of journalists. In just twenty months of war, over one hundred and fifty journalists were killed by Israeli forces, more than the combined total killed during World War I, World War II, the Korean War and the Vietnam War. Nearly all were Palestinian.

Many were killed while reporting from clearly marked press positions, or even after sharing their coordinates with the Israeli military. The Committee to Protect Journalists has described Gaza as the deadliest conflict for journalists in modern history.

This pattern cannot be dismissed as collateral damage. It reflects a deliberate attempt to silence witnesses, erase testimony and control the narrative of the war. Just as mass graves from 1948 were paved over and the Nakba denied, so today's atrocities are hidden beneath rubble and buried with the reporters who documented them.

In the logic of genocide, it is not enough to destroy a people. One must also destroy the evidence of their destruction.

**A Shattering Paradox**

For Palestinians, the report validated decades of testimony. For Israelis, it was dismissed as slander. For the world at large, however, the paradox was inescapable. The state created as a refuge after genocide now stood accused of committing one.

This inversion struck at the very heart of Zionism's legitimacy. From its inception, Zionism had been justified not only as a nationalist project but as a moral one. It was the answer to a world that had failed to protect Jews from extermination. Yet if Israel itself now practised exterminatory policies, what remained of that moral claim?

## Western Complicity

Western governments responded with a mixture of silence and denial. The United States dismissed the report as biased, the UK echoed Israeli talking points about self-defence, and European leaders urged restraint while continuing arms sales.

Yet this silence was not cost-free. Across Western societies, publics recoiled at the images from Gaza and the clarity of the UN's language. The gulf between governments and citizens widened. Demonstrations swept European capitals. University campuses became centres of protest. Churches, unions and civic groups began to call for boycotts and divestment.

The gap between elite complicity and popular outrage became a defining feature of the legitimacy crisis.

## The Role of the International Courts

Beyond the UN Commission, other institutions moved. The International Court of Justice issued provisional measures ordering Israel to allow humanitarian aid and refrain from genocidal acts, orders Israel largely ignored. The International Criminal Court opened investigations into Israeli leaders for war crimes and crimes against humanity.

While Israel and its allies dismissed these proceedings as politicised, the cumulative effect was unmistakable. The state that once demanded international law as protection was now the subject of its gravest accusations.

For diaspora Jews, the genocide charge was particularly wrenching. How could a people whose identity had been shaped by the memory of Auschwitz now be accused of inflicting genocide on others? For some, it was a moment of denial, and the charge was dismissed as antisemitism in another guise. For others, it was the breaking point, a moral line that could not be crossed. Synagogues and community groups fractured over the question. Families divided. The slogan *Never Again* was suddenly contested. Never again for whom?

### The Global South Steps Forward

While the West equivocated, the Global South was less hesitant. South Africa led the charge at the ICJ, framing Israel's actions as a continuation of colonial apartheid and demanding accountability. Latin American countries severed diplomatic ties. Arab states, long hesitant to confront Israel directly, seized upon the genocide determination to harden their stance.

This global shift further isolated Israel. What had once been framed as a Western-aligned democracy was increasingly seen as a rogue state, protected only by the shield of United States power.

The charge of genocide did more than condemn specific acts. It reframed the entire narrative of Zionism. If Palestinians were not simply victims of occupation but victims of genocide, then Zionism was not merely flawed. It was criminal. The vocabulary of debate shifted. No longer was this a question of disputed borders or failed peace processes. It was a question of whether a state could commit the very crime that had justified its creation.

The power of the word genocide lies in its irreversibility. A state accused of it cannot easily recover its moral standing, no matter how the war ends. The accusation lingers, shaping perception, law and memory.

For Israel, the charge marked the point at which its legitimacy crisis became existential.

## Section 6 – The Global Legitimacy Crisis

The charge of genocide did not exist in a vacuum. It reverberated across the globe, transforming the way Israel was perceived not only by its adversaries but also by its allies and once silent partners. For decades, Israel had enjoyed near automatic legitimacy in Western capitals, sustained by Holocaust memory, diaspora solidarity and the narrative of democracy under siege. By the mid 2020s, that legitimacy was collapsing.

### The Erosion of Western Support

The United States and the United Kingdom remained Israel's staunchest defenders. Successive administrations in Washington repeated the mantra of "Israel's right to self defence", while London's leaders, including Prime Minister Keir Starmer, tied their political identities to open support for Zionism. Yet beneath the rhetoric, cracks were visible.

In Congress, younger Democratic lawmakers openly challenged United States military aid. Trade unions called for divestment. University campuses erupted in protest, forcing leaders to confront dissent within their own constituencies. In Britain, massive demonstrations in London turned the city into a weekly centre of protest, often dwarfing government rallies of support.

The gulf between governments and citizens widened. Leaders clung to the old formulas. Publics moved on. Legitimacy in Western societies was no longer guaranteed from the bottom up but imposed from the top down, fragile, strained and increasingly unsustainable.

### Europe's Shifting Tone

In Europe, the shift was even clearer. Countries such as Ireland, Spain, Belgium and Norway recognised Palestine or pushed hard for recognition. The European Union, once reluctant to criticise Israel too directly, found itself forced to confront growing outrage among its citizens. European parliaments debated arms embargoes. Courts heard cases against companies complicit in occupation.

Even Germany, long Israel's most steadfast European ally, faced intense internal debate. While official policy remained protective, public opinion surveys showed a dramatic decline in sympathy for Israel, especially among younger generations. The weight of the genocide determination made silence harder to justify.

## The Global South Steps Forward

If the West equivocated, the Global South did not. South Africa led the case against Israel at the International Court of Justice, framing its actions as part of the wider struggle against settler colonialism and apartheid. Latin American countries, including Colombia and Chile, cut diplomatic ties. In Asia and Africa, solidarity with Palestine became a rallying point of resistance to Western double standards.

This alignment was not new. The Non Aligned Movement had long supported Palestinians, but the Gaza war of 2023 to 2025 gave it new urgency. Israel was no longer just seen as a regional aggressor. It was seen as a test case for whether international law applied universally or only to the powerless.

## Protest and Uprising from Below

The most visible sign of the legitimacy crisis was on the streets. From New York to Berlin, Johannesburg to Jakarta, millions marched in solidarity with Palestinians. In some cities, protests rivalled those of the anti Iraq War movement. In others, they were even larger. The images of children starving in Gaza, of journalists killed in record numbers, and of aid convoys bombed were too visceral to ignore.

Boycott, Divestment and Sanctions, once marginalised as a fringe campaign, found new mainstream resonance. Cultural figures, athletes and academics joined calls for isolation. University encampments became focal points of protest, echoing the anti apartheid struggles of the 1980s.

Israel, once a cause of admiration, had become a cause of outrage.

## Isolation and Defiance

Faced with this legitimacy crisis, Israel chose not compromise but defiance. Netanyahu and his far right allies framed the protests,

UN reports and international court rulings as part of a global conspiracy. They cast Israel as a fortress under siege not only from Hamas but from an antisemitic world.

This strategy found some resonance among allies and domestic supporters. However, globally it deepened the sense of isolation. A state that relied on moral legitimacy as much as military power now stood stripped of both.

**The Hollowing of Legitimacy**

The cumulative effect was stark. In the space of two decades, Israel had gone from being hailed as a miracle democracy to being accused of genocide and widely regarded as a pariah. Its legitimacy was no longer grounded in moral claim but in the raw shield of United States power.

This was not merely a shift in perception. It was a transformation in the global order. For the first time, Israel found itself on the wrong side of history not only in the Arab world but across much of the globe. Zionism's universal appeal, a story of survival, justice and rebirth, had given way to its universal condemnation as a story of domination, cruelty and decay.

**Section 7 – Conclusion: The Hollow State**

By the mid-2020s, the image of Israel as a vibrant democracy, a moral project, and a source of Jewish unity had all but collapsed. What remained was a state fractured within, brutal without, and increasingly isolated abroad. The fractures of Israeli society, between secular and religious, left and right, Jewish and Palestinian citizens, mirrored the fractures in its legitimacy across the world.

The language of democracy had given way to the language of dehumanisation. Palestinians were not neighbours but "animals," their cities not communities but "nests of terror." Violence in the West Bank and Gaza made clear that such words were not rhetorical excess but political intent. Pogroms and bombardments were not accidents; they were the lived reality of a movement that could no longer imagine coexistence.

The rupture with the diaspora deepened the crisis. Zionism had once claimed to speak for all Jews, to embody their hopes and guarantee their survival. Now it divided families and communities, as younger generations declared, "not in our name." The moral claim of universality, once central to the project, was collapsing from within.

The UN's determination that Israel was committing genocide sealed the transformation. The state that had been born in the shadow of genocide now stood accused of perpetrating it. Journalists were killed in record numbers, evidence was buried, and truth itself became a target.

Equally damning was the fate of aid workers. Convoys marked with red crosses and ambulances clearly identified as humanitarian were not spared. In one of the most shocking episodes, an ambulance crew was gunned down, their bodies loaded into the very vehicle that had carried the wounded, before Israeli bulldozers shoved the ambulance into a pit and covered it with earth. The evidence might have vanished but for mobile phone signals and leaked drone footage that exposed the crime. The world could no longer look away. To defend Israel was no longer to defend democracy but to defend atrocity.

Globally, Israel's shield narrowed to a handful of governments, above all the United States and the United Kingdom. Even there, legitimacy was fragile, imposed by political elites and rejected by growing majorities. In the Global South, Israel became a symbol of Western hypocrisy, the proof that international law was applied only selectively.

What emerged was a hollow state. Militarily powerful yet morally bankrupt, politically defiant yet internationally isolated,

Israel embodied the late-stage crisis of Zionism. It could dominate, but it could not persuade. It could survive, but it could not inspire.

This is the paradox of Zionism in the 21st century. Born as a movement of rebirth, it has become a movement of decay. Once claiming to restore Jewish dignity, it now brings shame and division. Once promising democracy, it now practises apartheid and flirts with authoritarianism. Once pleading "never again," it now stands accused of "again."

In the next chapter I will turn to the question of what comes after this fracture. If Zionism is hollowed out, what fills the void? Resistance movements, international solidarity, and alternative visions of justice are already shaping the debate. Chapter 11 will explore these possibilities, and the fears, hopes, and struggles that define the world after Zionism's legitimacy has collapsed.

# CHAPTER ELEVEN –
# Authoritarian by Design.

## Section 1 – Crisis Politics and the Permanent Emergency

Israel has always lived in the language of emergency. From its inception, the state framed its existence as precarious, surrounded by enemies, forever on the brink of annihilation. This sense of permanent threat was not only a reflection of geopolitical realities, it became a governing strategy. The politics of crisis allowed leaders to centralise power, silence dissent, and justify measures that in any other democracy would be intolerable.

### The Normalisation of Emergency

From the declaration of independence in 1948, Israel ruled under a legal state of emergency that has never been fully lifted. Emergency regulations inherited from the British Mandate, themselves colonial tools, were used to justify land confiscations, military tribunals, and restrictions on Palestinian citizens of Israel. What was meant to be temporary became permanent, embedding exceptional powers into the everyday structure of governance.

By the 21st century, this culture of emergency had metastasised. The constant invocation of existential threats, from Hamas rockets to Hezbollah raids, from Iran's nuclear ambitions to the spectre of "delegitimisation" abroad, created a political atmosphere in which any measure could be justified. Surveillance, detention without trial, censorship, and collective punishment were all defended as unfortunate necessities of survival.

### Netanyahu and the Politics of Perpetual War

No figure has embodied this strategy more fully than Benjamin Netanyahu. Facing corruption trials, electoral challenges, and deep divisions within Israeli society, Netanyahu repeatedly turned to war as his political lifeline. The Gaza campaigns of 2023 to 2025 were not only military operations; they were political gambits designed to preserve his premiership, rally his fractured coalition, and deflect attention from domestic scandal.

Netanyahu's genius, and his cynicism, lay in his ability to merge personal survival with national survival. His message was clear: to question him was to endanger the state itself. Thus, war became not just defence but a form of political theatre, a means of converting vulnerability into dominance.

**The Global Echo: Authoritarian Crisis Politics**

In this, Netanyahu was hardly unique. The strategy of ruling through crisis is a hallmark of authoritarian regimes. Viktor Orbán in Hungary invoked the "migrant crisis" to dismantle democratic checks and consolidate power. Recep Tayyip Erdoğan in Turkey exploited the failed coup attempt of 2016 to purge institutions and crush dissent. In 2025, Donald Trump in the United States, though constrained by constitutional limits, repeatedly framed immigration, crime, and pandemics as existential threats to justify exceptional powers.

Israel's difference lies in the duration and intensity of this strategy. While other regimes invoke crisis episodically, Israel has made it permanent. Every year, every election, every news cycle is saturated with the language of siege. This perpetual emergency blurs the line between democracy and authoritarianism, creating a system where normal politics is impossible because the state itself is always said to be on the brink.

The consequences of this strategy reach beyond politics into culture. A society conditioned to see itself as forever under attack becomes a society willing to accept cruelty as necessity. Palestinians are cast not as neighbours but as existential enemies; dissenters are branded as traitors; human rights organisations are accused of undermining national security.

In this way, the permanent emergency does not merely justify authoritarian measures. It shapes national identity itself. Israel is no longer simply a state that uses emergency powers; it is a state defined by them.

## Section 2 – The Architecture of Control

If crisis politics created the justification for authoritarianism, the architecture of control provided its machinery. Israel has constructed one of the most elaborate systems of domination in modern history, a lattice of laws, military decrees, surveillance technologies, and territorial fragmentation designed to ensure permanent supremacy over Palestinians. It is not incidental to Zionism; it is the very structure through which Zionism sustains itself.

### Military Law as a Permanent Fixture

In the West Bank, Palestinians live under military law that governs nearly every aspect of life. Permits are required to build a home, travel to work, harvest crops, or seek medical care. Military tribunals prosecute civilians, often children, with conviction rates exceeding 95 per cent. In contrast, Jewish settlers in the same territory live under Israeli civil law, enjoying full rights of citizenship.

This dual system, one law for Jews and another for Palestinians, has led international human rights groups, including Amnesty International and Human Rights Watch, to declare Israel an apartheid state. It is apartheid not as metaphor but as lived reality, enshrined in checkpoints, raids, demolitions, and bureaucratic harassment.

Palestinian citizens of Israel, nearly 20 per cent of the population, face a subtler but no less insidious framework. More than 65 laws discriminate in access to land, housing, education, and political expression. The 2018 Nation-State Law enshrined Jewish supremacy in constitutional form, declaring that only Jews have the right to self-determination in the land. Arabic, once an official language, was demoted.

These laws do not exist in isolation. They form a legal cage that signals to Palestinian citizens that they may reside within the state but never truly belong to it. The architecture of control operates not only in the occupied territories but also within Israel's recognised borders.

### Checkpoints, Walls, and Settlements

The physical landscape is equally instructive. Checkpoints carve Palestinian life into disconnected enclaves, reducing travel between cities into hours-long ordeals. The separation wall, eight metres high in places and cutting through neighbourhoods, farms, and even cemeteries, embodies the logic of exclusion in concrete. Settlements, illegal under international law, expand relentlessly, protected by soldiers and connected by highways Palestinians cannot use.

This geography is not accidental. It is designed to fragment Palestinian society, to prevent collective political action, and to normalise domination as the everyday condition of life.

### Technological Domination

If walls and checkpoints represent the old architecture of control, new technologies provide the updated model. Israel has pioneered sophisticated surveillance systems, including facial recognition software deployed in Hebron, predictive policing algorithms, and spyware such as Pegasus, sold globally but first tested on Palestinians.

These technologies create a digital panopticon in which Palestinians are constantly monitored, their movements tracked, and their communications intercepted. Artificial intelligence is even used to generate targeting lists for drone strikes, automating decisions about life and death.

The same tools are exported abroad, making Israel not only a practitioner of authoritarian control but also a global supplier of its instruments. From Latin America to Africa, regimes purchase Israeli surveillance technology tested on Palestinians, spreading the logic of occupation worldwide.

**Control by Design**

The cumulative effect is clear. Zionism has produced not a democracy with flaws but a system of control designed from the ground up. The legal frameworks, physical barriers, and technological apparatus are not temporary measures in response to crisis. They are permanent structures that define the state itself.

In this sense, Israel is not a democracy that occasionally slips into authoritarianism. It is an authoritarian state with democratic trappings for its Jewish citizens. For Palestinians, whether in Gaza, the West Bank, or within Israel itself, the reality is one of domination institutionalised into every layer of governance.

## Section 3 – Manufactured Enemies

Authoritarian regimes thrive on enemies. They require threats, internal and external, to justify their grip on power. In Israel, Zionism has institutionalised this logic, producing an endless cycle of manufactured enemies who serve to sustain the architecture of control. Some are real adversaries, others exaggerated, and still others conjured by rhetoric and propaganda. All serve the same purpose: to keep the state in a perpetual posture of siege.

**The Palestinian as the Eternal Enemy**

From the earliest days of the state, Palestinians have been cast not as neighbours with legitimate rights but as existential threats. This framing reduces every demand for dignity, from housing permits to the right of return, into an act of war. Children throwing stones are described as terrorists; farmers cultivating olive groves are accused of encroachment; protesters marching unarmed are branded as Hamas sympathisers.

The effect is to collapse all distinctions. Civilian and combatant, resistance and terrorism, grievance and threat, all are merged into a single category: the enemy. By stripping Palestinians of nuance, Israel sustains its narrative of eternal self-defence, even when it is the aggressor.

Externally, Iran has become the most useful enemy. For decades, Israel has portrayed Iran as a nuclear-obsessed aggressor intent on Israel's destruction. While Tehran's rhetoric often plays into this image, the threat has been amplified to serve domestic and diplomatic purposes. By presenting Iran as an existential danger, Israel not only justifies its militarisation but secures endless flows of U.S. aid and Western diplomatic cover.

The narrative of Iran as a looming apocalypse sustains the permanent emergency. Every Israeli government since the 1990s has invoked the Iranian threat, ensuring that security dominates politics and deflects attention from domestic inequality or corruption.

The enemy is not only at home or across borders; it is also abroad, in the form of international critics. Human rights organisations, UN investigators, diaspora dissenters, all are routinely smeared as antisemitic. The conflation of anti-Zionism with antisemitism is one of Israel's most effective tools, silencing criticism and painting dissent as bigotry.

This strategy manufactures an endless supply of enemies beyond Israel's borders. Activists in London, students in New York, parliamentarians in Dublin, all become part of a supposed conspiracy against the Jewish state. The result is to transform global accountability into another front in Israel's self-declared war of survival.

**The Necessity of Enemies**

This endless generation of enemies is not a side effect of Zionism; it is its lifeblood. Without existential threats, the justification for military domination, surveillance, and emergency governance would collapse. Enemies sustain the narrative of siege, and the narrative of siege sustains authoritarian power.

Other authoritarian regimes follow the same pattern. Orbán has migrants, Erdoğan has the Kurds, Putin has NATO, Trump had immigrants and "deep state" conspirators. Netanyahu has Palestinians, Iran, and critics everywhere. Each serves as proof that the state must remain on permanent war footing, that dissent is betrayal, and that domination is survival.

**A Society Shaped by Enmity**

The cost of this enemy-making is profound. A society conditioned to see itself surrounded by threats becomes incapable of imagining peace. Children grow up learning not about neighbours but about enemies. Politics is reduced to the management of fear. And leaders who might otherwise fall to corruption or incompetence survive by conjuring up new dangers.

Thus, the authoritarian design of Zionism is not sustained by force alone. It is sustained by fear, fear carefully cultivated through the manufacture of endless enemies.

## Section 4 – The Collapse of Democracy

This slogan was repeated so often that it became a mantra in diplomatic circles, in diaspora communities, and even in the language of Western leaders. By the 2020s, however, the façade had collapsed. What remained was not a democracy with flaws, but a deeply illiberal ethnocracy sustained by emergency powers, segregation, and authoritarian design.

## Judicial Reform and the Assault on the Rule of Law

The most visible crack appeared in 2023, when Netanyahu's government launched sweeping judicial reforms aimed at neutering the Supreme Court. The Court had long been Israel's only institution with even limited capacity to check government excesses. By curbing its power, Netanyahu sought to shield himself from corruption charges and give his far-right coalition freedom to legislate without constraint.

This assault triggered massive protests across Israel, drawing hundreds of thousands into the streets. Yet the protests, while dramatic, revealed the limits of democratic resistance. Many demonstrators waved Israeli flags and spoke passionately about saving democracy, but their vision of democracy was largely confined to Jewish Israelis. The occupation, apartheid laws, and the ongoing strangulation of Gaza were often absent from their rhetoric.

The Gaza war of 2023–25 provided Netanyahu with the perfect cover to push authoritarian consolidation further. Under the guise of wartime unity, critics were silenced, journalists detained, and political debate narrowed. Emergency regulations justified censorship, mass arrests, and the banning of Palestinian political organisations.

The very war that was presented as proof of Israel's democracy under siege became the instrument by which democracy was hollowed out. A state of perpetual emergency, already decades old, now fused seamlessly with open authoritarian practices.

## The Erosion of Legal Accountability

Netanyahu's corruption trials, once thought to threaten his political survival, faded into irrelevance amid the chaos of war. By entangling his personal fortunes with the fate of the nation, Netanyahu transformed legal accountability into a partisan question. To prosecute him was to weaken Israel, to oppose him was to embolden its enemies.

In this way, democratic institutions were not only undermined but delegitimised. Courts, prosecutors, and human rights defenders were cast as obstacles to survival. What began as the defence of a prime minister became the erosion of the very possibility of independent oversight.

**From Ethnocracy to Authoritarianism**

Some argue that Israel was never a full democracy, given its dual legal systems and institutional discrimination against Palestinians. Even by its own limited definition of democracy for Jews, the 2020s marked a turning point. What remained was an ethnocracy sliding openly into authoritarianism, in which loyalty to the state and its leaders mattered more than the rule of law, minority rights, or dissent.

The rhetoric of "the only democracy in the Middle East" now rang hollow. The international community could no longer reconcile that claim with images of journalists executed, aid workers bulldozed, or children starved. Democracy was not collapsing suddenly; it was being revealed for what it always was, a façade masking authoritarian design.

**The Global Comparison**

In this trajectory, Israel mirrored broader global patterns. Trump's America, Bolsonaro's Brazil, Modi's India, Orbán's Hungary, each showed how democracies can erode from within, how legal systems can be weaponised, and how emergency powers can become permanent. Israel's case, however, was more extreme. Its authoritarian drift was not a betrayal of Zionism; it was its fulfilment.

# Section 5 – Resistance Within Israel

Within Israel, movements emerged to challenge Netanyahu's corruption, judicial reform, and the erosion of civil liberties. These protests revealed that democratic instincts were not entirely extinguished, yet they also exposed the limits of resistance in a state built on occupation and exclusion.

**The Judicial Reform Protests**

In 2023, hundreds of thousands of Israelis took to the streets against Netanyahu's plan to weaken the Supreme Court. Week after week, demonstrators filled Tel Aviv and Jerusalem, waving Israeli flags and chanting about democracy. For many, it was the largest mobilisation in the state's history. The protests forced temporary pauses in the reform process and revealed the depth of unease with Netanyahu's power grab.

Yet the protests also carried contradictions. Many participants fought passionately for judicial independence but ignored or downplayed the Court's role in upholding the occupation and discriminating against Palestinians. Democracy, for much of this movement, meant preserving rights for Jewish Israelis rather than extending them universally. This selective vision limited the protests' transformative potential.

Resistance also emerged from within the military itself. During the height of the judicial reform crisis, hundreds of Israeli Air Force reservists threatened to refuse service, arguing that they could not fight for a government dismantling democracy. Their dissent was significant. The military is the bedrock of Israeli society, and open refusal hinted at cracks in the façade of unity.

However, this dissent too was circumscribed. While reservists objected to authoritarian governance at home, few extended their critique to the occupation or Gaza war. Their protest was framed as protecting Israel's internal democracy rather than challenging its external domination.

Palestinian citizens of Israel, nearly one-fifth of the population, continued to resist through political organisation, cultural expression, and solidarity with Gaza and the West Bank. Yet their voices were heavily policed. Political parties faced disqualification, activists were surveilled, and expressions of sympathy for Gaza were criminalised as support for terrorism.

Despite these restrictions, Palestinian citizens remained a vital counterpoint to authoritarian consolidation, challenging both Jewish supremacy and militarism. Their marginalisation within Israeli politics meant their resistance was often invisible to the majority.

### Human Rights Organisations Under Siege

Israeli human rights groups such as B'Tselem and Breaking the Silence continued documenting abuses, publishing reports on war crimes, and amplifying Palestinian voices. Their work gained international traction but came at a cost. They were branded as traitors, defunded, and targeted by smear campaigns.

The existence of such groups highlights that authoritarianism is not total. Yet the hostility they faced illustrates the shrinking space for dissent. Their persistence is remarkable, but their influence within Israel is limited by a political culture that increasingly equates criticism with betrayal.

Taken together, these movements reveal both the resilience and fragility of democratic instincts in Israel. Resistance exists in protests, in military dissent, in minority voices, and in civil society. But it is bounded by Zionism's core exclusion: the refusal to extend equality to Palestinians. As long as resistance defends only a democracy for Jews, it cannot address the deeper authoritarian design of the state.

The paradox of resistance in Israel is that it often defends a hollow democracy. Protesters demand checks and balances, but only within the ethnocratic framework. Soldiers refuse to serve for Netanyahu but not for the occupation. Human rights groups speak out but are dismissed as fringe.

Thus, resistance within Israel exposes the cracks in authoritarianism, but it also reveals the structural limits of what can be imagined inside the Zionist project.

## Section 6 – Conclusion: Authoritarianism as Destiny

The authoritarian turn in Israel is often described as a recent slide, a tragic departure from its democratic promise. But to see it this way is to misunderstand both the history and the design of Zionism. Authoritarianism in Israel is not an accident. It is not the product of one leader or one government. It is the logical outcome of a system built on exclusion, domination, and fear.

What we see in Netanyahu's Israel is not the betrayal of Zionism's ideals but their fulfilment. A state that privileges one ethnic group over another cannot be fully democratic. A state that rules millions under military law while granting full rights to others cannot sustain liberal norms. A state that defines survival through perpetual crisis cannot avoid centralising power.

The occupation, the siege of Gaza, the surveillance systems, and the endless invocation of enemies are not deviations from democracy. They are the architecture of authoritarianism, built into the project from its inception.

### The Illusion of Democracy

The protests of 2023, the judicial reform battles, and the international debates about "saving Israeli democracy" all cling to an illusion. They assume there was once a democracy to preserve. But the reality is that democracy in Israel was always partial, confined to Jews, and fragile even within that limited scope. For Palestinians, authoritarianism was never a threat on the horizon. It was the daily reality of checkpoints, raids, demolitions, and surveillance.

By the 2020s, the illusion could no longer be maintained. What remained was the revelation that Israel was not a democracy sliding into authoritarianism but an authoritarian state with democratic trappings for some of its citizens.

This trajectory places Israel alongside other late-stage authoritarian projects: South Africa under apartheid, Rhodesia before its collapse, and even colonial Ireland under British rule. Each justified domination through security rhetoric. Each claimed exceptionalism. Each eventually revealed the authoritarian core of its design.

Israel's distinctiveness lies in its success at exporting its model. Surveillance systems tested on Palestinians are now used worldwide. The politics of permanent emergency resonates with regimes from Hungary to India. In this sense, Israel is both a local authoritarian state and a global pioneer of authoritarian methods.

The conclusion is stark. Zionism's DNA — its exclusion of Palestinians, its reliance on perpetual crisis, and its construction of an ethnocratic state — makes authoritarianism inevitable. The mask of democracy may slip on and off depending on the audience, but the structure remains the same.

This does not mean resistance is futile. As we saw in the protests, in the diaspora, and in global solidarity movements, cracks in authoritarianism always exist. But it does mean that as long as Zionism defines Israel's foundation, authoritarianism is not a temporary deviation. It is destiny.

**Transition to Chapter 12**

So, the question then becomes: what comes after authoritarian Zionism? If the state is hollow, its legitimacy fractured, and its authoritarian design exposed, what alternatives begin to emerge? In Chapter 12, I will turn to the forces of resistance, Palestinian, Jewish, and international, that are shaping a different vision for the future, and the obstacles they face.

# PART III: The Reckoning

# CHAPTER TWELVE:
# Resistance, Reckoning and Renewal.

## Section 1 – The Roots of Resistance

If Zionism has been defined by domination, Palestinians have been defined by resistance. From the Nakba of 1948 to the Gaza wars of the 2020s, the Palestinian story is not only one of loss, but of survival through defiance. Resistance is not a side chapter in this history. It is the thread that binds generations, shaping identity, politics, and culture.

The Nakba was both catastrophe and catalyst. Hundreds of thousands were driven from their homes, entire villages erased, families scattered across camps in Lebanon, Jordan, and Gaza. Yet almost immediately, Palestinians began to organise, first through local committees, then through regional networks, eventually through the creation of the Palestine Liberation Organisation (PLO) in 1964. The PLO represented more than a political body. It was a declaration that Palestinians refused erasure. Where Zionism sought to bury their history under new names and settlements, the PLO insisted: *we are here, and we will not vanish.*

### The Evolution of the PLO

The PLO under Yasser Arafat grew into the most visible embodiment of Palestinian resistance. It carried the struggle onto the global stage, speaking at the United Nations, aligning with liberation movements from Vietnam to South Africa. It became both a military force and a diplomatic one.

But the PLO was also fraught with contradictions. Its armed operations drew international attention, but also gave Israel and its allies the language of "terrorism." Its attempts at diplomacy, most notably Oslo in the 1990s, brought recognition but also disillusionment, as settlements expanded and promises of statehood evaporated.

Still, the PLO set the precedent: Palestinian resistance would never be singular. It would take multiple forms, sometimes armed, sometimes political, sometimes cultural.

### The Rise of Hamas

Where the PLO faltered, Hamas emerged. Founded in 1987 during the First Intifada, Hamas combined social services with militant resistance, framing itself as both protector and provider. Its Islamist identity distinguished it from the secular nationalism of the PLO, appealing to those disillusioned by Oslo's failures and by the corruption of the Palestinian Authority.

For Israel, Hamas became the perfect foil, a convenient "terrorist enemy" that justified siege and war. Yet Hamas also represented genuine grassroots support, built on decades of poverty, blockade, and despair. Its rise was less about ideology than about the vacuum left by failed diplomacy.

### The Intifadas

The First Intifada (1987–1993) was a turning point, a largely grassroots uprising marked by boycotts, strikes, and civil disobedience. Images of children with stones facing soldiers with rifles reshaped global perception.

The Second Intifada (2000–2005) was bloodier, defined by suicide bombings and brutal crackdowns. It hardened Israeli opinion, militarised the occupation further, and deepened the divide between resistance and terrorism in Western narratives.

Both intifadas, however, revealed the central truth: Palestinians refused to accept subjugation as destiny. Each generation found new means to resist.

### Resistance as Survival

Palestinian resistance is not only armed or political. It is cultural, linguistic, and personal. Teaching children Arabic in refugee camps, preserving keys to lost homes, and writing poetry that refuses erasure are also acts of resistance. Figures like Mahmoud Darwish and Ghassan Kanafani gave voice to a struggle that is as much about memory as about territory.

In Gaza during the siege, survival itself became resistance: finding food, burying the dead, keeping schools open under bombardment. To exist in the face of attempted annihilation is to resist.

### Continuity Across Generations

What unites these forms of resistance PLO diplomacy, Hamas militancy, grassroots uprisings, cultural memory is continuity. Each generation has carried the struggle forward, adapting to new realities but refusing surrender.

This continuity unsettles Zionism. It reveals that no matter how many homes are demolished, how many villages erased, how many journalists silenced, the Palestinian refusal to disappear endures. Zionism promised to make Palestinians irrelevant; resistance ensured they remained central.

## Section 2 – Armed Struggle and its Dilemmas

Palestinian resistance has often been defined, especially in Western eyes, by its armed dimension. From fedayeen raids in the 1950s to the suicide bombings of the Second Intifada, from Qassam rockets in Gaza to tunnels under the border fence, armed struggle has been the most visible and the most controversial face of defiance. For Palestinians, it has represented the refusal to submit. For Israel and its allies, it has been the pretext for portraying all resistance as terrorism.

## The Logic of Armed Struggle

For a stateless, occupied people, armed struggle carries a certain logic. International law recognises the right of peoples under occupation to resist, including by force. Against the backdrop of military occupation, settlement expansion, and the denial of basic rights, violence has often been seen by Palestinians as the only language Israel cannot ignore.

The fedayeen raids of the 1950s and 1960s targeted military outposts and settler farms, symbolising a determination to contest the new state's expansion. Later, armed wings of the PLO and Hamas carried this forward, sometimes striking deep into Israeli cities.

## The Dilemmas of Violence

Yet armed struggle has always carried dilemmas. Tactics that target civilians blur the line between resistance and terrorism, alienating potential allies and giving Israel cover to intensify repression. Suicide bombings during the Second Intifada devastated Israeli society but also shifted global sympathy away from Palestinians. Rocket attacks from Gaza, though militarily ineffective against Israel's Iron Dome system, provided justification for massive retaliatory campaigns that destroyed whole neighbourhoods.

The ethical dilemma is stark: how to resist an overwhelming military power without reproducing cycles of civilian suffering? Some Palestinian leaders have argued that armed resistance is essential for dignity; others have warned that it plays into Israel's strategy of portraying the conflict as a war of equals rather than one of coloniser and colonised.

## Israel's Interest in Armed Resistance

Paradoxically, Israel has often benefited from Palestinian armed resistance. Hamas, in particular, has been used as a foil to delegitimise all Palestinian aspirations. By portraying the conflict as a fight against "terrorists," Israel deflects attention from occupation and settlements. Some Israeli officials even quietly admitted that a weakened Hamas was more useful than a strong, united Palestinian Authority that could negotiate effectively.

The dynamic is perverse: violence that emerges from desperation becomes the excuse for further domination.

### The Western Lens

In the West, armed resistance is almost always framed as terrorism. Palestinian rockets are highlighted, while Israeli airstrikes that kill thousands are explained as "self-defence." The asymmetry is profound: the violence of a state with one of the world's most advanced militaries is normalised, while the violence of the occupied is criminalised.

This framing obscures the imbalance of power. It implies two armies clashing when in fact the reality is a nuclear-armed state confronting a largely defenceless civilian population. The language of "war" itself becomes a distortion, suggesting symmetry where there is none.

### The Persistence of Armed Struggle

Despite its dilemmas, armed resistance persists because Palestinians see few alternatives. Negotiations have yielded nothing but more settlements. Nonviolent protests, such as the Great March of Return in Gaza in 2018, were met with sniper fire. In this context, armed struggle is not only a tactic but a symbol, a declaration that Palestinians will not disappear quietly.

For some, it is an act of desperation; for others, an act of dignity. For all, it is a reminder that domination breeds resistance, and resistance, however flawed, refuses surrender.

## The Unfinished Debate

The debate over armed struggle is far from settled. Some argue it is essential for maintaining leverage; others see it as a trap that perpetuates cycles of violence and delegitimises the cause internationally. What is clear is that armed resistance, whatever its dilemmas, is inseparable from the Palestinian story. It reflects the impossible choices forced on a people denied justice, and it underscores the urgency of finding alternatives that can break the cycle.

## Section 3 – Nonviolent Resistance and Global Solidarity

While images of rockets and raids dominate headlines, much of Palestinian resistance has been nonviolent. Boycotts, strikes, protests, hunger strikes by prisoners, and international advocacy have long been central to the struggle. Nonviolent resistance exposes the asymmetry of power more starkly than armed struggle and has often resonated more effectively with global audiences.

### The Legacy of Civil Disobedience

The First Intifada (1987–1993) was as much about boycotts and strikes as it was about stones. Palestinians refused to pay taxes, shut down businesses, and created underground schools when Israel closed theirs. This mass mobilisation showed the power of grassroots organisation in confronting occupation without weapons.

Though overshadowed in Western narratives by the violence of later years, the First Intifada remains a model of nonviolent defiance, demonstrating that ordinary people could challenge military occupation through collective action.

### The Great March of Return

In 2018, Gaza witnessed another landmark in nonviolent resistance: the Great March of Return. Thousands of Palestinians marched to the border fence each week, demanding the right of return for refugees and an end to the blockade.

The protests were overwhelmingly nonviolent. Yet Israeli snipers responded with live ammunition, killing over 200 demonstrators and injuring thousands, including medics and journalists. The world watched as unarmed protesters were gunned down, shattering Israel's narrative of "self-defence."

The Great March revealed both the power and the limits of nonviolent protest. It mobilised global sympathy, but it also exposed the reality that even peaceful resistance is met with lethal force.

**The Boycott, Divestment, Sanctions (BDS) Movement**

Launched in 2005 by Palestinian civil society, the BDS movement has become one of the most influential forms of nonviolent resistance. Inspired by the anti-apartheid struggle in South Africa, BDS calls for:

• Ending the occupation and dismantling the wall.
• Full equality for Palestinian citizens of Israel.
• The right of return for refugees.

BDS has grown into a global campaign, embraced by student groups, trade unions, churches, and cultural figures. Universities have divested from companies complicit in occupation; musicians have cancelled concerts in Tel Aviv; pension funds have withdrawn from settlement-linked firms.

Israel has treated BDS as a strategic threat, lobbying governments to criminalise it and branding it antisemitic. Yet the very ferocity of the backlash underscores its effectiveness. Like the boycott of apartheid South Africa, BDS has become a moral litmus test of the 21st century.

**Global Solidarity Movements**

Beyond BDS, solidarity has expanded in countless ways. Student encampments across U.S. and European universities called for divestment during the Gaza war of 2023–25, echoing the campus protests of the Vietnam era. Trade unions in countries from Ireland to South Africa passed resolutions refusing complicity.

Ireland in particular became a vocal supporter, drawing on its own colonial history to empathise with Palestinians. Dublin's parliament became the first in the EU to declare Israel guilty of de facto annexation of Palestinian land. Irish activists framed solidarity not only as politics but as memory, a recognition of shared histories of dispossession.

### Parallels with Other Struggles

The Palestinian cause resonates because it fits into a broader lineage of anti-colonial struggles. The parallels with South Africa's apartheid regime are striking: separate legal systems, restricted movement, demographic engineering, and international isolation. South African leaders, including Desmond Tutu and Nelson Mandela, explicitly linked the struggles, insisting that freedom for Palestinians was the unfinished business of global justice.

The Irish parallel is equally powerful. As in Palestine, Ireland endured partition, occupation, and suppression of national rights. Irish solidarity with Palestine is not abstract; it is born of lived experience.

### Nonviolence as Exposure

Nonviolent resistance does more than challenge Israel materially. It exposes the reality of domination in ways violence cannot. When unarmed protesters are shot, when boycott calls are criminalised, when hunger strikes force international headlines, the asymmetry of power is laid bare.

Israel has often tried to portray the conflict as a war between equals. Nonviolent resistance reveals the truth. This is not a war but an occupation, where one side holds overwhelming power and the other struggles to survive.

## Section 4 – Jewish Dissent and Alternative Visions

Resistance to Zionism has not come only from Palestinians or the Global South. Increasingly, Jewish voices themselves, within Israel and across the diaspora, have broken ranks with the ideology of Zionism. Their dissent carries particular weight, challenging the state's claim to speak for all Jews and reclaiming Judaism as a moral tradition distinct from the machinery of occupation.

### Diaspora Dissent

In the United States, where the largest Jewish population outside Israel resides, dissent has grown most sharply among the young. Organisations such as Jewish Voice for Peace (JVP) and IfNotNow have declared openly that "not in our name" will Israel wage war and commit atrocities.

These groups mobilise protests, disrupt political events, and provide an alternative moral compass, insisting that Jewish identity must not be conflated with the violence of the state. Their presence at mass demonstrations, often carrying banners reading Jews Against Genocide, punctures the narrative that all Jews stand behind Israel.

In the UK, groups like Na'amod have followed a similar path, calling for an end to occupation and a reimagining of Jewish solidarity grounded in justice rather than nationalism.

### Dissent Within Israel

Inside Israel, dissent has also persisted, though under increasing repression. Groups like Breaking the Silence, former soldiers testifying about the abuses they committed or witnessed, have exposed the brutality of occupation. B'Tselem, Israel's leading human rights NGO, has declared openly that the state is practising apartheid.

These organisations face smear campaigns, defunding, and threats. Yet their very survival is significant. They demonstrate that not all Israelis accept authoritarian Zionism and that seeds of alternative visions exist even in the heart of the state.

### Reclaiming Judaism from Zionism

For many dissenters, the struggle is not only political but theological. They argue that Judaism's core values—justice (tzedek), compassion, the memory of exile—have been betrayed by Zionism's ethnonationalism. Rabbis and scholars increasingly challenge the notion that Jewish safety requires Palestinian dispossession.

This is not new. Jewish opposition to Zionism existed long before 1948, from Orthodox communities that rejected secular nationalism to socialist Jews who saw Zionism as a distraction from global justice. What is new is the scale of this dissent in the 21st century, as the brutality of occupation forces a moral reckoning.

### Alternative Visions

Out of this dissent have emerged alternative visions for the future. Some call for a binational state, drawing on the writings of figures like Martin Buber, who imagined Jews and Arabs living as equals in one polity. Others advocate for a single democratic state across historic Palestine, with equal rights for all its citizens regardless of ethnicity or religion.

These visions remain marginal in official politics but resonate globally, especially among young Jews seeking to reconcile identity with justice. They signal the possibility of a post-Zionist future where Jewish life and Palestinian freedom are not seen as mutually exclusive.

### The Power and Limits of Dissent

Jewish dissent challenges one of Zionism's core claims: that Israel speaks for all Jews. By rejecting this monopoly, dissenters weaken Israel's moral shield and open space for new conversations about coexistence.

Yet the limits are real. In Israel, dissenting organisations are vilified as traitors. In the diaspora, activists are accused of betraying their community. The cost of dissent is high. Still, its very persistence matters. It proves that Zionism is not the inevitable expression of Jewish identity but one contested option, and increasingly, one in decline.

## Section 5 – International Law and the Global South

If Jewish dissent chips away at Zionism's moral monopoly, international law and the Global South strike at its political legitimacy. For decades, Israel enjoyed near-total protection from accountability, shielded by the United States and its Western allies. But as atrocities mounted in Gaza and the West Bank, and as the charge of genocide gained traction, global institutions and non-Western states began to push back.

### The Courts of Justice

The International Court of Justice (ICJ) became a central battleground. In early 2024, South Africa filed a case accusing Israel of violating the Genocide Convention. The ICJ issued provisional measures ordering Israel to allow humanitarian aid and prevent genocidal acts. Though Israel ignored these rulings, the very fact of the case transformed global discourse.

The International Criminal Court (ICC) followed, opening investigations into war crimes and crimes against humanity committed by Israeli leaders. Arrest warrants were rumoured for senior officials, creating unease even among Israel's staunchest allies.

These moves were symbolic as much as practical. Few expected Israeli leaders to be hauled before The Hague. But the symbolism mattered: Israel was no longer untouchable in the eyes of international law.

## The Global South Steps Forward

The most forceful challenges came from the Global South. South Africa's leadership in the ICJ case drew on its own experience of apartheid, framing Palestine as part of the unfinished struggle against colonial domination. Other African states joined in solidarity, recalling their own histories of occupation and racial subjugation.

In Latin America, countries like Colombia, Chile, and Bolivia severed diplomatic ties with Israel, citing war crimes and genocide. Across Asia, states condemned the Gaza siege as a violation of humanitarian norms.

This collective push marked a historic reversal. Where once Israel's legitimacy rested on Western backing, it now faced mounting pressure from the rest of the world.

## Europe's Hesitation, Ireland's Leadership

Europe remained divided. Germany, haunted by its past, clung tightly to unconditional support. The UK, under Keir Starmer, aligned even more openly with Zionism. But elsewhere, the tide shifted. Spain, Belgium, and Norway recognised Palestine. France wavered between solidarity marches at home and cautious diplomacy abroad.

Ireland, with its colonial memory and strong public support for Palestine, emerged as one of the loudest voices in Europe. Dublin's parliament condemned settlements, backed BDS measures, and became a moral outlier within the EU. For Palestinians, Irish solidarity offered not only practical support but symbolic affirmation that their struggle was understood as kin to Ireland's own history.

## The Disconnect with the United States

The United States remained the great exception. Successive administrations continued to block UN resolutions, provide military

347

aid, and defend Israel diplomatically. But here too cracks appeared. Younger Americans, including Jewish and progressive communities, increasingly supported Palestinians. Polls showed generational divides. While older voters remained staunchly pro-Israel, younger ones sympathised more with Palestinians.

This disconnect left Washington increasingly isolated, aligned with Israel at the state level but out of step with global public opinion and even with parts of its own society.

### International Law as a Mirror

What international law achieved, above all, was a reframing. The Palestinian struggle was no longer just a regional dispute but a test of whether the rules that govern the world would be applied universally or only to the weak. The ICJ and ICC may not stop Israeli bombs, but they expose the hypocrisy of a global order that claims universality while practising selectivity.

In this way, international law became both a tool and a mirror: a tool for Palestinians to press their case, and a mirror reflecting the double standards of the West.

## Section 6 – The Collapse of Myths

Every political project sustains itself through myths. Zionism, perhaps more than most, relied on stories that elevated its legitimacy beyond the reach of ordinary politics: myths of democracy, morality, survival, and exceptionalism. For decades, these myths insulated Israel from scrutiny, silenced dissent, and rallied diaspora support. By the mid-2020s, one by one, those myths had collapsed.

### The Myth of Democracy

Israel's claim to be "the only democracy in the Middle East" was once a powerful shield. Western leaders repeated it as a mantra, and journalists echoed it as fact. Yet the reality of dual legal systems, apartheid laws, and military rule over millions eventually broke through.

By the time Netanyahu moved to neuter the Supreme Court, and when Gaza's children were buried under rubble, the myth could no longer be sustained. Democracy, it turned out, applied only to some, and even then, only as long as they conformed to the state's narrative.

## The Myth of Morality

Equally potent was the myth of the "most moral army in the world." Israeli leaders insisted that no military exercised more restraint, that precision targeting spared civilians, and that humanitarian concern was central to operations.

But the evidence told another story: hospitals bombed, aid workers slaughtered, journalists killed in record numbers, and starvation used as a weapon. The UN's genocide determination stripped away the last veneer. To repeat the myth of morality was to defend atrocity.

## The Myth of Survival

Zionism framed itself as a desperate project of survival: a small state surrounded by enemies, forever on the brink of annihilation. Yet by the 21st century, Israel was not weak but one of the most powerful militaries on earth, armed with nuclear weapons, shielded by the United States, and integrated into global markets.

The rhetoric of vulnerability masked a reality of dominance. Palestinians, not Israelis, were the dispossessed. Gaza, not Tel Aviv, faced annihilation. The survival myth persisted in speeches, but the world increasingly saw it for what it was: propaganda for perpetual war.

## The Myth of Exceptionalism

Finally, Zionism rested on the claim of exceptionalism, that Jewish suffering, culminating in the Holocaust, justified unique measures. To criticise Israel was to deny Jewish history; to question Zionism was to invite accusations of antisemitism.

This myth worked for decades. But as Jewish dissent grew, and as diaspora communities rejected conflation with state violence, its grip weakened. The slogan "Not in our name" captured the shift: Jewish identity could no longer be monopolised by Zionism.

**The Ruins of Myth**

With these myths collapsed, Zionism stood exposed. No longer shielded by the aura of democracy, morality, survival, or exceptionalism, it was judged by its actions. And those actions—occupation, apartheid, genocide—left little room for illusion.

The collapse of myths did more than weaken Israel diplomatically. It transformed global consciousness. The story that once inspired admiration now provoked outrage. The movement that once claimed redemption now carried the stench of domination.

For decades, the Zionist project relied not only on military power but also on a set of powerful myths: the return of a people to their "promised land," the rebirth of a democracy "in the desert," the eternal security of the Jewish state. These narratives gave Israel international legitimacy, even when its actions on the ground contradicted its rhetoric. But by the third decade of the 21st century, those myths were collapsing under the weight of reality and, crucially, under the testimony of Israelis themselves.

In 2023, Ari Shavit, a well-known Zionist writer for Haaretz, published an essay under the haunting headline: "Israel Has Breathed Its Last." Shavit, hardly a radical, admitted that the country may have reached "the point of no return" and that it was no longer possible to "reform Zionism, save democracy, or divide the land." His words were less a call to arms than a lament, an acknowledgement that the occupation had metastasised into something terminal. He warned that Israel had become "a nuclear monster feeding on the money of American and European taxpayers," a project sustained by force rather than legitimacy, and concluded with a chilling possibility: that Israelis themselves would one day have to watch their state die from abroad, in Berlin, Paris, or San Francisco.

This moment of self-recognition matters because it marks the turning inward of the critique. For years, Israeli dissidents like Ilan Pappé and Gideon Levy warned that Zionism's contradictions would consume it. What makes Shavit's despair notable is that it comes not from the margins but from the heart of the mainstream Zionist intelligentsia. If a writer like Shavit can no longer find hope in reform, then the narrative of Israel as a democracy redeemable through partition has collapsed.

Archaeology has played its own role in dismantling Zionism's foundations. Israel Finkelstein of Tel Aviv University, one of the world's most respected biblical archaeologists, has long argued that many of the stories used to legitimise Jewish claims to Palestine are historically unsupportable. The idea that the Temple lies directly beneath Al-Aqsa, or that a continuous Jewish nation persisted in the land since antiquity, is exposed by Finkelstein's work as invention rather than fact. If the myths of return and divine promise were the moral scaffolding of Zionism, then the erosion of that scaffolding leaves only naked power.

What Shavit's confession and Finkelstein's research both reveal is that the Zionist edifice rests on sand. The myths no longer convince, even those who once told them. And when myth fails, only coercion remains, a truth increasingly visible to the world.

## Section 7 – Lessons of History

History rarely repeats itself neatly, but patterns do emerge. The collapse of Zionism's myths and the exposure of its authoritarian design do not exist in isolation. They echo the trajectories of other colonial and authoritarian projects that, for a time, seemed unassailable but eventually crumbled under their contradictions.

South Africa, Ireland, Algeria, Rhodesia each offers lessons for understanding both the endurance and fragility of Zionism.

### South Africa: Apartheid Unmasked

For decades, South Africa insisted it was a legitimate democracy, just one with separate "homelands" for Black Africans. Like Israel, it claimed security threats justified harsh measures. Like Israel, it enjoyed strong Western backing during the Cold War.

Yet apartheid collapsed when its moral bankruptcy became undeniable, when international solidarity movements turned isolation into unbearable pressure, and when internal resistance refused to break. The parallels with Israel are stark: two legal systems, segregated land, denial of political rights, and an elaborate architecture of control. The lesson of South Africa is that no system of racial supremacy can sustain itself indefinitely once the world names it for what it is.

### Ireland: Colonial Memory and Solidarity

Ireland's experience under British rule — dispossession, partition, suppression of language and culture — resonates powerfully with Palestinians. The Irish struggle demonstrates how a small nation, dismissed for centuries as unruly and inferior, could eventually secure independence through a combination of armed resistance, political negotiation, and international sympathy.

Ireland also teaches the importance of memory. Its history of famine and colonial exploitation fuels its solidarity with Palestinians today. Just as Ireland's experience reshaped its role in global politics, so too could Palestine's struggle, once resolved, reshape how the world understands decolonisation in the 21st century.

### Algeria: The Price of Liberation

Algeria's war of independence against France was one of the bloodiest anti-colonial struggles of the 20th century. Millions were displaced and hundreds of thousands killed. The French portrayed

Algerian resistance as terrorism, much as Israel brands Palestinian resistance.

Yet Algeria prevailed, proving that even entrenched settler-colonial projects can be overturned. The lesson here is sobering: liberation can come at immense human cost, but the determination of a colonised people can ultimately outlast even a powerful colonial army.

### Rhodesia: White Rule's Dead End

In Rhodesia, now Zimbabwe, a white minority declared unilateral independence in 1965, determined to preserve supremacy. For years, it seemed entrenched. But sustained guerrilla resistance, combined with international sanctions and shifting global norms, forced its collapse. Rhodesia's fate shows the limits of minority rule. Demographics matter, and when the majority refuses to acquiesce, systems built on exclusion eventually face either transformation or destruction.

### The Common Pattern

What unites these histories is not identical tactics but a common trajectory. Each system relied on myths of legitimacy, on violence to suppress resistance, on allies abroad to shield it, and on narratives of exceptionalism. Each eventually reached a breaking point when the myths collapsed, resistance persisted, and the world could no longer look away.

Israel today stands at a similar juncture. Its myths are crumbling, its violence ever more visible, and its allies increasingly isolated. History's lesson is clear: no colonial or supremacist project lasts forever once its contradictions are laid bare.

## Section 8 – The Vision Beyond Zionism

If the collapse of myths marks the end of Zionism's moral authority, the question that follows is: what comes next? History shows that endings, however bitter, also open space for new beginnings. The Palestinian struggle has never been only about resistance; it has also carried visions for what a just future might look like. These visions vary, one state, two states, confederations, but they share a common rejection of domination and a yearning for equality.

## The Two-State Mirage

For decades, the two-state solution was treated as orthodoxy by diplomats. Oslo enshrined it as the horizon of "peace." Yet even as politicians spoke of two states, settlements expanded, borders blurred, and the territory for a viable Palestinian state shrank to fragments.

By the 2020s, the two-state framework had lost credibility. It survived mainly as diplomatic cover, a way for Western leaders to appear committed to peace while avoiding the hard questions of apartheid and sovereignty. Palestinians increasingly saw it not as a solution but as a mirage, endlessly invoked to delay justice.

## The One-State Reality

In practice, one state already exists: Israel controls the territory from the Jordan River to the Mediterranean Sea. The issue is not separation but the terms of governance. Palestinians argue that if partition is impossible, then equality must be the answer, one state with equal rights for all its citizens, regardless of religion or ethnicity.

This vision is simple but radical, dismantling apartheid in favour of democracy. It terrifies Zionists because it undermines the premise of a "Jewish state." Yet it is also increasingly difficult to refute, as facts on the ground show permanent Israeli control.

## Confederal Models

Some propose a middle path: a confederation of two states with open borders, shared institutions, and joint governance of Jerusalem. This model attempts to reconcile the demand for national identity with the realities of interdependence. It recognises that Israelis and Palestinians cannot simply separate; their futures are intertwined.

Confederal ideas remain speculative but reflect a shift away from rigid separation toward creative coexistence.

### Justice as Foundation

Whatever the political form, the core principle must be justice. No settlement that ignores the right of return, equality under the law, or accountability for war crimes will hold. The lesson of South Africa is instructive: reconciliation without truth and justice risks papering over injustice. For Palestinians, justice is not negotiable.

### The Role of Jewish Dissent

Jewish dissenters play a critical role in articulating post-Zionist visions. Their insistence that Jewish safety does not require Palestinian dispossession opens pathways to futures beyond supremacy. By reclaiming Judaism from nationalism, they help to imagine a homeland that is shared, not stolen.

### Global Imagination

The vision beyond Zionism is not just for Israelis and Palestinians. It is a test of the world's imagination. Can the international community support decolonisation not only in rhetoric but in practice? Can the lessons of Ireland, South Africa, and Algeria be applied in Palestine? Can the West shed its double standards?

The answers remain uncertain. What is certain is this: Zionism's fall leaves a vacuum. Into that vacuum, new possibilities are being spoken, sung, and marched into existence.

## Section 9 – Conclusion: Renewal in the Shadow of Ruin

The story of Zionism in the 21st century is not only a tale of power and brutality but also one of exposure and reckoning. What began as a movement forged in trauma and survival became, over time, an instrument of domination that inflicted on another people the very dispossession it once sought to escape.

For decades, Zionism sustained itself through myths of democracy, morality, survival, and exceptionalism. These myths shielded it from scrutiny, bought it time, and won it allies. But as Gaza's towers fell, as hunger became a weapon, and as journalists and aid workers were buried in mass graves, the myths collapsed. What remained was naked power and the recognition that such power could not endure forever.

### Resistance as Continuity

Palestinians refused to disappear. From the camps of 1948 to the marches of 2018, from the armed struggle of the fedayeen to the cultural resistance of poets and teachers, they carried forward the refusal of erasure. Each generation inherited not only loss but defiance, proving that no bulldozer or airstrike could extinguish a people's will to exist.

This continuity of resistance is the central fact that Zionism could never overcome. It is why settlements multiplied but never erased Palestinian presence, why propaganda shifted but never silenced dissent, and why even in the ruins of Gaza, songs of return still echo.

### The Global Reckoning

What changed in the 21st century was not only Palestinian endurance but global recognition. The UN named genocide. The ICJ and ICC pursued accountability. The Global South rallied in solidarity. Diaspora Jews said "not in our name." Irish voices drew parallels with their own history. Students occupied campuses, churches divested, and unions took stands.

The world began to see clearly what Zionism had become: not a shield of survival but a system of domination. To defend it was no longer to defend democracy but to defend atrocity.

## Lessons of History

From South Africa to Algeria, history teaches that no system of supremacist rule can survive indefinitely. Zionism, like those before it, reached the limits of its contradictions. Its attempt to be both democracy and ethnocracy, both refuge and empire, proved unsustainable. The more it clung to power, the more it exposed its moral bankruptcy.

The lesson is not that Zionism was unique but that it was never exceptional. It followed the same arc as other colonial projects: rise, entrenchment, brutality, collapse. Its fall is not only a Palestinian story but a parable for the 21st century about the dangers of nationalism unmoored from justice.

## Renewal in the Shadow of Ruin

What remains is the question of renewal. Renewal will not come easily. The ruins of Gaza, the wounds of displacement, and the trauma of generations will not be healed overnight. But the possibility exists. It lies in visions beyond Zionism: in equality, coexistence, a shared homeland, and justice. It lies in the recognition that true safety cannot be built on another people's suffering.

The shadow of ruin is long, but within it, seeds of renewal can grow. If Palestinians and Jews are to share a future, it must be built not on supremacy but on justice. If the world is to have credibility, it must uphold its own principles universally, not selectively.

## Final Reflection

The rise and fall of Zionism is not only about one land or one people. It is a mirror held up to humanity. It asks whether trauma can justify domination, whether myths can excuse atrocity, and whether the world will tolerate genocide if it is carried out by allies.

The answers will shape not only Palestine and Israel but the future of global order itself. Zionism's collapse is not the end of the story but the opening of a new one, one that will test whether the world can choose renewal over ruin, justice over power, and humanity over supremacy.

# Epilogue – The Choice Before Us

The story of Zionism is not only written in the soil of Palestine. It is written in the conscience of the world. For decades, silence and complicity allowed myths to stand in place of truth. Today, those myths lie shattered. What remains is a question for all of us: having seen, will we act?

Palestine is more than a place. It is a test of whether humanity can learn from its history, whether we can choose justice over expedience, and whether we can refuse to repeat the cycles of domination that scar every century. The genocide in Gaza has shown us the cost of delay. Renewal will demand courage, solidarity, and imagination, not only from Palestinians and Israelis but from all who claim to care about the future of democracy and the dignity of human life.

In the ruins of Gaza, children still draw keys and olive trees. Their images carry a truth that tanks and drones cannot erase, and that another world remains possible. Whether we reach for it will be the measure of our time.

# References

**United Nations and International Law**

- United Nations Human Rights Council. *Report of the Independent International Commission of Inquiry on the Occupied Palestinian Territory, including East Jerusalem, and Israel.* Geneva: UN, 2024.

- International Court of Justice. *Application of the Convention on the Prevention and Punishment of the Crime of Genocide (South Africa v. Israel), Provisional Measures.* The Hague: ICJ, 2024.

- International Criminal Court. *Situation in Palestine: Report on Preliminary Examination Activities.* The Hague: ICC, 2021.

- United Nations Office for the Coordination of Humanitarian Affairs (OCHA). *Gaza Situation Reports, 2023–2025.* New York: UN OCHA.

**Historians and Scholarship**

- Morris, Benny. *1948: A History of the First Arab–Israeli War.* New Haven: Yale University Press, 2008.

- Pappé, Ilan. *The Ethnic Cleansing of Palestine.* Oxford: Oneworld, 2006.

- Shlaim, Avi. *The Iron Wall: Israel and the Arab World.* London: Penguin, 2014 (updated ed.).

- Segev, Tom. *1949: The First Israelis.* New York: Free Press, 1986.

- Khalidi, Rashid. *The Hundred Years' War on Palestine: A History of Settler Colonialism and Resistance, 1917–2017.* New York: Metropolitan Books, 2020.

- Said, Edward W. *The Question of Palestine.* New York: Vintage, 1992 (updated ed.).

**Human Rights Reports and NGOs**

- Amnesty International. *Israel's Apartheid Against Palestinians: Cruel System of Domination and Crime Against Humanity.* London: Amnesty, 2022.

- Human Rights Watch. *A Threshold Crossed: Israeli Authorities and the Crimes of Apartheid and Persecution.* New York: HRW, 2021.

- B'Tselem. *A Regime of Jewish Supremacy from the Jordan River to the Mediterranean Sea: This Is Apartheid.* Jerusalem: B'Tselem, 2021.

- Breaking the Silence. *Testimonies of Israeli Soldiers from the Occupied Territories.* Jerusalem: Breaking the Silence, ongoing.

**Key Political Speeches and Documents**

- Ben-Gurion, David. Quoted in *David Ben-Gurion: In His Own Words.* New York: Sabra Books, 1972.

- Netanyahu, Benjamin. Public speeches, 2015–2025. Israeli Government Press Office.

- Michaeli, Merav. Speech at Yisrael Hayom conference, 27 October 2022. Reported in *Times of Israel*.

**Journalism and Contemporary Accounts**

- *Haaretz* (various investigative reports, 2019–2025).

- *Al Jazeera English* (documentaries and coverage, 2018–2025).

- The Guardian. "Israel and Gaza Conflict Coverage," 2023–2025.

- The New York Times. "War in Gaza Special Reports," 2023–2025.

**Documentary and Testimony**

- Alon Schwarz (Director). *Tantura* [Documentary]. Israel/Germany, 2022.

- Kanafani, Ghassan. *Palestine's Children: Returning to Haifa and Other Stories.* Beirut: Institute for Palestine Studies, 1975.

- Darwish, Mahmoud. *Unfortunately, It Was Paradise: Selected Poems.* Berkeley: University of California Press, 2003.

# Further Reading & Resources

## On Zionism and Israeli History

- Herzl, Theodor. *The Jewish State.* Leipzig & Vienna: 1896.

- Penslar, Derek J. *Zionism: An Emotional State.* New Brunswick: Rutgers University Press, 2023.

- Sand, Shlomo. *The Invention of the Jewish People.* London: Verso, 2010.

## On Palestinian Struggle and Identity

- Masalha, Nur. *Expulsion of the Palestinians: The Concept of "Transfer" in Zionist Political Thought, 1882–1948.* Washington: Institute for Palestine Studies, 1992.

- Abulhawa, Susan. *Mornings in Jenin.* New York: Bloomsbury, 2010 (novel with historical basis).

- Said, Edward W. *Culture and Imperialism.* New York: Vintage, 1994.

## On Comparative Struggles

- Mandela, Nelson. *Long Walk to Freedom.* Boston: Little, Brown, 1994.

- Fanon, Frantz. *The Wretched of the Earth.* New York: Grove Press, 1963.

- Tutu, Desmond. *No Future Without Forgiveness.* London: Rider, 1999.

**On Contemporary Politics and Media**

- Sachs, Jeffrey. Public lectures and interviews, 2022–2025. Columbia University & UN Sustainable Development Solutions Network.

- Butler, Judith. *Parting Ways: Jewishness and the Critique of Zionism.* New York: Columbia University Press, 2012.

- Finkelstein, Norman. *Gaza: An Inquest into Its Martyrdom.* Chicago: University of Chicago Press, 2018.

- Hughes, Matthew. *Britain's Pacification of Palestine: The British Army, the Colonial State, and the Arab Revolt, 1936–39.* Cambridge: Cambridge University Press, 2019.

- Dáil Éireann. *Debate on Recognition of Palestinian Statehood.* Official Report, 22 May 2024.

- Government of Ireland. *Statement on the Recognition of the State of Palestine.* Department of Foreign Affairs, Dublin, 28 May 2024.

- Irish Times. "Ireland Formally Recognises Palestinian State." *Irish Times,* 28 May 2024.